RESTAURANT MANAGEMENT

RESTAURANT

MANAGEMENT

Nancy Scanlon

VNR VAN NOSTRAND REINHOLD
————— NEW YORK

Library of Congress Catalog Card Number 92-11375
ISBN 0-442-00834-1

I(T)P   Van Nostrand Reinhold is a division of International Thomson Publishing.
          ITP logo is a trademark under license.

Printed in the United States of America

Cover art: *Tables for ladies* by Edward Hopper
The Metropolitan Museum Of Art. New York, New York.

Van Nostrand Reinhold
115 Fifth Avenue
New York, New York 10003

International Thomson Publishing
Berkshire House
168-173 High Holborn
London, WC1V 7AA, England

Thomas Nelson Australia
102 Dodds Street
South Melbourne 3205
Victoria, Australia

Nelson Canada
1120 Birchmount Road
Scarborough, Ontario
M1K 5G4, Canada

16 15 14 13 12 11 10 9 8 7 6 5 4 3 2 1

Library of Congress Cataloging-in-Publication Data

Scanlon, Nancy Loman.
     Restaurant management / Nancy Scanlon.
          p.   cm.
     Includes bibliographical references.
     ISBN 0-442-00834-1
     1. Restaurant management.   I. Title
     TX911.M27S24 1992
     647.95'068--dc20

                                         92-11375
                                           CIP

Contents

Preface

The activity of restaurant management is often conducted as a secondary aspect of owning and managing a food service operation. Owner/managers are often chefs or service-oriented specialists who have entered the restaurant business to achieve a lifelong goal of "owning my own operation" or "being in business for myself." They bring to these newly founded businesses skills, talents, and experience in producing quality food or providing excellent guest service. Given the demands that their industry experience has made on their creative talents and energy, they are often untrained in the vital management skills that are necessary to keep their businesses operating profitably over a continuing period.

Management skills are the principles and practices that are being applied to the business functions of operating facilities in a wide range of settings and "for profit" outlines. These skills and principles provide the underlying framework of every type of business that functions successfully, regardless of the service provided or the product manufactured.

The primary function of a business is to produce profit for investors and owners. In a food service setting, food and service are the products that are sold to realize that profit. Unless business management principles are applied in every area of an operation, profit goals will not be realized.

Management in a food service operation is broken down into five major areas:

Purchasing

Distribution

Production

Service

Accounting

Within each of these areas are the common management concerns of managing:

Labor

Product

Profit

To manage each of the five major areas effectively, management must establish goals and objectives to be achieved over a determined period of time. For each objective, a series of plans which, when set in action, will control the three common concerns of management, labor, product, and profit is developed.

Restaurant Management has been developed as an introduction to the major areas of restaurant management concern. Styles of restaurant operations are identified to give the reader an understanding of the formats in which food service is offered and the ability to distinguish between independent and franchise ownership. The importance of market research to the success of both new restaurant ventures and ongoing marketing efforts is discussed. Market surveys and feasibility studies are important components of planning for restaurant businesses. Management's ability to analyze the potential or ongoing profitability of a restaurant operation requires a knowledge of how to read a profit and loss statement, determine a breakeven point, and lay out a feasibility study.

Menu development is an important area of management expertise. Management must be able to recognize how equipment and labor resources can affect a menu program, to develop a menu repertoire and to establish standards for the production of menu items. Pricing of menu items must combine accurate costing procedures with marketing techniques that respond to customer needs. Management must be aware of the variety of food costing and pricing methods available and know how to determine which will be most effective in a given operation. Beverage management can be a significant area of profit contribution. Management must understand how to establish standards and procedures for effective beverage management and establish a pricing program that best responds to the needs of the operation.

Purchasing and distribution challenge management to create a program that will meet the established profit goals and still provide a good product with minimum waste loss. Food and beverage cost control systems manage the production of a restaurant operation. Production controls and menu controls help management consistently produce an established quality and portion of food product at a cost that will result in menu prices that yield predetermined food cost percentages and profit margins.

Labor is a management concern that affects every area of a restaurant operation. The effective organization of employees at all levels from management to hourly wage staff determines how smoothly an entire operation functions. Management's ability to identify qualified employees through the interviewing process can affect employee retention and overall employee costs. Training programs are an important key to employee productivity and overall profitability. Management's ability to integrate computer food service systems into every area of a restaurant operation will contribute to both productivity and profitability.

Marketing is a management function that requires the application of market survey and competition analysis. Identifying customer needs, creating product/services to meet those needs, and generating customer interest in these products/services are challenging areas of management responsibility. Entrepreneurial management activities have traditionally marked the history of the development of the American restaurant. Management's ability to recognize opportunities and respond to them with profit-generating products and services will help every restaurant business to grow and be successful in the 1990s.

Students and industry professionals alike will find techniques and methods in these pages that they can apply to develop business plans, establish short- and long-term business goals and objectives, and create successful restaurant businesses.

Acknowledgments

A work such as *Restaurant Management* encompasses knowledge and expertise in management areas beyond the author's experience. The contributions of colleagues and friends are gratefully recognized, in particular, that of Paul Wise, director of the Hotel Restaurant Management program at the University of Delaware, who has been the consulting author on this text. His contributions and counseling have been invaluable. I am grateful to David A. Weiland for his contributions and organizational expertise in the chapters on profit analysis and food and beverage cost controls; to Richard Bonin, instructor at Johnson & Wales University, for his assistance in developing the chapter on purchasing and distribution; to the research library of the National Restaurant Association, for their assistance with material on restaurant law for the chapter on employee organization and restaurant management careers; to James Nystrom of the CRORD Group, Inc., for his continued contributions on computer food service systems; to Vince Freehan, vice president, Industry Relations of ECO-LAB, for the use of training materials.

1 *Styles of Restaurant Operation*

OBJECTIVES

1. To understand the basic formats in which food service is offered.

2. To be able to distinguish the differences between independent and franchise ownership.

3. To be aware of the changes that are taking place in restaurant development in the 1990s.

4. To realize the impact of national trends in health, the national economy, and ecology on the restaurant and food service industry.

CASE STUDY: THE OLIVE GARDEN

The Olive Garden restaurants represent a trend in the food service industry in which corporately owned restaurants are taking over the position and location of independent restaurants in local communities. At a time when competition for customers is at an all-time high, independent restaurants are struggling to stay in business. The Olive Garden restaurants are classified as casual restaurants serving Italian cuisine. The average unit has approximately 250 seats, which turn over twice at lunchtime on a corporate average. Originally a stand-alone concept from General Mills Corporation, the Olive Gardens are now paired with Red Lobster restaurants and located on major travel routes. An innovation currently being tested is a restaurant plaza that adds a third, noncompetitive concept restaurant, usually fast food, to create a destination location. Corporate purchasing power allows prices to be low. Hourly wages, salaries, and benefit packages draw local food service personnel. With the ability to mount a major advertising program, Olive Garden restaurants open to a curious community eager to try a new "not so fast" restaurant. The independent restaurant owner must sit back and hope that both help and customers return once the newness wears off.

Restaurant management in the 1990s offers a rich blending of traditional and entrepreneurial styles of restaurant operation and service. Through corporate takeovers a variety of chain and franchise operations have come under one parent company. The results of these meldings have been the restructuring of some restaurants and the partnering of others, such as the Olive Garden and Red Lobster by General Mills Corporation. In one franchise takeover a successful company, Al Copeland Enterprises, blended their floundering competition, Church's Fried Chicken, with the already successful chain Popeye's Famous Fried Chicken and Biscuits. The fast-food type of restaurant has been renamed *quick serve* in a direct response to customer demand for healthier foods and a wider range of menu items served in a timely fashion. Family-style service of the 1990s combines quick serve with casual sit-down dining. Full-service restaurants struggle against the drastic effects of economic downturns and changes in the spending patterns of both business and social customers. In the 1980s the need to provide restaurants that offered entertainment themes created the "concept" restaurant.

The "1991 Foodservice Forecast" published by *Restaurant & Institutions* magazine identifies twenty-seven different operational segments in the food service industry of the 1990s. Total forecasted sales for 1991 was $256,412,000,000 ($256 billion) generated from 696,292 units of food service operation.

Restaurant operational styles are of three major types: quick serve, family style, and full service. Within these three categories are restaurants which offer a wide variety of service styles from self-service to French service. Buffet, take out, and banquet service are some of the variations.

All of these categories of operational styles are operated as both independent and franchise businesses. To be better able to understand the development and current status of these restaurant operations as businesses it is important to understand the difference between an independently owned restaurant operation and a franchise restaurant operation.

INDEPENDENT OWNERSHIP

Independent ownership may be by an individual or a chain. Both individual and chain restaurants can be operated by a single independent owner. The distinction between individual and chain is the intentional duplication of a restaurant operation into more than one unit.

Many successful restaurateurs have taken a proven restaurant and found locations which will successfully support a duplicate of that operation. Early restaurant entrepreneurs such as Howard Johnson and Bill Marriott provide excellent examples of the successful application of this practice.

Howard Johnson found a highway intersection location to be highly successful. When major interstate roads replaced the original two-lane highways, his company moved quickly to provide roadside restaurants where customers had always found them, along major travel routes.

After founding the first Hot Shop in Washington, D.C., Bill Marriott and his wife, Allie, would locate major intersections in the Washington, D.C., area along routes which were heavily traveled. Opening Hot Shoppes in these locations provided the basis for the Marriott Corporation, which today operates hotels and restaurants internationally.

Independent restaurant operations are free-standing units. These operations may be owned and managed by individual owners or groups of investors. Owners may be involved in more than one operation and often borrow successful ideas and incorporate them into another restaurant, depending on the theme, cuisine, and location. Some owners choose to put all of their energies into one restaurant. The Hilltop Steak House in Saugus, Massachusetts (Figure 1-1), has consistently been one of the highest-volume single-unit operations in the United States. Averaging over $8 million annually, this restaurant seats 1100 and serves a limited menu which concentrates on high-quality beef dishes. Customers have been traditionally standing in line for a quality of food and service that they know will be consistent with their expectations. Independent restaurant operations are financially based on the resources of owners and/or investors who expect a percentage of any profits made as a return on their investment.

CHAINS

Corporate giants have found that takeovers of smaller corporations have often yielded a chain of restaurants. Depending on the primary objective of the corporation, the chain may be sold off or absorbed into the company. Food-related companies such as General Mills have developed their own restaurant chains and kept them under corporate ownership rather than turning them into franchises. The Olive Garden restaurants are a direct development of General Mills Corporation. These restaurants are financed by the parent company, which in turn receives all of the profits.

FIGURE 1-1   *Hilltop Steak House. Courtesy Hilltop Steak House, Saugus, Massachusetts.*

FRANCHISE

Franchising is a method of doing business whereby a parent company (the franchisor) grants (via a franchise agreement) an individual outlet owner (the franchisee) the right to market its products and services while using the parent's proven name, reputation and marketing techniques.[*]

Restaurant franchises are duplications of successful restaurant operations which are sold to individual owners or investors. An owner may have more than one franchise. Companies that sell franchises may also continue to own and operate some units for the parent company. These are called *company-owned units* and are not classified as franchises.

Popeye's Famous Fried Chicken and Biscuits began in New Orleans, Louisiana. A fast-food restaurant that specialized in high-quality fried chicken

---

[*]Thomas C. Kinnear and Kenneth L. Bernhart, *Principles of Marketing*, 2nd Ed., (Glenview, Scott Foresman & Co., 1984) p. 355.

quickly found success with southern customers. Adaptations of coatings and additional aspects of regional southern cuisine helped to expand the number of units in the Louisiana area. When Popeye's founder, Al Copeland, made the decision to offer this successful restaurant format to other interested investors, he retained the company's ownership in a number of units. Franchise owners are sold a complete duplication package consisting of a building structure, signage, equipment, decoration, training, paper supplies, and recipes. Franchise owners must agree to follow company guidelines to ensure consistent product quality and customer service. Failure to do so can result in their franchise licenses being legally revoked.

Financial arrangements generally include an initial franchise fee and require a cash investment by the investors. The parent company also receives a royalty on the earnings of each franchise. The amounts of fees and percentages of royalties range widely from one company to another, depending on each company's history of success.

RESTAURANT OPERATIONAL STYLES

Quick Serve

Quick serve is the 1990s food service industry term for what has traditionally been called fast food. In the 1960s and 1970s the development of the fast-food restaurant chains, McDonald's, Hardee's, and Burger King, specializing in a variety of hamburger items and french fries initiated a wave of self-service restaurant chains that included Taco Bell, Kentucky Fried Chicken, Long John Silver's, and a host of others representing specialty foods and cuisines.

These operations follow the basic format of providing limited seating in a casual atmosphere for customers who order at a self-service counter to "eat in or take out." In the 1970s drive-through windows (Figure 1-2) were added to many of these operations, allowing customers to order over an intercom system located in the parking lot and drive up to a pick-up window for their orders.

The growth of this segment of the industry was in direct relation to the growth of the population group represented by the "baby boomers," or post–World War II birth group. Today this group is about to become the senior citizen population of the United States and still represents the largest and most important consumer group in America. As the baby boomers began their families, the demand for inexpensive food served quickly in a casual atmosphere suited, for families with young children reacted very favorably to the fast-food restaurant style.

FIGURE 1-2   *McDonald's Drive-Thru.*

In the 1980s this same customer group now began to look for more variety in fast food menu offerings as well as healthier items and methods of preparation. Fast-food restaurants responded in part by producing salad bars and prepackaged salad items. In 1990 McDonald's Corporation was the largest purchaser of iceberg lettuce in the United States, according to the California Iceberg Lettuce Association, clearly showing the favorable reaction of the general public to these menu offerings. The McLean Deluxe hamburger, developed in cooperation with the National Beef Council, represents a major attempt by McDonald's Corporation to present food items in response to the needs of their customers. Chains such as Wendy's introduced a self-service buffet bar offering Mexican and Italian cuisine items as well as salads. Pizza Hut developed a line of pasta dishes to augment their traditional pizza/sandwich menu. Breakfast became an addition to many of the specialty hamburger and fried chicken chains in an attempt to recover slipping customer counts.

By the end of the 1980s the increase in two-income families dramatically changed the life-style of the American family, creating an increasing demand for foods to take out to eat in. The take-out window was, in many operations, doing as much volume as the walk-up counter. In Sharon, Pennsylvania, the

Quaker State and Lube Restaurant does close to $1 million of business annually in orders of chicken wings from their one drive-up window.

Fast-food restaurants were beginning to turn into casual family-style restaurants on their menu boards but remained self-service in their operations. As the industry began to recognize the impact of the development of the take-out segment of their operations and other trends, adjustments were made to the marketing plans of a number of restaurant chains:

1. *Quick-serve* was developed to define casual family-style dining which could represent fast-food, fast-food/family-style service combinations, or family-style service alone.

2. *Takeout* became a stand-alone restaurant concept.

3. Menu items that could be preprepared in a fast-food kitchen setting that also responded to the demand for healthy eating concerns were identified.

Pizza Hut Corporation has created a line of Carry-Out units which sell and deliver pizza as well as a selection of menu items from the red roof Pizza Hut restaurant menus. No customer seating is provided and drive-through windows are generally available. The company expects to have 3000 of these units located across the United States by 1995. In addition, Pizza Hut pizza will be made available to food service vendors in all segments of the industry from airlines to sports stadiums. This addition to their marketing strategy now allows the traditional Pizza Hut restaurant to concentrate on casual family-style service in a quick service setting with the fast-food line shifted to the Pizza Hut Carry-Out unit (Figure 1-3).

Family Style

Family-style restaurant operations are represented by food service operations offering booth and/or table service in a casual setting. A combination of buffet and table service can provide labor-cost-reducing opportunities while giving customers variety in visual presentation as well as menu offerings. Independent as well as chain and franchise restaurants incorporate this service style into their overall operations.

National chains such as Big Boy's and Howard Johnson's are examples of family-style operations. Theme and cuisine restaurants such as Chili's, the Ground Round, and Bennigan's are blends of family-style/casual dining. Family-style dining restaurants can offer alcoholic beverages but in the majority of cases do not. Operations that offer breakfast/lunch services are often operated as independent restaurants whose owners work as chef/managers. Delicates-

FIGURE 1-3   *Pizza Hut Carry-Out Unit.*

sens with table service, cafeteria-style steak houses, and coffee shops are also examples of the variety of family-style operations.

Full Service

Full-service restaurant operations are designated as those restaurants offering sit-down table service. A full-service restaurant is not defined by its price but by the type of service, atmosphere, and menu selection offered to the customer.

Menus in full-service restaurants generally offer a variety of course selections from appetizers to dessert and include alcoholic beverages. Pricing of menu items can range from mid/low to expensive, depending on the theme, cuisine, and location of the restaurant. Full-service restaurants are generally independently or chain owned. The Chart House is an excellent example of a chain-operated full-service restaurant (Figure 1-4). The company operated sixty-two units nationwide in 1989. These restaurants often confine themselves to dinner service only with location as a primary feature. They are located on a waterway whenever possible to emphasize the water navigation chart theme expressed in their signage, name, and menu cover. The atmosphere is casually upscale, and the menu offers a full course selection of regionally specialized

FIGURE 1-4   *Chart House Restaurant. Courtesy The Chart House Restaurant, Philadelphia, Pennsylvania.*

items. In Philadelphia, Pennsylvania, the Chart House is located on the Delaware River adjacent to the city. The architecture of the restaurant devotes all of the window space to water views. The lower level is a lounge and raw shellfish bar with dining on the upper level. Operation begins at 4:30 p.m. and caters to an after work and social clientele. The average check without alcohol is $15.

The economic recession of the early 1990s is affecting this segment of the restaurant industry more than any other. Full-service restaurants which flourished during the 1980s saw as much as a 50 to 60 percent decline in their customer counts in 1990 and 1991. Michael Hurst, former president of the

National Restaurant Association, noted that the roots of this severe downtrend lie in major changes in the dining out preferences of the baby boomers who represented a large percentage of the previous customer base for this restaurant style. Mr. Hurst noted, "Through the 1980's, this influential market segment sustained an interest in chic, experimental, high-priced dining establishments, but a variety of factors—aging, family building, a loss of confidence due to the 1987 stock market crash—has created another revolution in taste within this group. Today, baby boomers are looking for less elaborate meals in homelike surroundings and at lower prices."

The result of this change in customer needs and demands is a dining style called *casual style.* Full-service restaurants are adjusting their decors to reflect a less formal, comfortable atmosphere. Menu offerings are being revised to include simpler food items with less labor-intensive preparation. American regional foods prepared by "home-style cooking" methods are returning to full-service restaurant menus in place of highly developed food ingredient combinations and plate presentations.

This change in menu offerings has also allowed the menu pricing structure to be lowered to attract customers who are feeling the constraints on both business and personal spending for entertainment.

Healthier menu offerings include a wide variety of fresh seasonal greens and vegetables. Poultry has become the most popular low-cholesterol source of protein. Turkey and chicken are appearing in both traditional and experimental forms on restaurant menus. Cooking methods also reflect healthy dining concerns as stir-fry, steaming, and grilling take precedence over deep-fat frying, roasting, and use of heavy sauces.

Healthy dining programs for full-service restaurants are the result of the combined efforts of local hospitals and area restaurant associations around the United States. Restaurant menus indicate items which have been planned under the supervision of hospital dietitians to respond to a variety of dietary concerns, including low-cholesterol and low-sodium cooking (Figure 1-5). Restaurants provide nutritional breakdowns of the menu items for customers. This awareness of healthy dining concerns among restaurant customers responds to the basic needs of both middle-aged and senior citizen customer groups.

The baby boomer senior citizen groups will be healthier, wealthier, and longer lived than ever before in the history of the United States. This consumer group will have a major impact on the food service industry for the next 20 years and will require its needs and demands recognized through programs such as these. All phases of the industry will recognize the necessity of incorporating marketing techniques which will encourage the attendance of senior citizen customers.

Soups & Appetizers

CHICKEN SATAY 4.50
Marinated Wood Grilled Chicken with Peanut Sauce.

ORIENTAL STICKY WINGS 4.25
With Toasted Sesame Seeds.

WOOD GRILLED SHRIMP 6.95
With Cocktail Sauce and Cajun Remoulade.

GRILLED CHICKEN and HAVARTI QUESADILLA 5.75
With Black Bean Tomato Salsa.

MARYLAND CRAB CAKES 5.75
On Field Greens with Cajun Remoulade.

WARM TORTILLA CHIPS 3.25
With Salsa de Queso.

WISCONSIN CHEDDAR ONION
Cup 2.25   Bowl 2.75

CHEF'S DAILY SOUP
Cup 1.95   Bowl 2.50

Salads

FRESH GARDEN SALAD 2.25

CLASSIC CAESAR SALAD 3.25

CLASSIC CAESAR SALAD with GRILLED SHRIMP 4.50

SEASON'S SALAD 3.95
Fresh Lettuce tossed with Shrimp, Swiss Cheese, Fresh Tomato and Basil Vinaigrette.

Pasta

♦ FARFALLE
With Pesto, Scallops and Baby Shrimp.
(Fat 47.9 gm., Cholesterol 45 mg., Sodium 437 mg.)
Entree 12.95   Appetizer 6.95

PENNE PASTA
Baked with Four Cheeses, Fresh Tomato and Wood Grilled Chicken.
Entree 11.25   Appetizer 5.95

FETTUCCINI LATIN STYLE
Tossed with Garlic, Olives, Scallions, Black Beans and Lobster.
Entree 14.50   Appetizer 7.75

CHEESE FILLED EGG and SPINACH TORTELLINI
With Tomato Basil Sauce and Grilled Sausage.
Entree 11.95   Appetizer 6.50

Light Fare

POTATO PANCAKES 2.50   MASHED POTATOES 1.95   FRENCH FRIES 2.25

♦ STEAMED FRESH VEGETABLES in a BASKET 2.50
(Fat 2.25 gm., Cholesterol 0 mg., Sodium 32 mg.)

GARLIC CHEESE BREAD 2.95   BATTERED ONION RINGS 3.25

SEASON'S GRILLE BURGER 6.95
With Bacon and White Cheddar prepared with Pure Beef or Fresh Ground Turkey.

CLASSIC THREE DECKER CLUB 6.95

SEASON'S COBB SALAD 7.25   GRILLED SALMON COBB SALAD 8.50

♦ UNBELIEVABLE FRUITS 6.95
Freshest Available Seasonal Fruits with Yogurt
(Fat 15.25 gm., Cholesterol 20 mg., Sodium 188 mg.)

♦ HEALTHY ALTERNATIVES ♦

We have set the pace with our Healthy Alternatives menu program. We are committed to offering fresh fruits, steamed vegetables, decaffeinated beverages, whole grain breads, margarine and low cholesterol dressing and condiments. Selected items on our menu are prepared with your health in mind and are identified with a (♦)

Calculations of fat, cholesterol and sodium are based on approximate averages and should not be used to calculate or adhere to specific dietary guidelines.

FIGURE 1-5   *Courtesy St. Louis Marriott West, St. Louis, Missouri.*

CONCEPT DINING

In the 1980s the increased costs of entertainment combined with rising menu prices created a concept called the *destination restaurant*. Operators realized that customers were, for economic reasons, being forced to choose whether to go out for either dinner or entertainment rather than combining both in one evening. As a result, restaurants which offered both a dining and an entertainment package began appearing in a wide variety of themes and concepts. The Air Transport Command is one of a number of theme restaurants currently operated by Specialty Restaurants of Anaheim, California (Figure 1-6). The restaurant combines a casual-style, full-service restaurant with an entertainment lounge. In addition, the World War II theme of the restaurant incorporates a location adjacent to the runway at a small airport which allows diners to watch airport traffic. Nineteen forties music and memorabilia combined with interior design features complete a package which provides entertainment for families as well as couples over an extended dining time period.

FIGURE 1-6 *Exterior: Air Transport Command. Courtesy Air Transport Command, Wilmington, Delaware.*

Cuisine themes can also provide entertainment as well as a dining experience. Oriental restaurants which incorporate grill top tables into their facilities design offer guests the opportunity to watch their meal being prepared at the table (Figure 1-7). Table seating allows a number of guests to sit around one large table top so that customers are often seated alongside complete strangers.

Traditional full-service restaurants can incorporate light entertainment into their operations in a variety of ways. The Guest Quarters Hotel in Valley Forge, Pennsylvania, takes advantage of their bar area to promote late evening attendance by offering a piano lounge atmosphere adjacent to their dining room, providing popular music for easy listening and customer participation. A singing bartender adds more interest. This relatively low-key and inexpensive form of entertainment retains dining room customers for after-dinner drinks as well as drawing new customers for light late evening entertainment. The result is a steady volume of customers for a high-profit food and beverage area that might otherwise run high labor costs and low sales.

Developing a restaurant's destination possibilities can significantly increase overall business. There are, however, management and marketing considerations that must be evaluated. As managers and owners look to new ideas and concepts to increase their customer counts and profits, it is important to assess the needs of both customers and the local community. Creating a concept for

FIGURE 1-7   *Maijien Tableside. Courtesy Mai Jien Restaurant, Philadelphia, Pennsylvania.*

which there is no demand will have disappointing results. Customer needs must be defined before they are responded to with promotions and restaurant changes. In Chapter 2 the marketing process of defining customer needs is discussed.

SUMMARY

Restaurant ownership and management in the 1990s offer challenges in operating well-managed businesses which provide high-quality food and service to their customers.

The variety of formats in which restaurants can offer their services to the general public in the 1990s are the culmination of 50 years of innovative entrepreneurship and dedication to the customer, based on a tradition of food service professionalism.

It may seem impossible to develop more restaurant styles and formats than already exist. Fast food, quick serve, casual dining, and full service seem to cover the range of existing customer needs. Global communications and easily accessible travel have brought cuisines together from all over the world, offering a vast array of food tastes and presentations.

There are still exciting opportunities to be explored by the creative restaurant manager. An awareness of the need to eat healthier has created a revolution in restaurant menu planning, to which the food service community is only beginning to react. The life styles of the general American public will continue to change and their needs will have to be met. The demand for take-out foods will increase steadily in all categories of restaurant service. Changes in the environment and the availability of energy sources, food supplies, and water will affect the content of restaurant menus within the next few years.

Restaurant owners and managers will have to react to both economic fluctuations and the availability of qualified labor to operate their businesses successfully. The 1990s offer challenges to the ability of management to adapt to constantly changing conditions and customer demands while operating successful and profitable restaurant businesses.

CHAPTER QUESTIONS

1. List and discuss the three major categories of restaurant operational styles.

2. Identify the two primary business formats of restaurant ownership, defining the major differences between them.

3. Discuss the difference between a *chain* and a *franchise*.

4. What are the three major changes that have taken place within the fast-food restaurant segment?

5. What restaurant concept promises to become a major trend in developing restaurant businesses in the 1990s?

6. For what reasons was the term *quick serve* developed?

7. Define the outline of a full-service restaurant.

8. How are full-service restaurants being affected by changes in the American economy and life-style in the 1990s?

9. What impact will the healthy dining trend have on future restaurant business?

10. What advantages do destination restaurants have over other more traditional full-service restaurants?

ACTIVITIES

1. Identify an example of each of the operational restaurant styles in your community discussed in this chapter. Prepare a short case study on each, highlighting the services offered, seating capacity, type of cuisine offered, type of ownership, and theme or concept involved. Draw a conclusion as to how successful each operation is at attracting customers and maintaining customer volumes.

2. Investigate the differences between independent and franchise ownership. Select an operating restaurant business example of each and interview the owners as to their opinions of the ownership style that they selected. Determine which owner is more satisfied with his or her choice and why.

3. Identify an area of health, business, or environmental concern that will affect the restaurant industry in the 1990s. Research possible ways that restaurant managers will have to change their menu and/or operation to respond to these concerns. Present your findings to the class.

2 *Restaurant Development*

OBJECTIVES

1. To understand the importance of identifying a target market for a restaurant operation.

2. To be able to outline the four major points of a market survey.

3. To be able to interpret a market survey and apply the results to the management plans for a restaurant operation.

4. To be aware of how important local and national demographics are to effective restaurant planning and development.

CASE STUDY:
DEMOGRAPHICS OF THE 1990s

Demographics are the data and statistics of a population group that identify segments and trends in patterns of work, family life, geographic distribution, income spending, and other areas. These factors often influence the future development of business and are used to forecast trends and identify needs that customers do and will experience. New products and services are then developed to satisfy these needs, in hopes of financial success.

Major demographic trends that are currently affecting the food service industry in the United States are described in the following sections.

Two-Income Families/Working Mothers

Increased financial pressures as well as desire to reenter the work force have caused approximately 47 percent of the female population of the United States to work outside the home. The resulting two-income families have now increased their optional spending income and significantly decreased the amount of time available for recreation as well as fulfilling basic daily needs such as food preparation.

Single-Parent Families

Changes in the pattern of family life creating single-parent families place pressure on one person to fulfill all of the family's basic living needs as well as to provide an income. The amount of time available in most cases for food shopping and preparation is minimal.

Aging Population

The population group in the United States aged 35 to 54 will grow by 32 percent to 11.3 million by the year 2000.[*] As a group they will be healthier, wealthier, and longer lived than any earlier generation. An unprecedented purchasing power combined with a need for food prepared outside the home make this group an ideal target market for a wide range of food service products. All three of these demographic trends are offering creative opportunities to identify areas of the food service industry and create products and services that will best answer the needs of these customer groups.

It is elementary to the success of any restaurant business that owners and managers define a target market and develop a customer profile. This step is necessery for both established restaurants and start-up businesses in the planning stages. A *target market* is that segment of the pool of available customers who have been identified as the strongest potential customer base for a business and toward whom all sales efforts are aimed.

Determining a target market requires the preparation of a market survey to outline the geographical community and its population with the objective of identifying a pool of customers. These prospective customers are then analyzed to identify needs within the group that will be met in the format of a restaurant business.

---

[*]Source: "1991 Foodservice Forecast," Bureau of Foodservice Research, *Restaurant & Institutions*, 1990.

A market survey is made up of individual surveys of four major areas of the market:

1. Community

2. Customer

3. Competition

4. Labor pool

As each of these four areas will have a major impact on the success of a restaurant business, it is necessary that management be aware of the profile of each area and how it will affect the business. In this chapter we will discuss the aspects that must be reviewed to interpret the market survey information successfully.

Interpreting the market survey requires management to identify targeted segments of each area of the market that will be relevant to their restaurant business. Management then determines needs of the targeted segments that can be met within the format of the restaurant. Having identified these needs, management surveys the competition and develops objectives and plans to meet them. Successfully developing and analyzing a market survey allow owners and managers to make their efforts more effective in realizing the primary objective of making a profit.

Although developing a market survey can often be a difficult and tedious task, successful financial and marketing efforts will more than justify the effort. This part of the development process can be turned over to outside professionals such as consultants and agencies who are experienced in developing market surveys.

IDENTIFY THE MARKET

The initial phase of developing a market survey requires a knowledge of the statistics that make up the four areas of a market survey:

1. Community

2. Customer

3. Competition

4. Labor pool

It is necessary to research the demographic statistics of the community in order to obtain this information.

Demographics is the statistical study of the population of a community with reference to its size, density, population distribution, and vital statistics. This information is available in town and city halls and has been compiled from the national census that is conducted in the United States every 10 years. Additional updated information is sometimes available from the Chamber of Commerce and the local libraries.

The information most helpful to owners and managers of food service operations for developing effective surveys and customer profiles is

1. Population

2. Sizes of age groups

3. Average family sizes

4. Breakdown of income averages within the general population

5. Major trends in growth and development in the community

The demographic survey format shown in Figure 2-1 can be easily incorporated in a market survey which outlines the areas for which demographic information is necessary. The statistical information in Figure 2-1 can usually be obtained from the library, city or town hall, or Chamber of Commerce of the community.

The general economic health of the community is a major factor in the future success of a restaurant business. Communities forecasting a healthy continuance of businesses which employ significant numbers of the population will offer a steady restaurant customer base. Communities suffering from difficulties in retaining or attracting businesses offer uncertainties in employment opportunities for prospective customers and an unsteady customer base.

It is important to understand the profile of the business community in your area. The type of products and/or services provided by these businesses can often determine the forecasted stability of the business community. In the United States, 75 percent of all businesses produce and/or provide services to the general population. Only 25 percent of businesses in the United States produce manufactured goods. Labor strikes, shortages of raw materials and energy supplies, and major changes in the demands for manufactured goods can close plants within weeks.

An example of the effects of the closing of major sources of employment is provided by the statistics which accompanied the announcement of the closing of some military bases.

Total loss of jobs: 6158

Loss of military jobs: 1958

Loss of civilian jobs: 2700

Loss of related contract jobs: 1500

Total loss of income to community

Annual wage tax revenue: $1,000,000

Total loss impact on retail sales, real estate, and supporting services annually: $750,000,000

---

1. Area population growth over last 5 year period:
2. Estimated population growth/decline in next 5 years:
3. Number of households in area:
4. Household income scale:

$75,000 or more	_____ %
$50,000 to $75,000	_____ %
$35,000 to $50,000	_____ %
$25,000 to $35,000	_____ %
$15,000 to $25,000	_____ %
$ 7,500 to $15,000	_____ %
Below $7,500	_____ %

5. Average household size:
6. Per capita income:
7. Population by age   Marital status

18–25	_____ %M	_____ %S
25–35	_____ %M	_____ %S
35–40	_____ %M	_____ %S
40–50	_____ %M	_____ %S
50–65	_____ %M	_____ %S
65–70	_____ %M	_____ %S
70–80	_____ %M	_____ %S

8. Community businesses   % of Total

Number of service businesses	_____	_____ %
Number of manufacturing businesses	_____	_____ %
Total number of businesses	_____	

FIGURE 2-1 *Demographic Survey Information Form. Source: Menu for Profit, Profit Enhancement Programs, 1991, Section II, p. 1.*

It can be seen that the loss of 1,958 military jobs involved the additional loss of 2,700 jobs for civilian support staff. The impact on the community is the total overall loss of income for 6,158 employees.

Employment income becomes revenue in the community dispersed on both necessary and disposable services and goods from food and clothing to appliances and automobiles. Job loss and income reduction also affect the stability of the housing market and dramatically influences the overall economic health of the community.

Full-service restaurant businesses are often among the first to feel the effects of reduced customer spending. Quick-serve restaurants generally thrive in this type of economic climate when customers need to be able to purchase prepared food outside the home but can compromise on the style of restaurant they patronize.

Events that can affect a restaurant's success often occur outside the local community. Energy supplies for the United States are subject to international events such as the Persian Gulf War in 1990. This event threatened to reduce the flow of imported oil into the United States sharply. This reduction would have affected every major business area from transportation to food production. During the 6-month period of this international conflict, restaurant businesses suffered severe cutbacks in customer counts. In addition, future food sources and supplies were questionable and prices fluctuated in reaction to this uncertainty. This was coupled with a national economic recession that had been affecting the country for an extended period before the Persian Gulf conflict. Many restaurant operators were unable to sustain their businesses under the strain of both major national events and were forced to sell out or declare bankruptcy. Those who survived this period recognized the necessity of applying basic business management principles to their operations, directing their efforts toward providing their target markets with the products and services that were most needed to retain customers.

LABOR

The availability of qualified labor is one of the major problems facing restaurant managers in the 1990s. The demographics of the United States indicates a population whose largest group is represented by the baby boomers. The age group 24 years old and under, which traditionally provides the majority of food service employees, is the smallest population group.

The result of this reversal of population group size is a dramatic decrease in the available labor pool for the majority of food service operations. As a result, managers will have to expand into nontraditional labor pools to recruit the balance of their employees. This labor search will be concentrated on the senior citizen population, who are healthier and are expected to have a longer life span than ever before.

Training programs for both of these labor source groups are necessary to produce a qualified labor pool. The food service industry has been and will continue to be one of the strongest growth industries in the United States. Changing family patterns are continuing to increase the opportunities for growth in food service businesses. Communities that provide job-training opportunities for these businesses offer managers a labor pool that has the asset of being knowledgable about their jobs and the benefit of training in a variety of food service job-related skills.

Competition for these employees is forcing restaurants to increase their pay scales and offer benefit packages. Job sharing and other adjustments in work schedules provide more employment flexibility for two-income and single-parent families. Day care programs, continued education, health plans, and even profit-sharing programs are encouraging employees to break the traditional pattern of short-term employment in this industry.

The labor analysis form in Figure 2-2 gives a breakdown of the sources of labor in your community. In addition, this form requires that you identify the types of employees that you will require according to the style of your restaurant operation and the level of service and cuisine that you are offering or will offer.

Competition

"Know your competition" has always been a major component of successful marketing effort. Identifying and understanding the competition and what products and services they offer are first steps in restaurant development.

Competition can be identified as any restaurant business that offers a majority of food and beverage products and services that are directly competitive with those provided by your operation. Similarities in pricing structure are especially important to determine. Location, size, number of seats available, variety of facilities provided, theme, and cuisine are major factors that are surveyed in analyzing the competition.

The first step in establishing the competition is to determine a geographical radius in which the competition generally falls. There are always examples, however, of restaurants which, because of location or theme, are outside the general geographical radius but provide competition for your customers' business. Overall factors that affect this radius are urban or rural setting, transportation routes or facilities, travel time, and location of your restaurant in relation to these factors.

This information is available from libraries, city or town halls, chambers of commerce, and vocational schools and colleges.

1. Size of employable labor pool:

2. Increase and/or decrease in last five years:

3. Forecasted increase or decrease in next five years:

4. Labor population by age   Level of Education

14–18	_____	_____%	_____
18–25	_____	_____%	_____
25–35	_____	_____%	_____
35–40	_____	_____%	_____
40–50	_____	_____%	_____
50–65	_____	_____%	_____
65–70	_____	_____%	_____
70–75	_____	_____%	_____
75–80	_____	_____%	_____

5. Availability of food service training programs:

   Vocational High Schools:

   Post Secondary Restaurant & Culinary Programs:

   Community College Programs:

   4 Year College Programs:

6. Availability history of food service employment:

7. Local Restaurant & Food Service Organizations:

FIGURE 2-2   *Labor Source Analysis Form.*

It has been determined that the average customer will generally confine travel time to a restaurant to 30 to 45 minutes, resulting in a roundtrip time of 1 to 1 ½ hours. Laws concerning driving under the influence of alcohol have a major impact on the travel time some customers will allow when selecting a restaurant.

The competition survey sheet in Figure 2-3 has a format that analyzes the location, physical appearance, and special features of a restaurant or food service outlet.

INTERPRETING THE MARKET SURVEY

Understanding the key factors to be assessed in interpreting market survey information is essential to use this major marketing tool effectively.

Community Needs

Primary to any decision involving developing or changing a food service operation is accurately determining the need for a new restaurant or changes in a restaurant in the community as a whole. The general economic health of the community is an essential indicator of what the response to different styles of food service operations will be. Using the information gathered on forms such as the one in Figure 2-1, the following questions can assess the current and future economic health of the community:

1. Was there a decline or increase in population growth within the past 5 years?

2. Is the population growth in the next 5 years expected to decline or increase?

3. Are the majority of households families or single persons?

4. What is the average family size?

5. How many two-income families are there?

6. What is the percentage of family households with three or more persons in comparison to the number of two-income families?

7. In what range does the highest percentage of household incomes fall?

8. In what range does the highest percentage of the married population fall?

9. What is the largest population group by age?

10. What is the average per capita income?

COMPETITION SURVEY SHEET

Restaurant or Foodservice Outlet _____

Address _____

Date _____

Completed by _____

1. LOCATION
    A.   *Where is the community in the restaurant located?* _____
    B.   *Access from major roads* _____
    C.   *Parking* _____
    D.   *Sign Visible* _____ *lighted* _____
    E.   *Access from public transportation* _____
    F.   *Availability of public transportation* _____
    G.   *Location features and liabilities* _____

2. PHYSICAL APPEARANCE
    A.   *Architectural style* _____
    B.   *Outstanding features* _____
    C.   *General exterior condition* _____
    D.   *General interior condition* _____
    E.   *Types of dining areas* _____

3. SERVICE FEATURES
    A.   *Days open   (weekly)* _____ *(yearly)* _____
    B.   *Hours open (daily)* _____ *(weekly)* _____
    C.   *Seating capacity* _____
    D.   *Turnover (per dining area and meal service)* _____
    E.   *Average check (per meal)* _____ *(overall)* _____
    F.   *General cuisine* _____
    G.   *Meals provided (breakfast)* _____ *(lunch)* _____ *(dinner)* _____
    H.   *Beverage services (lounge)* _____ *(beer and wine only)* _____
          (bar) _____ *(full beverage list)* _____
          (wine list) _____ *(attached)* _____
    I.   *Service (good)* _____ *(mediocre)* _____ *(poor)* _____
    J.   *Additional facilities* _____
    K.   *Entertainment* _____
    L.   *Community acceptance* _____
    M.   *Apparent problems* _____
    N.   *Menu attached (yes)* _____ *(no)* _____
    O.   *Floor layout (provide description or sketch)* _____
          _____

FIGURE 2-3   *Competition Survey Form. Source: Nancy Scanlon, Marketing by Menu 2nd Ed., New York, Van Nostrand Reinhold, 1991.*

The answers to these questions will tell you whether the population is increasing or declining and in what income level and age range the largest customer pool lies. These answers, combined with an analysis of the competition within the community, will produce an overall picture of the prospective business climate.

Customer Needs

As discussed previously, demographic information on a potential customer base can be broken down into the following demographic categories:

1. Age

2. Average income

3. Family size

4. Sex

5. Marital status

6. Occupation

7. Level of education

Segmentation is the breakdown of information into categories. It allows management to identify key factors about potential customers which would make them a more effective target market. To complete the exercise, management determines some common characteristics which identify their customer base. For example, customers may be light or heavy alcoholic beverage drinkers, sports-oriented, frequent travelers, casual or sophisticated in their dining habits.

The combination of consumer characteristics and demographic information will create a customer profile that will identify a target market profile:

Customer profile + Demographic information = Target market.

This target market profile can now be broken down further into a segmentation of the frequency of customer use.

The frequency with which a customer will return to a restaurant is a good indication of his or her reaction to marketing efforts. The pattern of use of a restaurant also provides additional marketing information for the customer profile. Tools for measuring this information are often indicated by the method of payment that is most commonly used and the purpose of the customer's use of the restaurant.

Restaurant operators who develop customer mailing lists can qualify their users by categories and target specific mailings and promotional activities to them. The three general categories are: heavy user, medium user, and light user. By combining such additional information as family size, average check amount, beverage consumption, and purpose of visit these customers can be targeted for specific marketing efforts.

A major identification of a segment of the market concerns what customer needs management can identify and create products and/or services to fulfill. As discussed in Chapter 1, the fastest-growing segment of the food service industry is takeout. A combination of changes in the family profile, work patterns, and eating styles has increased the demand for high-quality food products that can be purchased fully or partially prepared and taken home for consumption. The profile of this customer might be the following:

Family size: 2–4

Average age: 35

Sex: female

Average income: medium to upper

Frequency: heavy user

Method of payment: check or credit card

Profession: career-oriented

Management can also use this information as the basis for future plans and decisions about changes in concepts, promotional activities, menu programs, hours of operation, and staffing.

Labor

By completing the labor source analysis form in Figure 2-2 you will identify the availability of various labor pools in your geographical area. By comparing increases or decreases in availability of labor with forecasts you will also be able to perceive how well you will be able to fill the labor requirements of your restaurant.

The percentages of available labor within age ranges indicate the type of average employee you will have. High school students turn over quickly but have a high energy level. College students are seasonal and transient. Older employees are reliable and interested in their jobs. Their employment records are stronger than those of the other two groups. This population group is also more receptive to lower wage scales because this is a second income in many cases supplementing pensions and social security payments. Training programs provide an instant pool of employable personnel as well as a resource for training your employees.

Figure 2-4 provides a format to identify the qualifications needed by your potential labor pool. By comparing these needs with the available labor pool, management can make a realistic analysis of whether the demands of the restaurant will be met by available workers. If these needs cannot be met, then management must adjust the operation of the restaurant to match the available skills of the labor market.

Competition

In addition to the information on the competition survey form in Figure 2-3, management can look to the recent development of other restaurant operations as indicators of the needs of customers and the community as well as trends in economic health. The current trend toward company-owned units of corporate chains rather than franchises provides professional marketing information to independent owners and managers. Southwest Cafes, Inc., offers five different Mexican theme restaurants. Each restaurant concept answers the need of a different target market. Some offer higher-priced menu items and full service dining. Others offer midrange pricing with an appropriate menu item selection. Yet another offers a quick-serve atmosphere with low-range menu pricing. Interior decor and seating match the level of menu item selections and range of pricing. By recognizing which market this company is trying to reach in establishing new restaurants, management can incorporate this information into their new development strategies.

A thorough survey of the competition also allows management to compare menu item listings and prices. This comparison often reveals market saturation of cuisine trends, dining styles, and theme concepts. By comparing the number of available customers with the current competition management can assess how competition could affect future business and decide whether the community will support the restaurant concepts and changes being envisioned. Market saturation of direct theme and menu ideas provides management with the opportunity to create a different approach to the original plans or change to different dining styles and levels of cuisine. It is also possible to identify a window of need that the competition is not filling and develop a concept to answer that need.

SUMMARY

The essential task of identifying a target market requires management to make a thorough evaluation of the community, customers, competition, and available

---

LABOR NEEDS & SOURCES

Fill in the qualifications that you need your personnel to have in order to run your operation effectively.

Identify sources for qualified labor in your market area.

QUALIFICATIONS OF PREPARATION PERSONNEL

1. Executive chef _____

_____

2. Sous chef _____

_____

3. Line cooks _____

_____

4. Preparation personnel _____

_____

5. Baker (Pastry chef)_____

_____

6. Dishwasher(s) _____

_____

QUALIFICATIONS OF SERVICE PERSONNEL

1. Dining Room Manager _____

_____

2. Captain(s) — Host/Hostess _____

_____

3. Servers _____

_____

4. Bus persons _____

_____

5. Cashiers _____

_____

6. Bartenders _____

_____

LABOR SOURCES IN YOUR MARKET AREA

_____

_____

_____

_____

Are the personnel available in your market area capable of carrying out the level of food production and service that you are offering?

FIGURE 2-4   *Labor Needs and Sources. Source: Menu for Profit, Profit Enhancement Programs Inc., 1991, Section II, p. 4.*

labor pool. If this step is taken before any other major planning functions, owners and managers will have accurate information on which to base their planning efforts. A realistic interpretation of findings in all four areas of the market can enable management to recognize segments of the market that have specific needs that can be filled.

Owners and managers often steadfastly insist on carrying through ideas even though competition surveys show that a sufficient number of other businesses provide this service for the number of available customers. The result is that their efforts are in direct competition and that by diluting the potential customer market they are placing themselves in a highly vulnerable position. If, on the other hand, efforts are concentrated on providing this same customer pool with a new service for which a need has been indicated, management will be approaching a customer pool which should be highly receptive.

FIGURE 2-5. *Southwest Cafes Ad. Courtesy Southwest Cafes, Dallas, Texas.*

Competition in the 1990s for the food service customer will be more intense than ever before. Owners and managers must apply traditional business and management techniques to areas of their business which historically have been casually treated. The food service industry has offered a unique area of business development for highly creative individuals, who have often disregarded basic business principles and allowed high customer volumes and cash flows to influence their decisions. Unfortunately rising costs in all areas of a food service operation combined with shrinking customer counts and increased competition have ended this era of casual business management. The current trend in restaurant development by major corporations such as General Mills and independent restaurant companies representing a number of company-owned units is a direct reflection of the success of the application of management principles to restaurant businesses. Market survey results are applied to location site selection, menu item choices and pricing, theme and concept development, as well as marketing strategies.

CHAPTER QUESTIONS

1. Explain the importance of determining a target market for restaurant development.

2. Identify the four major areas that a market survey must address and give a short definition of each.

3. Why is determining customer needs such an important phase of restaurant planning and development?

4. Define the term *demographics*.

5. Discuss the elements of a community's economic profile that should be evaluated in relation to restaurant development.

6. How have recent population trends affected the traditional patterns of availability of labor to the food service industry?

7. Why is the availability of food service training programs in a community important to owners and managers?

8. Define the term *competition* as it relates to restaurant businesses.

9. Which two areas of information combine to identify a target market?

10. Explain why market segment identification is necessary to produce effective marketing programs.

ACTIVITIES

1. Complete the survey forms for demographics, labor, and competition provided in this chapter. Use the suggested sources of information as the basis of your investigations.

2. Develop a profile of the available senior citizen labor pool in your community. Survey a selection of senior citizens at community centers and retirement residences to assess their willingness to participate in jobs in various levels of restaurant styles from fast food to fine dining. From this information create a profile of skills, education, and interest level of this segment of the labor pool.

3. Identify trends in both local and national demographics that are affecting the planning and development of restaurants in the 1990s. Give examples of and discuss restaurant themes and concepts which present restaurant business opportunities in response to these trends.

4. Define an area of restaurant development and create a competition profile using your community as a basis for the surveys. From the results identify a need indicated by local and national trends which is not being met by the competition.

3 *Profit Feasibility*

OBJECTIVES

1. To understand the concept of feasibility as it applies to profit-making (-producing) restaurant operations.

2. To be able to determine an average check on the basis of market survey information.

3. To be able to outline the four aspects of profit and discuss their individual importance to the overall success of an operation.

4. To be aware of the importance of establishing profit goals in the planning of a restaurant operation.

CASE STUDY: GRAND CONCOURSE, STATION SQUARE, PITTSBURGH, PENNSYLVANIA

The profitability of restaurant operations in the 1990s is often determined by management's ability to develop cost centers and marketing programs to maximize facility use. *Cost centers* are those individual areas of an operation that generate sales independently of one another. The Grand Concourse restaurant is the renovated main waiting room of a former city train station. The floor plan includes the central dining room area pictured in Figure 3-1 as well as a casual side dining area and raw bar for a total of two cost centers. Figure 3-1 is the promotional flyer marketing the formal central dining area as a location for wedding

35

FIGURE 3-1   *Grand Concourse Restaurant. Courtesy Grand Concourse Restaurant, Pittsburgh, Pennsylvania.*

receptions. Because of the unique setting that the restaurant provides it is very popular for weddings and private parties. The natural division of the two dining areas allows regular restaurant activity to continue at the same time that a private party occupies the central dining room. This extension of the operation's business provides needed sales revenues that help to balance off slow restaurant volume periods caused by the recessionary economic climate of the early 1990s.

Making a profit is the primary goal of any "for profit" business regardless of the service or the product offered. Nonprofit businesses are community-service-oriented and must apply business techniques to break even, or create enough revenue to cover the costs incurred.

Profit can be defined as

1. The excess of returns over expenditures in a transaction or series of transactions

2. The excess of the selling price of goods and services over all related costs

3. Net after-tax income, usually for a given period

Profit feasibility is the predetermination by owners and managers of the probability for excess returns over expenditures. In order to determine profit feasibility it is necessary to outline all the operational activities of the planned business and estimate their individual costs and sales volumes. From these figures one can accurately calculate the feasibility of probable income and profits. In an ongoing operation this process is done by analyzing the statement of income and expense.

Calculating the break-even point for a restaurant business is one of the first steps in profit analysis. The *break-even point* is that point in business operations where revenue equals cost. Anticipated profit can be projected from that point on.

In establishing a new business operation it is necessary to follow the outline of a feasibility chart. In an ongoing operation this same chart should be developed to make sure that management is aware of the information necessary to establish the feasibility level of proposed profit goals accurately.

Cost is made up of three major segments:

1. Food cost

2. Labor cost

3. Overhead cost

Each of the three primary areas of cost has a major impact on the success of a restaurant business. Management should be aware of the profile of each area and how it can affect the overall profitability of the operation.

DIRECT AND INDIRECT COSTS

Costs are those expenses which are both direct and indirect expenses of operating a business. The general guideline for distinguishing costs is that *direct costs* are any expenses directly related to providing the product and/or service to the customer and are normally affected by volume, whereas *indirect costs* are those expenses which are necessary to maintain the operating business and are not affected by changes in the volume of business. In addition, a subcategory of direct costs breaks out the major expenses entailed in the direct production and service of the product. The following listing identifies the various expense areas of direct and indirect costs:

Direct operating expenses

    a. Linen, china, glass, and flowers

    b. Costs of cleaning and associated supplies

    c. Employee uniforms and laundry costs

    d. Cooking equipment, utensils, and kitchen tools

    e. Restaurant decorations, including flowers

    f. Menus, wine lists, and other promotional material

    g. Licenses and permits

Utility expenses

    a. Heat, light and power, including any type of energy use (gas, oil, electricity, and other canned or bottled fuel used in restaurants)

    b. Water, ice, and trash removal

Administrative expenses

Costs directly related to the operation of the business management of the restaurant, including

    a. Telephone services and equipment rental

    b. Computer and data-processing costs

    c. Office supplies and printed materials used in the business management of the operation

    d. Insurance costs not related to either employee benefits or building occupation costs

e. Management fees, such as accountanting and property management

f. Security services

g. Professional dues and expenses

Advertising expenses: promotional costs, including

a. Advertising through any of the media

b. Costs of advertising or public relations agencies

Repairs and maintenance expenses: costs associated with the physical maintenance of the restaurant property, including

a. Interior or exterior design costs

b. Maintenance of furniture, upholstery, and window hangings

c. Repairs to furnishings, floor coverings, and building structure

d. Repairs to refrigeration, air conditioning, plumbing, heating, kitchen and dishwashing and sanitation equipment

Occupation expenses: expenses that do not change regardless of the volume of the restaurant's business

PRIMARY AREAS OF COSTS

Primary costs are the expenses for labor and the purchase of food and beverages. The following are the three primary cost areas:

1. Food cost: direct costs related to the purchase of any food-related product used in a restaurant

2. Beverage cost: direct costs related to the purchase of any beverage-related product, alcoholic or nonalcoholic, used in a restaurant

3. Labor cost

a. Wages and salaries, including vacation pay, overtime, commissions, and bonuses paid to employees

b. Costs of the following employee benefits

Social Security

Federal and state unemployment taxes

TABLE 3-1 Statement of Income and Expense*

| | All Restaurants | | | | | |
| | Amount Per Seat | | | Ratio to Total Sales | | |
	Lower Quartile	Median	Upper Quartile	Lower Quartile	Median	Upper Quartile
Sales						
Food	$2,385	$3,723	$5,512	80.0%	94.4%	100.0%
Beverage	202	552	1,199	6.7	14.0	25.9
Total Sales	2,800	4,342	6,022	100.0	100.0	100.0
Cost of Sales						
Food	832	1,232	1,754	28.0	33.9	39.8
Beverage	46	140	335	22.0	26.0	32.8
Total Cost of Sales	944	1,397	1,945	28.0	32.3	38.4
Gross Profit	1,820	2,876	4,084	61.6	67.7	72.0
Other Income	11	26	71	0.3	0.6	1.4
Total Income	1,858	2,908	4,288	62.2	68.3	72.7
Controllable Expenses						
Payroll	730	1,050	1,495	20.4	24.8	29.3
Employee Benefits	27	51	117	0.6	1.1	3.3
Direct Operating Expenses	120	190	299	2.9	4.6	7.1

Music and Entertainment	4	13	33	0.1	0.3	0.8
Advertising and Promotion	57	144	296	1.4	3.4	6.0
Utilities	110	155	190	2.6	3.4	4.4
Administrative and General	46	86	193	1.2	2.4	5.1
Repairs and Maintenance	42	75	115	1.1	1.7	2.4
Total Controllable Expenses	1,233	1,899	2,745	36.9	44.9	52.1
Income Before Occupation Costs	507	930	1,549	14.2	22.6	31.3
Occupation Costs						
Rent	159	256	406	4.2	6.0	8.5
Property Taxes	15	33	61	0.4	0.9	1.7
Other Taxes	14	60	138	0.3	1.3	4.3
Property Insurance	38	65	121	0.9	1.5	2.7
Total Occupation Costs	206	355	550	5.9	8.1	11.3
Income Before Interest and Depreciation	189	586	1,089	5.4	13.7	23.4
Interest	10	43	110	0.2	1.2	3.2
Depreciation	57	.117	214	1.5	3.1	5.3
Restaurant Profit	$52	$368	$945	1.4%	9.2%	19.4%

*Limited-Menu Tableservice.
Statement of Income and Expenses— All Restaurants.**
**All ratios are based as a percentage of total sales except food and beverage costs, which are based on their respective sales.

Source: Restaurant Industry Operations Report '90. National Restaurant Association and Laventhol and Horworth Washington D.C.

State health insurance tax

Workmen's Compensation insurance premiums

Welfare payment plans

Pension plans

Insurance for health, accident, hospitalization, Blue Cross, Blue Shield, and other group policy premiums

Expenses directly related to the well-being of the employee, such as meals, transportation, education, and employee activities

Managing these costs requires that standards for purchasing as well as specific procedures for receiving, distribution, billing, and accountability be established throughout an operation. The margin for error between breaking even and making a profit in today's highly competitive and high cost market is minimal. Management's ability to recognize fluctuations and overruns in all areas of cost is essential to the success of any business in the 1990s.

Statement of Income and Expenses

Before investors, owners, and managers can attempt to determine profit feasibility for a new or ongoing operation it is necessary that they outline all of these costs in an organized manner. The statement of income and expense in Table 3-1 was developed by the National Restaurant Association in cooperation with the hospitality accounting firm of Laventhol and Horwath as a guide for restaurateurs, offering sales and expense terminology that applies directly to their businesses. When accurate information is used to complete the form, feasible and/or accurate profitability can be calculated. The dollar figures are also translated into percentages of cost and income. This format breaks down expenses into manageable areas of accounting which are often more relevant to restaurant managers than traditional accounting terminology.

As discussed earlier in this chapter, expenses are direct or indirect, depending on their relationship to the production of the product and/or service. In this worksheet the assignment of costs to one category or another goes a step further by designating some expenses as either controllable costs or occupation costs. This further designation allows management to identify costs that might possibly be decreased. Controllable costs are the following:

Payroll

Employee benefits

Direct operating expenses

Music and entertainment

Advertising and promotion

Utilities

Administrative and general

Repairs and maintenance

The labor costs listed under primary costs, itemize the breakdown of costs that are included in both payroll and employee benefits. Other primary cost areas are itemized under expense categories, such as direct operating expense, utility expense, administrative expense, advertising expense, and repairs and maintenance expense.

Occupation costs are the following:

Rent

Property taxes

Other taxes

Property insurance

Additional information required on this worksheet is listed under supplemental operating information as

Sales per seat

Food	$ _____
Beverage	$ _____
Average receipt (check) per seat	$ _____

Daily seat turnover (turnover rate)

This information is needed to develop a feasibility chart which is the basis for profit analysis accurately.

Understanding the importance of the ratio of cost to sales expressed as a percentage is an essential management skill. The breakdown of the restaurant industry dollar in Table 3-2 from the *Restaurant Industry Operations Report* for 1990 published by the National Restaurant Association is an example of the ratio of cost to sales for the type of full-service restaurant indicated in the upper quartile category of the statement of income and expense in Table 3-1.

TABLE **3-2**   The Restaurant Industry Dollar*

	Full-Menu Tableservice
Where It Comes From	
Food Sales	79.9
Beverage Sales	18.2
Other Income	1.9
Where It Went	
Cost of Food Sold	26.9
Cost of Beverage Sold	4.8
Payroll	27.9
Employee Benefits	5.3
Direct Operating Expenses	6.5
Music and Entertainment	0.5
Advertising and Promotion	2.3
Utilities	2.9
Administrative and General	4.8
Repairs and Maintenance	2.0
Rent	4.5
Property Taxes	0.5
Other Taxes	0.4
Property Insurance	1.2
Interest	1.4
Depreciation	2.9
Other Deductions	1.3
Net Income Before Income Taxes	3.9

*The operating ratios listed in this chart are based on responses from 1,223 establishments throughout the United States.

Source: Restaurant Industry Operations Report, 1990, National Restaurant Association.

A comparison of this information with the statement presented in Table 3-3 gives a more concise picture of the distribution of costs and expenses of the average restaurant surveyed. *Profit* in this chart is designated as net income before income taxes.

Table 3-3 is the statement of income and expenses from the combined restaurant and bakery operation La Brasserie and La Belle, Inc., in Washington, D.C.

Sales on this statement are represented as a total revenue of $2,095,610. *Costs* are broken down into three major areas: cost of sales, operating expenses, and administrative expenses. This format offers an additional subtotal, cost of sales, at $1,246,064, which, when deducted from revenue, yields a gross profit of $849,546. Operating expenses totaling $390,336 are now deducted from gross profit for a balance of $519,210. As shown in Table 3-4, administrative expenses

TABLE 3-3   Income statement: La Brasserie and La Belle, Inc.*

Revenue:** $2,095,610	

Cost of Sales:

Flowers	$9,611
Salaries and wages	$586,081
Liquor	$126,400
Food	$346,201
Tips	$158,955
Bar supplies	$9,765
Subcontractor	$9,051

Total Cost of Sales $1,246,064	
Gross Profit $ 849,546	

Operating Expenses:

Rent	$95,835
Laundry/supplies and linen	$40,557
Telephone	$9,907
Sales tax	$138,041
Credit card charges	$41,676
Utilities	$29,223
Rental and leasing	$15,097

Total Operating Expenses $390,336

Administrative Expenses:

Compensation to officers	$106,060
Repairs and maintenance	$23,207
Advertisement	$16,234
Insurance	$82,362
Payroll taxes	$55,325
Interest expenses	$17,250
Property tax	$20,733
Administration and other expenses***	$130,273

Total Operating/ Admin $451,444	
Net Income (loss) $ 7,766	

*Consolidated statement of income and expenses for the year ending October 31, 1990.
**The figures include LaBrasserie restaurant and LaBelle, Inc. bakery. The bakery accounts for about $100,000 in revenue.
***Other expenses includes travel & entertainment, office expenses, life insurance, legal & accounting & depreciations.

Source: LaBrasserie
Source: Phyllis Richman, "La Brasserie: Accounting for Taste," *The Washington Post*, November 26, 1990.

TABLE 3-4   Net Income Chart

Revenue		$2,095,610
−	Cost of Sales	$1,246,064
	Gross Profit	849,546
−	Operating Expenses	$ 390,336
	Adjusted Gross Profit	519,210
−	Administrative Expenses	$ 451,444
	Net Income (Loss)	$ −7,766

of $451,444 are deducted, causing the original gross profit of $849,546 to be reduced to a net loss of $7,766.

To identify areas of cost that resulted in a net loss for La Brasserie and La Belle, Inc., each area of cost on the statement of income and expense must be analyzed. Profiles of the areas where La Brasserie and La Belle, Inc., costs ran over industry norms are apparent. Management can investigate these areas to determine the changes necessary to decrease costs and increase profits. The percentages of cost, indicated as parts of the restaurant industry dollar in Table 3-2, indicated by the National Restaurant Association (NRA) figures can be compared to percentages derived from the La Brasserie figures in Table 3-3.

La Brasserie & La Belle Inc.: labor costs	50.0%
Industry norm: labor costs	34.2%
Cost overrun	15.8%

This translates into $906,421 in labor costs for La Brasserie & La Belle, Inc.:

La Brasserie & La Belle total revenues	$2,095,610
La Brasserie & La Belle total labor costs	$906,421
Balance for expenses and profit	$1,189,589

All other expenses appear to be in line with national restaurant norms. To the observant manager it would be obvious that labor is the area of cost that is causing the greatest drain on profit.

The most obvious area where costs for La Brasserie and La Belle exceed industry norms is labor. In Table 3-5 labor costs are listed under cost of sales and administrative expenses:

TABLE 3-5   Percentage of Labor Costs to Revenue

Cost of sales	
Salaries and wages	$586,081
Tips*	158,955
Administrative costs	
Compensation to officers	106,060
Payroll taxes	55,325
Total labor costs**	$906,421
% of revenue represented by labor costs	50%

*Under IRS laws tips paid to servers by credit card are subject to social security. The restaurant must also pay the credit card fee on the charge.
**This total does not include employee benefits such as insurance.

BREAK-EVEN POINT

It is important to remember that costs include both indirect and direct costs. Direct costs are incurred in direct proportion to sales. This allows management to determine a level of feasibility called the *break-even point*. Break-even points are generally charted on a graph and calculated by estimating the point at which revenues will equal the cost of doing business. Break-even points compare sales revenues to cost of sales. Cost of sales fluctuates, depending on customer volumes, labor costs, and food costs. Indirect costs that have been incurred to make both product and service available are computed by adding direct costs to the base cost. Figure 3-2 illustrates a break-even graph.

The following steps outline the process of constructing a break-even graph.

Step One

Draw a horizontal line across the graph at the point which represents fixed costs ($336,656.25).

Step Two

Draw a line on a 45-degree angle from the bottom right-hand corner (0) to the top left-hand corner. This line represents sales revenue.

Step Three

Mark the point on the graph which represents the approximate total of fixed and variable costs.

BREAKEVEN GRAPH

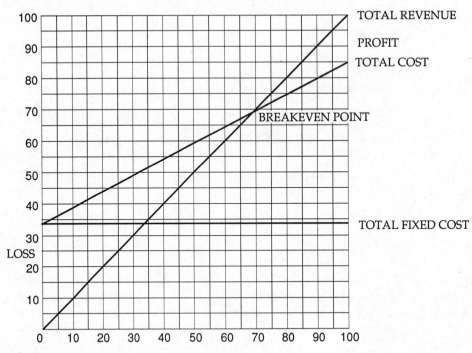

FIGURE 3-2   *Break-Even Graph*

Step Four

The point at which the two lines intersect represents the point at which revenue will equal costs; the *break-even point*.

Using the costs, revenues, and statistics from the feasibility chart in Table 3-6 the break-even point for this operation is calculated as follows:

Total fixed cost:	$336.656.25
Variable cost:	276,806.25
Total cost:	$613,462.50
Total revenue:	$748,125.00
Break-even point:	$680,000.00

Management now knows that the point at which revenue (sales) will equal the cost of doing business (direct and indirect costs) is $680,000. It will be at this point that the business is operating with costs in direct proportion to sales.

TABLE 3-6   Feasibility Chart

Total estimated operating costs for one year:	1,000,000.00
20% of total costs as calculated profit margin:	200,000.00
Total sales needed to cover costs and profit:	2,000,000.00

Restaurant Statistics
  Number of meal services: 2
  Anticipated seating turnover
    Lunch: 2.5
    Dinner: 1.5
  Seating Capacity: 250
  Number of days open annually: 307
  Total number of customers served daily: 1,000
  Adjusted average number of customers served daily,
    based on projected 75% occupancy: 750
  Total estimated number of customers served annually, based
    on 75% occupancy: 230,250
  Average lunch check: $6.00
    Daily lunch revenue: $469 \times 6.00 = \$2,814$
  Average dinner check: $15.50
    Daily dinner revenue: $281 \times 15.50 = \$4,355.50$
    Daily lunch and dinner revenue: $7,169.50
  Total estimated annual revenue: $2,201,036.50
  Total sales needed: $2,000,000.00

Customer volumes and other flexible factors will not necessarily affect the ability of the business to operate. The size of the profit margin will depend on additional sales, as shown on the break-even graph in Figure 3-2.

THE FEASIBILITY CHART

Before establishing the probability of profit it is necessary to outline all of the operational activities of a restaurant business. This can be done by using the format in Table 3-6. If a statement of income and expense has been developed, total amounts for operating costs can be entered on the feasibility chart. In this example, total operating costs have been estimated at $1,000,000.

Using a desired gross profit percentage of 20 percent, the calculated profit margin ($200,000) can be entered along with total sales needed, in order to cover both costs and profit goals.

Management now lists the known restaurant statistics and determines a realistic percentage of occupancy for a 1-year period. In an ongoing operation this percentage can be developed by referring to past sales history. In a new operation the percentage of occupancy can be estimated by analyzing the competition, location, and projected customer base demographics as discussed in Chapter 2.

The average check information is established for a new operation by using the current menu prices of the direct competition as a guideline. To find the average check amount that customers must spend in order to produce enough income to cover the costs and anticipated profits, divide the number of customers annually into the combined costs and desired profit totals.

Total annual costs	2,000,000
20 percent gross profit	<u>200,000</u>
Total:	2,200,000
Total customers annually	230,250

$$2,200,000 \div 230,250 = \$9.55 \text{ (average check)}.$$

In Figure 3-2 the average check would be $9.55. To determine the feasibility of expecting this average check to be a realistic figure, this amount must be compared to average checks for each meal service at the current direct competition. Customers cannot be expected to pay a much higher menu price for similar menu items than they are currently paying. Management can, however, increase average checks by promoting different areas of the menu, a marketing technique which is discussed in Chapter 12.

Once the average checks have been determined, daily meal service revenues can be multiplied by anticipated customer counts (ACC) to find daily revenue totals.

Average lunch check

Daily lunch revenue: × ACC = $ Lunch Period Revenue Total

Average dinner check

Daily dinner revenue: × ACC = $ Dinner Period Revenue Total.

Daily lunch and dinner revenue: $ Daily Revenue Total.

These figures are then multiplied by the number of days open to determine probable annual revenue figures. This figure is now compared to the total sales needed to cover both costs and profit.

Total estimated annual revenue: $

Total sales needed: $

The application of the break-even point can be used by management as an additional tool by which to judge feasibility:

Total estimated annual revenue: $

Total sales needed: $

Breakeven point: $

The feasibility of this operation is determined by whether or not enough sales can be generated to cover costs and desired profit. In this example, estimated sales exceed the amount needed by a specific amount. This indicates that if the income and expenses hold true and the figures used to calculate percentage of occupancy and average checks are accurate, this operation can produce a feasible profit for investors and owners. In addition, enough sales are possible above those needed to ensure a safety cushion against changes in the numbers in those areas which can directly affect revenues.

The decision as to whether a restaurant business is feasible is significantly different from the decision that profit is feasible. We know from the break-even point analysis that the business is feasible. Profit feasibility will depend on variable costs and revenue. Investors, owners, and managers will have to determine the acceptable profit goal before making a final decision to proceed with the business.

PROFIT GOALS

The profit goals owners and managers establish must be based on an accurate assessment of the feasibility of the operation and include an analysis of profit percentages from operations in the same category of restaurant operation. An example of this analysis information is seen in Table 3-7.

These dollar figures and percentages represent restaurant operations classified into lower (quick service), median (casual-family style), and upper (full service). Actual dollar profit is calculated per seat. Dollar profit is converted to the percentage of total sales that it represents. Comparing both the dollar profit and the percentage of each category yields the following conclusions:

TABLE 3-7   Restaurant Profit Percentages

	Lower	*Median*	*Upper*	*Lower*	*Median*	*Upper*
Restaurant profit	$52	$368	$945	1.4%	9.2%	19.4%

1. Full-service style generates more income per seat.

2. Casual-family style generates approximately one-third of the income per seat that full service does.

3. Quick-serve generates less dollar profit per seat but higher volume profit.

A quick overview of this analysis might lead to the assumption that full-service restaurants are more profitable than quick serve. This assumption is proved incorrect, however, when the percentages of profit are multiplied first by the actual profit dollar and then by the percentage of seat occupancy:

$$\text{Purchase} \times \% \text{ Profit} \quad = \text{Total Sales} \qquad = \% \text{ Seat Occupancy}$$

$$\$ \ 52 \times 1.4\% \ = \$ \ \ \ 728.00 \times 75\% = \$5,\!460.00$$
$$\$368 \times 9.2\% \ = \$ \ 3,\!385.60 \times 50\% = \$16,\!928.00$$
$$\$945 \times 19.4\% = \$18,\!333.00 \times 35\% = \$6,\!416.55$$

Guidelines for gross profit margins range widely from 4 percent for quick serve to 20 percent for ambitious full-service restaurants as industry standards. Where owners and managers choose to set their goals along this range totally depends on their interpretation of the many aspects of their operation that we have discussed here.

SUMMARY

In order to determine profit feasibility it is necessary to understand the total operation of any business completely. Every cost must be outlined, whether direct or indirect. To do this, management must go through the accounting exercise of developing a statement of income and expenses. For an ongoing business the figures for this statement are based on past operating history and known factors. For a business in the development stage figures are based on information gathered from similar restaurant operations available through associations such as the National Restaurant Association and accounting firms specializing in hospitality-related businesses.

The statement of income and expenses is the basis for the feasibility chart. Outlining the basic operational figures for the restaurant operation, the feasibility chart provides the means to calculate customer counts, average check, and revenue on an annual basis. These figures, when combined with total estimated annual costs, can be used to determine the profit feasibility of an operation.

The decision to carry out business plans is not always dependent on projected profitability. Calculating the break-even point can often help owners and managers establish the point at which a business will generate enough revenue to cover the costs of operations and production. The feasibility of a business operation's ability to function is based on owners' and managements' understanding of exactly where they stand in their business operations in relation to the break-even point and how long they are willing to maintain that level without making sizable profits.

Determining profit feasibility requires management to determine profit goals. It is essential that these goals be based on realistic interpretations of the capabilities and resources that the business has available to it if the overall financial objectives of the operation are to be met.

CHAPTER QUESTIONS

1. Explain the importance of determining the feasibility of an operation.

2. Identify the four aspects of cost, giving a short definition of each.

3. Outline the calculations necessary to determine an average check. Identify the major factors of an operation that must be known in order to make the calculation.

4. Discuss the various definitions that can be given to the term *profit* and how they apply to a restaurant operation.

5. Explain the difference between direct and indirect costs. Give operational examples of each.

6. How do prime costs differ from direct and indirect costs?

7. Outline the costs and levels of profit from revenue to net income.

8. Explain the term *break-even point*. Why is it important for management to know where this point is in their business operations?

9. What factors must be known to calculate a break-even point?

10. Discuss the difference between profit feasibility and business feasibility. What must management base their profit goals on?

ACTIVITIES

1. Using the breakdown of the restaurant industry dollar in Table 3-2, compare current percentages of cost with those of a currently operating restaurant.

2. Analyze the income statement for La Brasserie & La Belle to determine areas of cost that exceed industry norms. Using the format for the statement of income and expenses, try to assign the costs from the income statement into the categories of controllable expenses and occupational costs to get a more accurate accessment of the problem areas for this restaurant operation.

3. Determine a break-even point for La Brasserie and La Belle, using the figures offered in their statement of income and expense.

4 Menu Development

1. To understand the importance of a well-developed menu program to the success of a restaurant operation.

2. To be able to recognize how equipment and labor resources can affect a menu program.

3. To be able to develop a menu repertory for a variety of restaurant operations.

4. To be aware of the importance of establishing standards in the production of menu items.

CASE STUDY: AMERICAN CUISINE

The 1970s saw an explosion in the United States of an interest in food, for both home and restaurant consumption. American Cuisine broke loose as a new breed of American-born chefs entered the restaurant scene. These young chefs brought a driving interest in regional American cuisines and fresh native ingredients to the American public, who responded with overwhelming enthusiasm.

By the 1980s experiments at all levels of dining were adding Cajun spices to fast food chicken and juniper berries in raspberry purée to fine dining. The "age of material consumption," as the 1980s has often been called, created a level of consumer spending in the middle- and upper-class levels of American society that produced a startlingly successful decade for fine dining restaurants. What you ate became almost as important as where you ate.

The most important management area of any restaurant operation is the menu program. It is the major key to the profitability and success of an operation. The menu program involves every aspect of an operation from purchasing to accounting and directly affects the quality of both food products and guest service. It consists of all of the elements of the planning, production, and sales analysis of menu items, including the printed menu. In this chapter we will discuss how cuisine, equipment, labor, and operating standards affect the menu program.

Once the style of restaurant operation and average check have been determined, management can begin to plan the basic content of the menu so that the selection of kitchen equipment, facilities design and layout, pricing and cost controls, purchasing and distribution plans, labor requirements, training programs, and computer food service systems can take place.

An essential ingredient in the menu program is cuisine. *Cuisine* is the style or manner in which food is prepared and is usually associated with a specific nationality or region of a country. The style of restaurant operation determines a level of service and food preparation. Cuisine selection directly affects cooking methods and purchasing requirements for the food products needed.

Equipment availability determines the type of method that can be used for food preparation. The *cooking load,* or amount of food product that can be prepared at any one time, is determined by the variety of cooking equipment available in a kitchen.

Labor resources in a community are a major factor in the selection of both a style of restaurant operation and the sophistication of the preparation methods planned for menu items. As one of the major areas of concern facing restaurateurs in the 1990s, labor and food service skill level availability is of primary importance to a menu program.

The *menu repertory* is an index of all of the food items that could be prepared in a restaurant and serves as a major quality control factor in daily operations. The selection of food items is controlled by the availability of food product and the capacity of the restaurant to store it properly to ensure the least amount of waste through spoilage and theft.

Establishing standards becomes a management priority for an ongoing restaurant operation. Two basic standards relate to food quality and service. Standards of food quality include a variety of concerns regarding food purchasing, storage, distribution, preparation, presentation, and costing. Standards of service include wait service, customer service, and restaurant presentation, important aspects of a successful operation.

CUISINE

The diversity of cuisines offered in the American restaurant of the 1990s is a direct result of the food service customer of the 1980s. Their demand for more diversity in cuisine offerings at all levels of restaurant styles from quick service to fine dining resulted in the current range of menu offerings.

Combinations of food products and cooking methods in the 1980s were highly experimental as chefs competed for customer attention. One interesting combination of cuisines is this ingredient listing for a Dallas Antipasto from the Four Seasons Hotel in Dallas, Texas.

DALLAS ANTIPASTO

Dallas Mozzarella

Grilled Quail

Barbequed Lamb Rib

Smoked Shrimp

Black Bean Relish

Pickled Okra

Jalapeños stuffed with Goat Cheese

Food and Wine magazine in April 1988 said of the American public's passion for change, "Trends, especially food trends, seem to come and go with the speed of light, and culinary passions last about as long as a Hula-Hoop or Pet Rock." Six major cuisine and dining trends that dominated the 1980s have become firmly rooted in restaurant practices for the 1990s.

American Nouvelle Cuisine

What began as a return to regional native American foods and food combinations has become an eclectic combination of fresh food products, cultures, and cuisines. The layering of one cuisine on another is producing menu combinations which are at times as startling for their diversity as the variety of tastes and presentations that they produce. It is not uncommon to find a full service restaurant offering menu selections in all categories from appetizer to dessert that represent a gathering of a half dozen American and international cuisines. The menu in Figure 4-1 is representative of the restaurant serving basic "American cuisine" with an average check of approximately $25. The entrée selection

Farmhouse Favorites & Today's Fresh Fish

Appetizers

SHRIMP COCKTAIL 7.95

ESCARGOT IN MUSHROOM CAPS 6.95

FRIED ZUCCHINI 3.95

COMBINATION PLATTER 9.95
Escargot, crab stuffed mushrooms with zucchini, calamari and potato skins

CRAB STUFFED MUSHROOMS 7.95

FRIED CALAMARI 4.95

POTATO SKINS 5.95
With cucumber sauce

STEAK TARTARE 8.95
Traditional garni

Salads

GARDEN GREENS
With choice of dressing

CAESAR SALAD
With homemade croutons and dressing

BIBB LETTUCE
With crumbled blue cheese and vinaigrette dressing
A La Carte 2.95

Soups

FRENCH ONION SOUP

BEER CHEESE

A La Carte
Cup 2.45 Bowl 3.45

Entrees

All entrees are served with fresh baked cracked wheat bread, soup and salad and your choice of baked potato, rice pilaf, fresh vegetable, French fries or buttered noodles

Specialties Maison

LEMON VEAL 16.95
Prime veal medallions sauteed in butter, white wine, lemon and finished with a hint of demi-glace

FARMHOUSE CHICKEN 13.50
Grilled breast topped with smoked ham, jack cheese and mushroom bordelaise sauce

SHRIMP LINGUINI PACIFICA 16.95
Shrimp, snow peas, broccoli and peppers sauteed in extra virgin olive oil with garlic and basil-parsley clam sauce

CHICKEN MOUTARDE 13.95
Sauteed chicken breast with mushrooms blended with cream, brandy and dijon mustard

CALF'S LIVER 13.95
Pan seared and topped with sauteed onions

JUMBO SHRIMP STIR FRY 15.95
Stir fried in sesame oil with Oriental cut fresh vegetables and cashews, with our tangy Oriental sauce

SEAFOOD IMPERIAL 15.95
Crab, scallops and shrimp baked in a white wine and cheese sauce

SCAMPI CHARDONNAY 16.95
Jumbo shrimp sauteed in garlic herb butter with chardonnay wine

COLDWATER LOBSTER TAIL 22.95
A firm sweet coldwater tail broiled and served with drawn butter

CHICKEN STIR FRY 14.95
Stir fried in sesame oil with Oriental cut fresh vegetables and cashews, with our tangy Oriental sauce

---

PRIME RIB OF BEEF, AU JUS
Hand selected, three weeks aged midwest beef, slow roasted and served with au jus and creamed horseradish sauce

Regular Cut 14.95   Large Cut 17.95

FILET MIGNON   Petite Cut 14.95   Regular Cut 17.95
The tenderest steak in beefdom

STEAK RICKENBACKER 16.95
Aged New York steak seared with three color peppers, mushrooms and onions

PRIME TOP SIRLOIN STEAK 15.95
U.S.D.A. prime beef, center-cut steak three weeks aged. Our most flavorful cut

TERIYAKI TOP SIRLOIN 16.95
Our prime center-cut top charbroiled and basted with homemade teriyaki sauce

PEPPERCORN STEAK 16.95
Seared with fresh cracked black pepper, served over a sauce with brandy, cream, demi-glace and green peppercorns

NEW YORK STEAK 17.95
The king of steaks, well-aged and marbled

BROCHETTE OF BEEF 13.95
Charbroiled cubes of marinated filet mignon skewered with peppers, onions and mushrooms

Combinations

STEAK AND LOBSTER 29.95
A petite filet mignon paired with a coldwater lobster tail. Served with drawn butter

PRIME RIB AND SCAMPI 18.95
A lighter cut of prime with jumbo scampi style shrimp

STEAK AND SCAMPI 19.95
Petite filet mignon served with jumbo jumbo scampi style shrimp

PRIME RIB AND LOBSTER 28.95
A lighter cut of prime with a broiled coldwater lobster tail. Served with drawn butter

Beverages

FRESH BREWED CUSTOM BLEND COFFEE, DECAFFEINATED, OR TEA 1.25

*Sales tax will be added to the price of all food and beverage items.
We reserve the right to refuse service. Not responsible for lost or stolen articles.*

FIGURE 4-1 *Air Transport Command. Courtesy air Transport Command, Wilmington, Delaware.*

offers cuisine selections ranging from Italian to Oriental to French to traditional American.

Figure 4-1 offers casual dining with a menu that highlights a variety of cuisine offerings. The Marketplace menu (Figure 4-2) also concentrates on items which can serve as quick meals or offer a range of small food items that can be ordered to make up an entire meal. This combination is seen under the menu category California Platters, a pizza dough variation with toppings from a variety of cuisine themes.

Southwestern/Mexican Cuisine

The southwestern/Mexican cuisine trend began across most of the United States with basic food items such as tacos, burritos, and enchiladas. The restaurant chain Chili's has expanded these menu offerings to include a variety of frahitas and sizzling steak platters in a casual dining setting. Grilling over mesquite coals also became popular in the 1980s, and although the use of mesquite as a cooking fuel has tapered off, grilling as a cooking method has become increasingly popular. Many restaurants have developed grill kitchens that allow customers to watch the cooking activity around the grill top. Barbeque has burst out of the deep South and Southwest and has fostered popular rib houses such as the one offering the menu in Figure 4-3, which includes beef, lamb, and pork barbequed ribs.

Other menus combine barbeque cooking styles with traditional menu items such as prime rib of beef, pork chops, and chicken. The menu in Figure 4-4 offers a combination of southwestern and southern cuisine items.

HEARTFUL DINING

Called by many names, "healthly eating" has become a firmly established menu concept of the 1990s and one that should influence every menu. Originally this trend responded to customer needs for foods prepared with cooking methods that did not involve frying or use of heavy sauces and were low in sodium and free of preservatives. Today it has become a major concern of the American dining public. A 1990 survey of restaurant customers concluded, "Almost half (45.8%) of all consumers in the country are 'very concerned' with nutritious eating."[*] The pie graph in Figure 4-5 illustrates the level of consumer concern.

---

*Source: Restaurant & Institutions 1990 Taste of America Study.

Ribs

With salad, garlic toast, baked potato, lyonaise potatoes or fries.
ST. LOUIS STYLE RIBS — *Barbequed - delicious* 7.95
BARBEQUED CHICKEN & RIBS 8.95
RIBS AND BARBEQUED SCAMPI — *a house favorite* 8.95

RIB SAMPLES

CHICKEN FINGERS AND RIBS 5.25
ONION RINGS AND RIBS 4.50
FRIED CHEESE AND RIBS 4.95
RIBS & SKINS — *Skins can be Mexican, American or Pizza* 4.75
JUST RIBS 3.50

South of the Border

BEEF BURRITO 4.95
A flour tortilla stuffed with shredded beef, cheddar and jack cheese, topped with diced lettuce, tomato, and black olives. Garnished with sour cream and served with nacho chips.
CHICKEN BURRITO 4.95
Just like the beef burrito but with diced chicken.
SHRIMP BURRITO 5.95
Served like the other two with a generous portion of shrimp.
MEXICAN COMBO — *Any two of our 3 burritos* 6.95
TACO SALAD 4.50
A flour tortilla shell with lettuce, avocado, tomato, cheddar cheese, olives and beans topped with diced chicken and sour cream.

Rachel's Better Side

With baked potato, lyonaise potatoes or fries, salad and a croissant.
STEAK TERIYAKI — *Char-broiled and basted with our teriyaki glaze*..... 7.95
SIRLOIN STEAK — *With mushroom sauce* 7.95
FILET MIGNON SLICES — *Served on garlic toast* 9.95
SMOTHERED CHICKEN — *Chicken breast smothered with* 7.95
grilled peppers and onions topped with mozzarella cheese in a Poupon wine sauce.

With a cup of soup, salad, and croissant or garlic bread.
FETTUCINI ROMANO WITH SCAMPI 10.95
Scampies and broccoli in a garlic butter tossed with Romano cheese over a bed of homemade fettucini noodles.
SHRIMP SCAMPI — *Sauteed in garlic butter* 8.95
Served over wild rice (a house favorite).
SEAFOOD FETTUCINI 7.95
Scallops, baby shrimp, bacon and mushrooms, sauteed in a rich seafood sauce over a bed of spinach fettucini.
CHAR-BROILED CHICKEN 7.95
Two flavors — lemon or oriental with rice pilaf.

With baked potato, lyonaise potatoes or fries, soup, salad, and a croissant.
STEAK OSCAR — *8 oz. filet mignon topped with crab*,................ 13.95
bearnaise sauce, and asparagus spears.
NEW YORK STRIP — *14 oz. - a real meal* 13.95
FILET MIGNON — *8 oz. char-broiled to order* 11.95
PETITE FILET — *6 oz. char-broiled to order* 9.95
(For those who prefer a smaller filet.)
SEAFOOD COMBINATION — *Broiled and always fresh* 8.95

California Platters

Light and Fluffy Dough Laced with Parmesan Cheese with all your Favorite Toppings! .... mmmmm!

SHRIMP	MEXICAN	CAJUN	PALM SPRINGS	VEGGY	EARTH QUAKE
Shrimp Scallions, Garlic Butter, Feta Cheese, Topped with Monterey Jack	*Refried Beans, Guacamole, Olives, Jalapeno Peppers, with Monterey Jack*	*Our Spicy Cajun Greens Smothered with Monterey Jack Cheese.*	*Scallions, Artichoke Hearts and Monterey Jack Cheese.*	*Broccoli, Onions, Tomatoes, Feta Cheese and Monterey Jack.*	*Onions, Mushrooms, Poupon Mustard Ground Beef, and Colby Cheese.*
5.50	5.25	5.25	4.95	4.95	4.95

California Platter Samplers		
Any Half Platter with your choice of the following:	RIBS............5.95 FRIED CHEESE . 4.10 ONION RINGS......3.95 ONION LOAF 3.95	POTATO SKINS .... 4.75 *(Mexican, American or Pizza)* CHICKEN FINGERS 5.25

Her Sweet Side

CHEESECAKE — *Topped with cherries or strawberries* 1.95
HOT FUDGE OR CHOCOLATE SUNDAE.................... 1.75
BUTTERSCOTCH SUNDAE 1.75
RAINBOW SHERBET.................................... 1.75
MUDD PIE — *Coffee ice cream in a chocolate cookie crust* 1.95
topped with hot fudge, whipped cream and chopped walnuts.

FIGURE 4-2 *Marketplace Restaurant. Courtesy Marketplace Restaurant, Erie, Pennsylvania.*

FIGURE 4-3 *Rib It Menu. Courtesy Rib It Restaurants, Media, Pennsylvania.*

61

BEGINNIN'S (Cold)

Our Famous Crab Claws 4.95

Oyster Shooters–Oysters served in a shot glass with pepper vodka 1.95 each

Fresh Shucked Oysters, half shell 1/2 doz. 4.95

Peel 'n' Eat Shrimp with cocktail sauce* 4.50

Spicy Peel 'n' Eat Shrimp* 4.75

*we peel – $1 extra

BEGINNIN'S (Hot)

Peel 'n' Eat Garlic Shrimp* 4.95

Peel 'n' Eat – Hot 'n' Spicy Shrimp from Hell* 4.95

Peel 'n' Eat BBQ Shrimp* 4.95

Baked Oysters Blue Bayou 5.95

Aunt Hattie's Voodoo Chicken Wings 4.25

Mayberry BBQ Sampler– Selection of Our Famous BBQ for 4 or More Persons per person 3.95

Deep-Fried Soft-Shell Crab with Cajun Tartar Sauce 5.25

BBQ Potato Skins 4.75

Dixie-Fried Chicken Fingers with BBQ Dip 4.95

*we peel – $1 extra

SOUPS 'N' GREENS

Sweet Corn and Ham Chowder 2.25

Delta Fish Gumbo 2.95

Po'k Salad–Annie's Mixed Greens 2.50

Memphis Blues BBQ Salad– BBQ Chicken, Oranges, Almonds, Lettuce, and a Poppyseed Dressing– Enough for a Whole Meal 4.25

SIDES

Corn Bread .95

Giant Stuffed Baked Potato Sour Cream, Cheddar, Butter and Chives 1.95 With BBQ Pork or Chicken 2.75

Co' Slaw .95

Billy's Smashed Potatoes 1.50

Homemade French Fries 1.50

BBQ Baked Beans 1.50

Hush Puppies 1.00

Corn on the Cob .95

Collard Greens 1.50

Buster's Red Beans 'n' Rice 1.50

Potato Salad 1.50

MEALS (5-STAR)

BUSTER'S GIANT TEXAS BBQ PRIME RIB With Razorback BBQ Onions, French Fries or Baked Potato 10.95 Tuesday Nights Only!

FLOYD'S FAVORITE BBQ PORK CHOPS Slo-Smoked Then Grilled, Served with Baked Beans and Co' Slaw 7.95

SPIT-ROASTED HALF CHICKEN With Fire-Roasted Vegetables and Potatoes 6.95

ALL-AMERICAN CHICKEN POT PIE Made by Buster Himself! Only 7.95

SMOKED BBQ (Slow)

North Carolina Style Pulled Pork 8.25

Slab of Memphis Style Ribs Half order 7.95 Full order 12.95

BBQ 1/2 Chicken 6.95

Rib and Pulled Pork Combo 9.95

Brisket and Rib Combo 9.25

Slo-Smoked Texas Brisket Platter 7.95

BBQ Rib and Chicken Combo 8.50

BBQ Sampler – Ribs, Pork, and Brisket 9.95

BBQ Beans, Corn Bread and Co' Slaw Accompany All BBQ Platters
Your Choice of Regular, Sweet, Hot BBQ Sauce or Spiced Vinegar

BROTHER BOBBY'S SEAFOOD BASKETS

All of our seafood is fried in cholesterol free Canola Oil

Fried Clams 7.95

Fried Oysters 7.95

Fried Shrimp 8.95

Fried Catfish 7.95

Fried Schrod 7.95

Fried Scallops 7.95

Combo Basket 8.95
Shrimp, Clams, Catfish and Scallops

Baskets Include Hush Puppies, French Fries and Co'Slaw

FIGURE 4-4 Buster's American Barbeque. Courtesy Buster's American Barbecue, Saugus, Massachusetts.

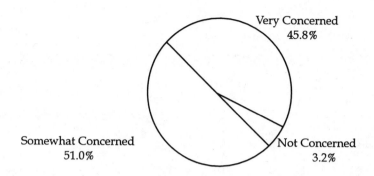

FIGURE 4-5 *Concern with Nutritious Eating.*

The variety of salad item selections offered in the dinner and luncheon menus in Figure 4-6 is a direct management response to customer needs. These menus are from a Guest Quarters Hotel dining room, which caters to a heavy business clientele for luncheon and weekday evenings and a local social clientele for weekends.

As discussed in Chapter 2, area hospitals and restaurant associations have been joining together to offer healthy eating programs to the general public, responding to a wide variety of medical as well as health concerns of the rapidly growing senior citizen population in the United States.

QUICK MEALS

A definite change in eating patterns, called "quick meals," has evolved. This trend is appearing both in the daily meal pattern for individuals and in the way in which menu items are selected from a menu to make up a meal.

The traditional pattern of three major meals a day is changing to five or six small meals, or quick bites, consumed in the following general time pattern throughout the day:

7:00 a.m.: Light breakfast

10:30 a.m.: Midmorning snack

2:00 p.m.: Light lunch

5:30 p.m.: Small meal

9:00 p.m.: Late evening snack

The major characteristic of food items for small meals is a reduction in the portion size of the main item and a change in the selection of the surrounding

Appetizers

Spiced Smoked Salmon
orange cranberry sauce
$8.25

Asparagus L'Dente
raspberry vinaigrette
$5.95

Asparagus Louisienne
warm cajun hollandaise
$5.95

Chester County Mushrooms
clam stuffing topped with blend of cheeses
$6.50

Lobster Tail "Vert Pre"
dill, watercress and parsley mayonnaise
$12.50

Ale Battered Shrimp
warm honey pepper sauce
$6.95

Snails in Puff Pastry
garlic lemon butter
$5.95

Shrimp Cocktail
Gulf Jumbo Shrimp with zesty cocktail sauce
$8.25

Soups

Seasonal Soup
prepared daily by our chef
$2.95

Baked French Onion Soup
A blend of Spanish, sweet and Bermuda onions, baked with Provolone and Swiss cheeses
$4.50

Seafood Bisque
Crabmeat and lobster blended with sherry
$3.95

Salads

Bibb Lettuce Brazilla
Hearts of Palm, Sauce Banana
$5.25

Caesar Salad
The traditional
$3.95

Seafood Salad Louie
Lumpcrab crab and lobster salad with Louie dressing
$12.95

Salad Fromaggio
Sweet Gorgonzola with sliced tomato and Balsamic vinegar
$3.95

The Grille Salad
A delightful mixture of Radicchio, Belgian Endive, Boston Bibb and Chesterbrook Vinaigrette Dressing
$3.95

Welcome To The
Grille at Chesterbrook

For your dining pleasure, we are proud to offer a new and exciting concept. Whether you are looking for a leisurely lunch, or one that fits a hectic schedule, the Grille at Chesterbrook can accommodate both. Choose from the a la carte menu offering popular luncheon favorites or our special buffet.

The Grille Buffet ... $10.50
Our express buffet! Featuring soup of the day, salad bar, pasta and fresh shrimp, stir-fry, entree, vegetable, carving station and dessert bar

Salad and Dessert Bar ... $7.75
Featuring soup of the day, assorted cold salads with fresh and peel shrimp and our complete dessert bar

The Dessert Bar ... $3.95
Sumptuous display of our fresh baked cakes and pies

Soups / Appetizers / Salads

Chef Selection of Seasonal Soup ... $2.95
Prepared daily by our Chef

Baked French Onion Soup ... $4.50
A blend of Spanish, sweet and Bermuda onions, with baked Provolone and Swiss cheese

Seafood Bisque ... $3.75
Crabmeat and lobster blended with sherry

Steak & Caesar ... $7.25
The traditional salad with Julienne Sirloin Strips

Taco Salad ... $5.75
A delightful blend of special meats, cheese and greens on an edible shell

Cobb Salad ... $7.25
Romaine gently tossed with chicken, avocado and bacon strips with special cobb dressing

Tossed Salad ... $2.50
Mixed greens, tomatoes, cucumbers and sliced mushrooms

Chesterbrook Salad ... $8.25
Cajun seafood salad

Cold Poached Salmon ... $10.50
Cucumber dill sauce

Fresh Fruit Salad (Seasonal) ... $6.95
Fresh sliced fruit with your choice of cottage cheese or sorbet

FIGURE 4-6 *Guest Quarters Menus. Courtesy Guest Quarters Hotel, Great Valley, Pennsylvania.*

items such as heavy starches and sauces. Food manufacturers are responding to consumer needs on the supermarket level by providing a wide variety of preportioned and preprepared small meals that can be microwaved.

On the restaurant level, "quick bites" involve choosing two or three appetizers, soups, and/or salads to make up the major portion of the meal rather than the traditional appetizer with main course and surrounding items. Menu items are often shared by diners, making the meal an entertainment function. Table 4-1 is an example of a menu selection for two customers from Paolo's menu in Figure 4-7, showing the variety of tastes, textures, and flavors that can be achieved with this quick bites style of menu item selection. Paolo's menu concentrates on Italian cuisine items cooked in a wood burning oven or on an open grill. Restaurant managers have found that this trend in menu selection often produces the same check or a higher average check than the traditional format.

Equipment Capacity

Ongoing restaurants have equipment which must either be incorporated into food preparation methods or replaced with more functional pieces. Before making any menu selections a complete evaluation of current equipment and its capabilities should be made. The format in Figure 4-8 outlines the basic equipment currently in place in an existing kitchen. Management must now look at the food preparation methods most commonly applied to the production of menu items in the style and level of cuisine that they have selected. An evaluation of what equipment will be needed in addition to that already in place will help management to determine the feasibility of any changes in the current menu offerings.

TABLE 4-1   Quick Meal Menu Selection

Diner One	Diner Two
Minestrone soup	Mussels marinara
Fried calamari	Carpaccio Milanese
Roman chicken	Ravioli
Caesar salad	Paolo's salad
Chocolate mousse torte	Kiwi lime sorbet
Espresso	Cappuccino
Total check, $26.05*	Total check, $29.30*

*Does not include alcoholic beverages.
Paolo's Menu (Courtesy Paolo's Restaurant, Inner Harbour, Baltimore, Maryland).

Appetizers

ROMANO CRUSTED BREAST OF CHICKEN Marinated boneless breast of chicken gratinéed with romano cheese and fresh herbs. 5.95

MINESTRONE Fresh vegetables simmered in a rich veal and chicken broth. Touched with pesto. 3.95

FRIED CALAMARI Lightly seasoned calamari served with lemon and Paolo's marinara. 4.95

MUSSELS MARINARA Fresh cultivated mussels, garlic, white wine and a touch of marinara. 5.95

CARPACCIO MILANESE Shaved fresh sirloin served with romano cheese, calamata olives and homemade basil vinaigrette. 7.95

TORTELLINI Tomato and spinach pasta filled with pesto and gorgonzola, served with prosciutto, sun dried tomatoes, mushrooms and sauce rose. 5.95

FRESHLY FILLED RAVIOLI Ricotta, fontina and romano cheeses wrapped in fresh pasta. Served with a saute of smoked salmon, garden vegetables and chive butter sauce. 5.95

Pizza

SAVOR THE FLAVOR OF THE CITY'S FINEST WOOD BURNING PIZZA OVEN

FRESH MOZZARELLA AND FINE HERBS Paolo's classic red sauce, sun dried tomatoes and fresh plum tomatoes. 7.95

ITALIAN SAUSAGE Our classic red sauce, quattro formaggi, roasted red peppers, calamata olives and Italian sausage. 8.95

WHITE PIZZA Roasted red peppers, roasted garlic, fresh herbs and quattro formaggi. 6.95

PAOLO'S Smoked salmon, quattro formaggi, roasted red peppers and fresh herbs. 8.95

PIZZA ANGELO Topped with Italian sausage, pepperoni, mushrooms, quattro formaggi and Paolo's red sauce. 8.95

GRILLED CHICKEN Crusted pizza dough brushed with pesto, topped with oak grilled chicken, roasted red peppers and goat's cheese. 8.95

YOURS! Pick three items from our Chef's selection of traditional and innovative ingredients to create your own pizza! 8.95

PAOLO'S CALZONE Our crusty pizza dough wrapped around a hearty filling of Italian sausage, goat's cheese and fresh spinach. 8.95

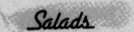

Salads

PAOLO'S SALAD Romaine, radicchio and arugula, tossed with a raspberry champagne vinaigrette, gorgonzola cheese, calamata olives, plum tomatoes, and freshly toasted pine nuts. 2.95

CAESAR SALAD A small plate offering of a wonderful classic. 2.25

FIGURE 4-7 *Paolo's Menu. Courtesy Paolo's Restaurant, Baltimore, Maryland.*

EQUIPMENT EVALUATION CHART

MENU ITEM   *COOKING METHOD*   *EQUIPMENT NEED*

_____

_____

_____

_____

_____

_____

_____

_____

_____

_____

_____

_____

_____

KITCHEN EQUIPMENT IN PLACE   *ADDITIONAL EQUIPMENT NEEDS*

_____

_____

_____

_____

_____

_____

_____

_____

_____

FIGURE 4-8   *Equipment Evaluation Chart. Source: Menu for Profit P.*

TABLE 4-2 Precut Yield/Use Chart

Item	Prod. No.	Pack	Guar. Shelf Life	Yield	Conversion Bulk/Precut	Uses	Approx. Serv. Per Case
Carrot sticks			14 days	100%	50 lb. jumbo carrots	School menu item Salad bar item Catering Dips	Rand.: 880 stks
Random pack	33	4/5 lb bags per carton			0.50 1 case case = 4/5 lb. random		
Precision pack	31	4/4.5 lb trays per carton			0.53 1 Case Case = precis.	Portion control	Prec.: 460 stks
Shredded carrots	30	4/5 lb bags per carton	14 days	100%	0.47 Case = 1 case carrot and raisin salad	Salad bar item Baking ingredient	64 Cups

Product	Code	Pack / Cut Size	Shelf Life	Yield	Conversion	Uses	Count
Julienne carrots	82	4/5 lb bags per carton Cut Size: 1/8" × 1/8" × 1-1/2"-2"	14 Days	100%	0.49 Case = 1 case	Side of plate garnish Stir fry Salads	60 Cups
Celery sticks	51	4/5 lb bags per carton	14 days	100%	0.83 Case = 1 case 6.5 lb	School menu item Salad bars	560 Stks
	52	6/5 lb bags per carton				Catering Bloody Marys Dips	840 Stks
Broccoli florettes		4/3 lb bags per carton	14 Days	100%	22 lb 18 bunches 1.3 Case = 1 Case 4/3 lb. Flor.	Salad Bar Stir fry	880 Flor.
		3/3 lb bags per carton			1.0 Case = 1 case 3/3 lb flor.	Dips Baked potato topping	660 Flor.

Source: Bud of California from Dole.

Labor needs are as important to equipment selection as food preparation. The skill levels of available food production employees in your community often determine the type of preparation equipment that is needed. The amount of preprepared product that is incorporated into purchasing specifications will also help to reduce equipment needs. For example, a buffalo chopper, or spinning bowl food cutter, can in one minute process six heads of cabbage or six pounds of celery or five pounds of onions. The equipment requires kitchen space of 33 by 24 inches. Processed produce will need to be washed, trimmed, and cut to size for chopping and slicing. Kitchen staff will need to be able to prepare produce with a minimum of waste and a maximum of product left for processing.

The alternative is a wide variety of high-quality precut and sliced vegetables, which are packaged without additives, have a good shelf life, and are ready for immediate use in a wide variety of recipes. Table 4-2 features a breakdown of information on precut celery, broccoli, and carrots. The chart indicates yield at 100 percent and a guaranteed shelf life of 14 days for all products. The conversion column compares the amount of bulk product that was used to make a case of precut product. Carrots are available in stick form, shredded, or julienne cut. These products provide management with food cost and labor cost savings, mimimizing waste and labor time for preparation. In addition, portion standards for these products are much more controllable.

Equipment can also offer management the ability to develop menu items using product that is high in both food cost and prepreparation labor costs. An excellent example of this is shrimp. Regardless of the size, shrimp needs to be preprepared by deveining and often shelling. Individual handling of shrimp breaks down the product and is labor-intensive. The alternative is to use a shrimp peeling and deveining machine, which is cost-effective when 500 pounds of shrimp a week are put into production. The comparison of machine production rates versus hand peeling in Table 4-3 shows the obvious advantages of prepreparation by machine.

Using the peeling and deveining machine allows management to purchase at bulk prices when buying large quantities of shrimp and take advantage of fluctuating prices on various sizes of shrimp. Menu items can be developed to offer a variety of shrimp recipes, as illustrated by the menu in Figure 4-9. A total of ten menu items on this page offer some form of shrimp as an ingredient.

LABOR CAPACITY

The capacity of labor to produce the menu items selected for a restaurant menu is a major management concern. Without the professional culinary skills to

TABLE 4-3 Shrimp Production Rate by Pounds per Hour

Shrimp Count (Number per Pound)	Pounds per Hour
16/20	210–275
36/42	100–120
51/60	70–85
Shrimp Production Rate by Hand for Skilled Worker	
43/50	1 lb per hour
Time per shrimp	1 ¼ shrimp per minute
Labor cost based on $5.50 per hour rate	11 cents per shrimp

prepare and produce menu items management is forced to select items which can be prepared with a maximum amount of preprepared food products. The cooking methods required for these menu items must also utilize equipment such as microwave and convection ovens and fryalators.

In many cases a skilled chef is available, but the remainder of the kitchen crew has little or no training. In this situation management must select menu items and ingredients that allow the chef to concentrate on those aspects of preparation and presentation that create an important menu item. Effective planning for this labor situation can result in a menu which blends uncomplicated listings with recipes that can become signature items, highlighting the experienced chef to the benefit of the restaurant.

THE MENU REPERTORY

As stated earlier, the menu repertory is an index of all of the food items that could be prepared in a restaurant and serves as a major quantity control factor in daily operations. In each category any item that the restaurant can prepare is listed. Additional recipe and cost card files are created to merge with this listing so that management can select menu items at any time that have been evaluated as to their potential success in both customer satisfaction and profitability. These items are chosen on the basis of a selection process outlined in the following list:

Menu repertory selection outline

  A. General item selection

  B. Problem identification

  C. Repertory item selection

  D. Final menu selection

"SHRIMP HAPPENS"

BROILED ROCK SHRIMP 10.99
broiled and served with hot drawn butter
...for the real rock shrimp lover, a full pound **13.99**
HOUDINI'S GREAT SCAMPINI 11.99
Gulf shrimp, sauteed in sweet butter, fresh garlic and herbs
... it disappears before your eyes
SHRIMP-SHRIMP 12.79
broiled rock shrimp, along with jumbo fried shrimp. A delectable duo!
ROCK SHRIMP and CRAB LEGS 13.99
over 1/2 lb. of Alaskan crab legs, along with a "school" of rock shrimp
served with hot drawn butter
ARNIE'S GOLF FRIED SHRIMP 11.99
beer battered, deep-fried and served with cocktail sauce - good for puttin'
BROILED ROCK SHRIMP and STEAK 13.99
Rock shrimp with chargrilled sirloin steak
STIR FRY SHRIMP 10.99
a sauté of shrimp, fresh mushrooms, snow peas, broccoli,
onions, peppers and water chestnuts splashed with soy- ahoy
DELICATELY SKEWERED SHRIMP
basted with Louisiana Licker sauce and chargrilled
full skewer with garlic toast **5.99**
two skewers, complete dinner **10.99**
ALFREDO'S SHRIMP ALFREDO 10.99
tender Gulf shrimp served in Alfredo's rich sauce atop his bed of linguine
Chardonnay and shrimp - to keep away the blimp!

CHICKEN

"OPEN" SESAME CHICKEN STIR-FRY 9.59
tender chicken breast, sautéed with broccoli,snow peas, mushrooms, sesame seed and soy
GARLIC ED'S CHICKEN GRILLE 8.99
Ed's garlic sauce is basted on a chargrilled boneless chicken breast
MARIA'S MARINATED CHICKEN 8.99
chargrilled chicken breast with South-of-the-Border flair ... muy bieuno!
Chicken and chablis will make you say oui!

U.S.D.A. BEEF STEAKS

NEW YORK STRIP special cut, well trimmed and charbroiled 10 oz. **14.99**
KANSAS CITY FILET MIGNON our finest cut **14.99**
CHICAGO SIRLOIN STEAK preferred top sirloin; our most savory steak 7 oz. **9.99**
U.S.A. STEAK and LOBSTER sweet and tender lobster with choice sirloin steak **19.99**
with 8 oz. filet mignon add **6.99**
ALASKAN CRAB and STEAK 14.99
chargrilled top sirloin steak with over 1/2 lb. of Alaskan crab legs
served with hot drawn butter
STEAK and ROCK SHRIMP 13.99
preferred top sirloin steak with a "school" of rock shrimp
with hot drawn butter
We've got Parducci's cabernet to go with steaks today!

SALAD PIER

a whole fishing pier full of salads ... **included with all entrées**
as MAIN ENTRÉE   **4.99**
with **wings & sandwiches** 2.59
salad pier & chowder 5.99
FRESH HOUSE SALAD 1.49

A 15% gratuity will be added to all tables of 8 or more

FIGURE 4-9   *Shrimp Menu. Source: Quaker State Lube Restaurant, Sharon, Pennsylvania.*

Step A is the listing of any food item that could be prepared in the restaurant under the guidelines of restaurant style, cuisine, equipment, and labor availability.

Step B in the repertory selection process identifies any items for which there may be a problem finding product, preparing, or serving. This category also requires that management evaluate the costs of the food products and the resulting menu price. If the price will be too high to balance with the other menu items, then it must be eliminated.

Step C chooses a number of menu items for each category which offers an interesting but compatible selection from which management can choose a final menu. Those items not listed on the printed menu now become available as menu specials and backup items to utilize seasonal ingredients and reconstitute leftover food. These items can also be test marketed through the menu "specials" program that registers customer reaction to menu items. Favorable reactions indicate that the items can be developed for the next series of menu changes.

Step D, the final menu selection, identifies a balance of menu items in each category of the menu that offers the customer a blend of texture, taste, and color. These items also fulfill the requirements of production, service, and cost that management must consider in order to operate a successful restaurant.

STANDARDS

Standards are the measures of performance that management sets in order to establish objectives that can help to achieve the overall goals of the business. In food production those standards are

1. Standard recipe card

2. Standard cost card

3. Standard purchasing specification

4. Standard portion

5. Standard plate presentation

If the established standards are met in all five areas, the objectives of high-quality food production and established food cost percentages will be attained. When any one or more of these standards are not met, the objectives for the entire menu program are jeopardized.

If, for example, the portion size of a menu item is arbitrarily changed in food production by the use of the wrong size serving spoon, food costs will increase.

This will now set off a chain reaction that results in an increased food cost percentage for this menu item. At the same time the kitchen is mistakenly using an 8-ounce boned chicken breast instead of a 6-ounce portion. As chicken is costing $0.14 per ounce, the food cost on this item has just increased by $0.28. The customers will also expect that menu item to be served with the same size chicken breast the next time that they order it. The server will have to overcome this expectation created by the improper portioning of food product. If this pattern continues, menu items will be presented inconsistently to the customer time after time, creating dissatisfaction. Food costs will be inconsistent, creating a problem for management in monitoring problem areas so that waste factors can be corrected and food costs brought back into line.

SUMMARY

A well-developed menu program offers management the ability to select the most effective menu items that can be consistently produced to meet the objectives of high-quality food production and customer service.

Restaurant management must determine a style of cuisine in order to begin selecting menu items. Equipment needs are determined by the style and level of cuisine as well as the preparation methods required for production. The availability of skilled labor often determines the type of food products that can be incorporated into the menu plan and the equipment needed for food production.

Established standards of operation are essential to a successful business. In food production, standards begin with a recipe card and continue through each production step to plate presentation. Meeting these standards will ensure a high quality of food production and an established food cost percentage.

QUESTIONS

1. Define the term *menu program*. List all of the components of a menu program.

2. How does the selection of a style of cuisine affect a menu program?

3. What cuisine trends are currently influencing the restaurant industry?

4. Why does labor play such an important role in the process of menu development?

5. How does labor availability determine the type of food products utilized in food production?

6. Define the term *menu repertory.*

7. Outline the four steps in the item selection process of a menu repertoire. Discuss why this process is important to the overall menu program.

8. What effect does equipment capacity have on the selection of menu items in an ongoing restaurant?

9. Define the term *standard* as it is discussed in this chapter.

10. Identify the two basic standards for a restaurant operation. List those additional standards that apply to food production.

ACTIVITIES

1. Select a style and level of cuisine to be incorporated into an ongoing restaurant operation. Using the Air Transport Command menu in Figure 4-1 as a guideline, identify a selection of menu items for each menu category. Document the elimination of items by the use of the menu repertoire selection outline in the chapter.

2. Choose one of the four cuisine trends discussed in this chapter. Identify a restaurant in your community that uses that cuisine in their operation. Interview the management to determine how successful the trend is within their menu program.

3. Investigate the validity of the customer percentage figures concerning nutritious eating offered in Figure 4-5. Draw up a questionnaire. Identify a location which would provide you with a large number of food customers to interview and conduct a market survey. Compare your results with the ones in the figure.

4. Select a restaurant in your community whose cuisine style and menu indicate that a large percentage of preprepared product should be used. Interview the chef (a) to find out exactly how much preprepared product is being used and (b) to identify areas where preprepared product could be incorporated to make the menu program more productive and profitable.

5 *Menu Pricing*

OBJECTIVES

1. To understand the importance of developing a policy of menu pricing that combines accurate costing procedures with marketing techniques.

2. To be able to calculate food cost percentages and menu prices using a number of food cost formulae and accounting methods.

3. To be aware of a variety of menu pricing methods and the ways in which they can be combined.

4. To be able to identify and discuss the four components of pricing.

CASE STUDY: MELROSE DINER

The Melrose Diner in Philadelphia, Pennsylvania, is located in the heart of the city's Italian district. It is a 24-hour operation with a wide base of customers whose needs vary according to the time of the day and the week. The Melrose Diner has a complete printed menu for each day of the week as well as late evening and breakfast menus. Daily specials are chosen according to the sales mix for that particular day of the week. Monday's and Tuesday's menus have items with lower selling prices on the specials menu. Friday's, Saturday's, and Sunday's menus have the highest prices of the week on the specials menu.

The pricing method used in this operation incorporates food cost percentage, contribution to profit, and prime cost method. The basic menu is priced according to food cost percentage and adjusted up or down from that point.

Management uses the food cost percentage method to establish a base foundation that they know will produce the profit goal. Onto this base they can now add other pricing methods to achieve a variety of results. For example, filet mignon is placed on the dinner menu as the high end item at a selling price of $12.50. This price is well below the price of $16.95 that is needed to meet the overall desired food cost percentage. It is on the menu solely for customer satisfaction. Approximately six portions are sold a day. The filet steak is also used on the breakfast menu as a small butterflied tenderloin steak, where it is again the high end item. There are other menu items such as chopped steak which produce a much higher profit and are priced below the desired food cost percentage to encourage volume sales.

Appetizer and dessert items run higher food costs than main menu items. Appetizers are priced at a 45 percent food cost and desserts at a 55 percent food cost. Management's theory is that the sales goals for the operation are based on main menu item sales. Appetizer and dessert sales are additions to this revenue and although they must be priced high enough to generate a profit, the selling price should encourage volume sales, not volume revenue.

Labor is a major consideration in the selection of menu items. A taco salad that was originally tested for menu use had excellent food cost and good customer response. However, the labor involved to prepare the variety of ingredients, fry the taco shell, and put the salad togeather was so high that the item was eliminated from the menu selection. Management found that they would have to add another person to the line to answer the production demand for the menu item.

Customer perceived value is often considered in menu pricing. A customer preference for stews has resulted in the development of four different stew bases: chicken, seafood, beef, and lamb. However, customers perceive stews as having a low value, regardless of the contents. In order to fulfill the customer demand for stews and still meet food cost percentage needs, different stews are coordinated with daily menus according to price. Chicken and beef are offered on the days which feature lower menu prices. Seafood and lamb appear on the higher-priced menus. The result is that customer needs are met at prices which simultaneously meet the costing needs of the operation.

Recognizing the individual needs of a restaurant operation is important in establishing the method of menu pricing to be used. This example of combined methods has evolved over a period of years with careful attention paid to the increases in food and labor cost as well as customer needs.

The daily menu selection from the Melrose Diner is an example of the application of three of the menu pricing methods discussed in this chapter (Figure 5-1). The methods and their applications are analyzed in the sections that follow.

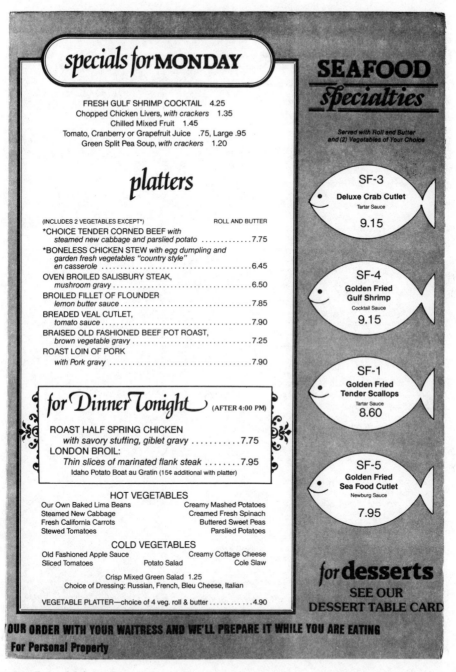

specials for MONDAY

FRESH GULF SHRIMP COCKTAIL 4.25
Chopped Chicken Livers, *with crackers* 1.35
Chilled Mixed Fruit 1.45
Tomato, Cranberry or Grapefruit Juice .75, Large .95
Green Split Pea Soup, *with crackers* 1.20

platters

(INCLUDES 2 VEGETABLES EXCEPT*)	ROLL AND BUTTER
*CHOICE TENDER CORNED BEEF *with* *steamed new cabbage and parslied potato*	7.75
*BONELESS CHICKEN STEW *with egg dumpling and* *garden fresh vegetables "country style"* *en casserole*	6.45
OVEN BROILED SALISBURY STEAK, *mushroom gravy*	6.50
BROILED FILLET OF FLOUNDER *lemon butter sauce*	7.85
BREADED VEAL CUTLET, *tomato sauce*	7.90
BRAISED OLD FASHIONED BEEF POT ROAST, *brown vegetable gravy*	7.25
ROAST LOIN OF PORK *with Pork gravy*	7.90

for Dinner Tonight (AFTER 4:00 PM)

ROAST HALF SPRING CHICKEN
with savory stuffing, giblet gravy 7.75
LONDON BROIL:
Thin slices of marinated flank steak 7.95
Idaho Potato Boat au Gratin (15¢ additional with platter)

HOT VEGETABLES

Our Own Baked Lima Beans   Creamy Mashed Potatoes
Steamed New Cabbage   Creamed Fresh Spinach
Fresh California Carrots   Buttered Sweet Peas
Stewed Tomatoes   Parslied Potatoes

COLD VEGETABLES

Old Fashioned Apple Sauce   Creamy Cottage Cheese
Sliced Tomatoes   Potato Salad   Cole Slaw

Crisp Mixed Green Salad 1.25
Choice of Dressing: Russian, French, Bleu Cheese, Italian

VEGETABLE PLATTER—choice of 4 veg. roll & butter 4.90

SEAFOOD Specialties

*Served with Roll and Butter
and (2) Vegetables of Your Choice*

SF-3
Deluxe Crab Cutlet
Tartar Sauce
9.15

SF-4
**Golden Fried
Gulf Shrimp**
Cocktail Sauce
9.15

SF-1
**Golden Fried
Tender Scallops**
Tartar Sauce
8.60

SF-5
**Golden Fried
Sea Food Cutlet**
Newburg Sauce
7.95

for desserts
SEE OUR
DESSERT TABLE CARD

...OUR ORDER WITH YOUR WAITRESS AND WE'LL PREPARE IT WHILE YOU ARE EATING

For Personal Property

FIGURE 5-1 *Melrose Diner Menus Day 1. Courtesy Melrose Diner, Philadelphia, Pennsylvania.*

specials for TUESDAY

FRESH GULF SHRIMP COCKTAIL 4.25
Chopped Chicken Livers, *with crackers* 1.35
Chilled Mixed Fruit 1.45
Tomato, Cranberry or Grapefruit Juice .75, Large .95
Swiss Potato Soup, *with crackers* 1.20

platters

(INCLUDES 2 VEGETABLES EXCEPT*)   ROLL AND BUTTER

*OVEN ROASTED FRESH PORK CHOPS (2) *with*
  sauerkraut and glazed fresh apple slices 7.60
BAKED SCROD *with Creole sauce* 7.15
BONELESS CHICKEN BREAST CUTLET
  PARMESAN *with tomato sauce* 7.25
FRIED SEAFOOD CUTLET, *newburg sauce* 7.95
*CHOW MEIN *with Chicken & Mushrooms on Bed of*
  Crisp Chinese Noodles with saffron rice
  en casserole 6.45
*OLD FASHION BEEF STEW *with garden*
  fresh vegetables en casserole 6.45
BRAISED TENDER SWISS STEAK,
  brown vegetable gravy 7.50
ROAST CHOICE SIRLOIN OF BEEF, *au jus* 7.25

for Dinner Tonight (AFTER 4:00 PM)

BAKED FILLET OF FLOUNDER *stuffed with*
  crabmeat imperial, tasty sauce 8.95
LONDON BROIL:
  Thin slices of marinated flank steak 7.95
ROAST SLICED TURKEY BREAST *with savory*
  stuffing, giblet gravy, cranberry sauce 7.15
  Idaho Potato Boat au Gratin (15¢ additional with platter)

HOT VEGETABLES

Glazed Fresh Apple Slices   Fresh Cauliflower au Gratin
Our Own Baked Beans   Creamy Mashed Potatoes
Buttered Sweet Peas   Mixed Vegetables
Sauerkraut   Buttered Rice

COLD VEGETABLES

Old Fashioned Apple Sauce   Creamy Cottage Cheese
Sliced Tomatoes   Potato Salad   Cole Slaw

Crisp Mixed Green Salad 1.25
Choice of Dressing: Russian, French, Bleu Cheese, Italian

VEGETABLE PLATTER—choice of 4 veg. roll & butter 4.90

SEAFOOD specialties

*Served with Roll and Butter
and (2) Vegetables of Your Choice*

SF-3
Deluxe Crab Cutlet
Tartar Sauce
9.15

SF-4
**Golden Fried
Gulf Shrimp**
Cocktail Sauce
9.15

SF-1
**Golden Fried
Tender Scallops**
Tartar Sauce
8.60

SF-5
**Golden Fried
Sea Food Cutlet**
Newburg Sauce
7.95

for desserts
**SEE OUR
DESSERT TABLE CARD**

UR ORDER WITH YOUR WAITRESS AND WE'LL PREPARE IT WHILE YOU ARE EATING
For Personal Property

FIGURE 5-1 (*continued*) *Melrose Diner Menus Day 2. Courtesy Melrose Diner, Philadelphia, Pennsylvania.*

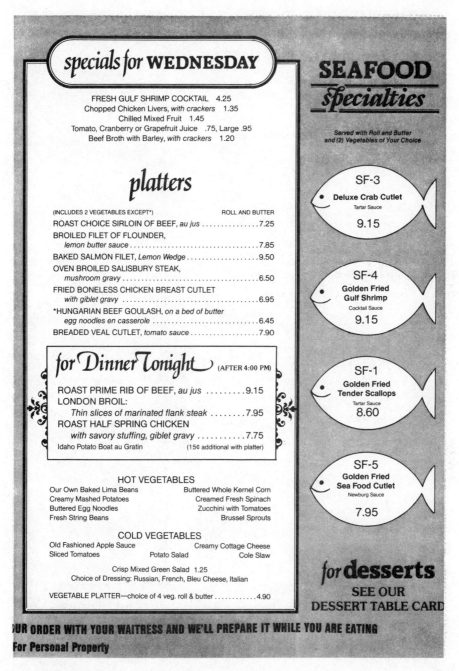

specials for WEDNESDAY

FRESH GULF SHRIMP COCKTAIL   4.25
Chopped Chicken Livers, *with crackers*   1.35
Chilled Mixed Fruit   1.45
Tomato, Cranberry or Grapefruit Juice   .75, Large .95
Beef Broth with Barley, *with crackers*   1.20

platters

(INCLUDES 2 VEGETABLES EXCEPT*)   ROLL AND BUTTER

ROAST CHOICE SIRLOIN OF BEEF, *au jus* 7.25
BROILED FILET OF FLOUNDER,
   lemon butter sauce 7.85
BAKED SALMON FILET, *Lemon Wedge* 9.50
OVEN BROILED SALISBURY STEAK,
   mushroom gravy 6.50
FRIED BONELESS CHICKEN BREAST CUTLET
   with giblet gravy 6.95
*HUNGARIAN BEEF GOULASH, *on a bed of butter
   egg noodles en casserole* 6.45
BREADED VEAL CUTLET, *tomato sauce* 7.90

for Dinner Tonight   (AFTER 4:00 PM)

ROAST PRIME RIB OF BEEF, *au jus* 9.15
LONDON BROIL:
   Thin slices of marinated flank steak 7.95
ROAST HALF SPRING CHICKEN
   with savory stuffing, giblet gravy 7.75
Idaho Potato Boat au Gratin   (15¢ additional with platter)

HOT VEGETABLES

Our Own Baked Lima Beans   Buttered Whole Kernel Corn
Creamy Mashed Potatoes   Creamed Fresh Spinach
Buttered Egg Noodles   Zucchini with Tomatoes
Fresh String Beans   Brussel Sprouts

COLD VEGETABLES

Old Fashioned Apple Sauce   Creamy Cottage Cheese
Sliced Tomatoes   Potato Salad   Cole Slaw

Crisp Mixed Green Salad 1.25
Choice of Dressing: Russian, French, Bleu Cheese, Italian

VEGETABLE PLATTER—choice of 4 veg. roll & butter 4.90

SEAFOOD Specialties

*Served with Roll and Butter
and (2) Vegetables of Your Choice*

SF-3
Deluxe Crab Cutlet
Tartar Sauce
9.15

SF-4
**Golden Fried
Gulf Shrimp**
Cocktail Sauce
9.15

SF-1
**Golden Fried
Tender Scallops**
Tartar Sauce
8.60

SF-5
**Golden Fried
Sea Food Cutlet**
Newburg Sauce
7.95

for desserts
SEE OUR
DESSERT TABLE CARD

...UR ORDER WITH YOUR WAITRESS AND WE'LL PREPARE IT WHILE YOU ARE EATING
For Personal Property

FIGURE 5-1 (*continued*)   *Melrose Diner Menus Day 3. Courtesy Melrose Diner, Philadelphia, Pennsylvania.*

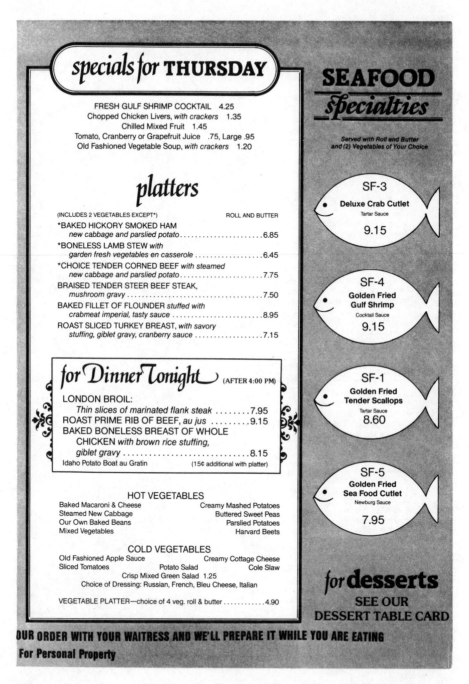

specials for THURSDAY

FRESH GULF SHRIMP COCKTAIL   4.25
Chopped Chicken Livers, *with crackers*   1.35
Chilled Mixed Fruit   1.45
Tomato, Cranberry or Grapefruit Juice   .75, Large .95
Old Fashioned Vegetable Soup, *with crackers*   1.20

platters

(INCLUDES 2 VEGETABLES EXCEPT*)   ROLL AND BUTTER

*BAKED HICKORY SMOKED HAM
    new cabbage and parslied potato 6.85
*BONELESS LAMB STEW *with*
    garden fresh vegetables en casserole 6.45
*CHOICE TENDER CORNED BEEF *with steamed*
    new cabbage and parslied potato 7.75
BRAISED TENDER STEER BEEF STEAK,
    mushroom gravy 7.50
BAKED FILLET OF FLOUNDER *stuffed with*
    crabmeat imperial, tasty sauce 8.95
ROAST SLICED TURKEY BREAST, *with savory*
    stuffing, giblet gravy, cranberry sauce 7.15

for Dinner Tonight   (AFTER 4:00 PM)

LONDON BROIL:
    Thin slices of marinated flank steak 7.95
ROAST PRIME RIB OF BEEF, *au jus* 9.15
BAKED BONELESS BREAST OF WHOLE
    CHICKEN *with brown rice stuffing,*
    giblet gravy 8.15
Idaho Potato Boat au Gratin   (15¢ additional with platter)

HOT VEGETABLES

Baked Macaroni & Cheese   Creamy Mashed Potatoes
Steamed New Cabbage   Buttered Sweet Peas
Our Own Baked Beans   Parslied Potatoes
Mixed Vegetables   Harvard Beets

COLD VEGETABLES

Old Fashioned Apple Sauce   Creamy Cottage Cheese
Sliced Tomatoes   Potato Salad   Cole Slaw
          Crisp Mixed Green Salad 1.25
    Choice of Dressing: Russian, French, Bleu Cheese, Italian

VEGETABLE PLATTER—choice of 4 veg. roll & butter 4.90

SEAFOOD Specialties

*Served with Roll and Butter
and (2) Vegetables of Your Choice*

SF-3
Deluxe Crab Cutlet
Tartar Sauce
9.15

SF-4
**Golden Fried
Gulf Shrimp**
Cocktail Sauce
9.15

SF-1
**Golden Fried
Tender Scallops**
Tartar Sauce
8.60

SF-5
**Golden Fried
Sea Food Cutlet**
Newburg Sauce
7.95

for desserts
SEE OUR
DESSERT TABLE CARD

OUR ORDER WITH YOUR WAITRESS AND WE'LL PREPARE IT WHILE YOU ARE EATING
For Personal Property

FIGURE 5-1 (continued)   *Melrose Diner Menus Day 4. Courtesy Melrose Diner, Philadelphia, Pennsylvania.*

Menu pricing is a management skill that requires a thorough knowledge of an operation's costs and profit goals and a realistic appraisal of what the market (customer) will bear in menu prices.

Profit in a restaurant operation is generated by revenues. Revenues are produced directly by sales of menu items. The statement of income and expense from La Brasserie and La Belle (Table 3-3) clearly illustrates that in order to generate a profit, the expense incurred in operating a restaurant must be less than the revenue generated by the sale of the menu items.

Menu item pricing is based on four pricing formats in which the menu may be presented. These four formats place menu items together in pricing groupings. Management must establish the general pricing format to be used to establish an average check.

Four components of pricing must be considered in order to achieve menu prices that accurately reflect the needs of the operation in order to produce a desired profit for owners and investors:

1. Food cost

2. Labor cost

3. Overhead cost

4. Profit

These four elements of the pricing structure together represent 100 percent of the selling price.

Pricing formulas are a series of mathematical equations that offer management a variety of options as to how they price menu items. Each formula represents a technique of food service accounting and reflects a different theory of restaurant management.

MENU PRICING

Menus have traditionally been priced according to four basic formats. The initial pricing structure was termed *à la carte,* or "from the carte," the bill of fare or listing of what was being served for the day. On an à la carte menu every item is priced separately. With the advent of hotels and hotel dining rooms, the *table d'hôte,* or "table of the hotel," system originated, offering one price for a full meal. From both of these pricing formats arose the need for variations, semi à la carte and semi table d'hôte. The four formats are the following:

1. *À la carte:* all menu items are priced separately.

2. *Semi à la carte*: menu items are priced separately in most areas of the menu and grouped together in others.

3. *Table d'hôte*: all menu items offered for a meal service are included in one price. This is often called *prix fixe*, French for "fixed price."

4. *Semi table d'hôte*: menu items are grouped under one price in some areas of the menu and priced separately in others.

Menu pricing requires the application of marketing as well as accounting skills. *Marketing skills* are those techniques that help to promote the sale of the item. *Accounting skills* are those methods used in establishing a cost for the product and determining the selling price on the basis of the desired food cost percentage.

Before determining a final menu price the following factors should be established:

1. What is the competition charging for the same or a similar menu item? Same or similar means that the same portion size that you are planning for is being served.

    When competitors' prices are reviewed, it is important that whoever is carrying out this function determine exactly what is included in the price. Does the price include an accompaniment such as french fries, lettuce and tomato, and/or vegetables? The price must be evaluated on the basis of the additional items. Portion sizes must also be approximately the same in order for a price comparison to have any value.

    For example; the competition is selling a fried shrimp item that includes six number 16 shrimp while your item includes six number 30 shrimp. The menu items are only similar, not the same: number 16 shrimp are more expensive than number 30s.

2. How important is this menu item to your menu mix? Is this item a loser or a leader? Will higher volume sales allow the menu price to be lower and still create a profit?

    The menu mix is the ranking of menu items in each category of the menu by sales volume and contribution to profit. A menu item with a high sales volume may not necessarily contribute to overall profit. On the contrary, it may be draining profit, depending on its food cost percentage and sales price. Items that both contribute to profit and have a high sales volume are called leaders. Items that have a low sales volume and do not contribute to profit are called losers. There are also items which have a high food cost and high volume sales as well as those which have a low food cost and low volume sales. Management will need to set a balance among these factors. The total menu is reviewed for the overall effectiveness of the pricing of all of the items. (Management will sometimes make a decision to run a high food cost item at a lower food cost percentage in order to attract customers, knowing that volume purchasing will help to reduce food cost and that customers will buy surrounding food and beverage items that will help to offset the loss of profit on the promotional item.)

3. What will the market (customer) bear as a price that reflects the perceived value of the item?

Determining what the market will bear is a marketing technique that requires evaluating the past history of menu item sales for an ongoing restaurant. It also requires an accurate analysis and assessment of the competition's volume sales of these items. Using a review of competitors' prices as a basis for pricing is only valid if all of the factors are known. In this case, it is necessary to have a substantial estimate of item sales.

Customer price acceptability is also based on the perceived value of the product to the customer. For example, prime rib of beef has a higher perceived value for many customers than does broiled breast of chicken. Stuffed lobster tail has a higher perceived value than poached filet of flounder. Management must take perceived value into consideration in setting menu prices. If the price is above or below customers' perceived value, then they will not buy it. In some cases, management is able to establish a menu price that will create more profit than the actual price in terms of food cost percentage. On other occasions, management will have to run a lower food cost percentage than desired in order to respond to customer demand and offer the menu item.

4. Is the menu price of this item compatible with the menu prices for other items in that menu category?

Pricing on the overall menu must keep within a certain dollar amount range in all categories. Entrée prices should be held to within an $8 to $10 range of least expensive to most expensive. When customers are offered too wide a range of menu prices, they are faced with a decision to buy in the lower or higher range of prices. The results are confusion and a tendency to select menu items in the lower price range. By limiting the range of prices, customers feel comfortable about buying at either end of the pricing scale.

An entrée selection with a pricing range from high to low of $8.00, beginning at $9.95 and ending at $16.95, is presented in Figure 5-2. An entrée selection with a pricing range of $10 is presented in Figure 5-3.

Pasta

PENNE BOLOGNESE   Quill shaped pasta with hand-milled Capri tomatoes in a spicy Italian meat sauce. 9.95

FETTUCCINE SMOKED SALMON   Fresh ribbon pasta tossed with smoked salmon in a light garlic cream sauce and topped with a touch of fresh salmon caviar. 9.95

ANGEL HAIR WITH SHRIMP AND SCALLOPS   Jumbo shrimp and Bay scallops sautéed in white wine, shallots and a herb butter sauce. 13.95

PENNE CON VODKA   Quill shaped pasta with prosciutto, red peppers, onions and mascarpone cheese tossed in a vodka rose sauce. 9.95

TORTELLINI ROSÉ   Filled with pesto and gorgonzola then sautéed with prosciutto, sun dried tomatoes, mushrooms and sauce rose. 9.95

DUCK SAUSAGE LASAGNA   Layers of tomato pasta filled with our homemade duck sausage, sun dried tomatoes, garlic roasted mushrooms and ricotta cheese. Served on a bed of creamy rosemary sauce. 13.50

FETTUCCINE CARBONARA   Gorgonzola, pancetta and fresh sage tossed in a garlic cream sauce with spinach and egg fettuccine. 9.95

LOBSTER CASSEROLE   Fresh lobster, wild mushrooms, carrots and ginger in a sauce rose topped with quattro formaggi. 15.95

RAVIOLI BOLOGNESE   Our fresh pasta is filled with a rich combination of Italian cheeses and served with Bolognese sauce and spinach agli olio. 10.95

GRILLED PEPPERED SIRLOIN   Sliced, oak wood grilled sirloin served on fettuccine tossed with pesto, roasted red peppers, grilled Bermuda onions and mushrooms. 13.95

MARINATED AND GRILLED BREAST OF CHICKEN   Oak wood grilled breast of chicken served with saffron linguine tossed with fresh pesto and plum tomatoes. 11.95

Oak Wood Grill

THESE SPECIALTIES ARE COOKED ON OUR OAK WOOD FIRED GRILL

WARM GRILLED CHICKEN SALAD   Served on a bed of seasonal greens with fresh mozzarella, plump ripe tomatoes and a walnut vinaigrette. 8.95

GARLIC FENNEL SAUSAGE   Grilled italian sausage served with red peppers and onions over saffron linguine with marinara sauce. 9.95

MIXED GRILL   Spicy Italian sausage and herb chicken are served with Chef's pasta and fresh vegetables. 10.95

BEEF TOURNEDOS GERARDA   Center cut tenderloin medallions prepared with a wild mushroom, pink peppercorn and Marsala wine sauce. 16.95

HERB GRILLED CHICKEN BREAST
Marinated with fresh rosemary, sage, extra virgin olive oil, lemon & Balsamic vinegar.
Served in its natural juices   12.95
Served with sun dried tomatoes, mushrooms and red peppers in a rosemary scented sauce. 13.95

NATURE WHITE VEAL
Ala Mozzarella   Tender oak grilled veal medallions layered with mozzarella, romano and our marinara sauce. 16.95
Anthony Style   Grilled with wild mushrooms and capers in a light lemon butter sauce. 16.95

GRILLED JUMBO SHRIMP   Marinated with fresh rosemary, sage, extra virgin olive oil, lemon and Balsamic vinegar. Served over saffron linguine tossed with fresh pesto and plum tomatoes. 15.95

FRESH SEAFOOD   The finest, freshest seafood the market has to offer each day.
Market Price

FIGURE 5-2   *Paolo's Entrée List. Courtesy Paolo's Restaurant, Baltimore, Maryland.*

Entrees

Shrimp Quixote $19.95
Spanish Rice & Saffron Sauce

Chicken Breast Chevré $14.75
Spinach, Wild Mushrooms, & Bacon in a Montrachet Sauce

Steamed Vegetables L'Dente $12.95

Maryland Style Crab Cakes $19.95
Fresh Lump Crabmeat on Pepper Coulis

Grille Specialties

Salmon, Swordfish or Mahi Mahi $17.50
Seasonal Variety of Fresh Chutneys

Filet Mignon $19.50
Sauce Beurre Rouge

Lamb Chops $19.95
Double Boned, Garlic Sauce

New York Strip Steak $18.95
Cafe D'Paris

Chicken Calypso $14.75
Blends of Exotic Spices & Fresh Vegetables in Orange Pernod

Sauteed Delicacies

Tri Seafood Medley $18.95
Trio of Salmon, Swordfish & Mahi Mahi
Chef's Special Sauces

Breast of Duckling Tahitienne $16.95
Raspberry Rum & Coconut Orange Sauces

Veal Chesterbrook $18.95
Fresh Asparagus Tips in a Light Curry Sauce

Wiener Schnitzel Hölstein $17.95
Vienna's Traditional Veal; Egg, Capers & Anchovies

All Entrees are Presented with our Chef's Selection of Fresh Vegetables or Mousses.

Desserts

A Premium Selection of Desserts & Cordials, Featuring
Ben & Jerry's Ice Cream, is the Perfect Ending to Your Dining Experience.

FIGURE 5-3 *Guest Quarters Entrée Menu.* *Courtesy Guest Quarters Hotel, Great Valley, Pennsylvania.*

Menu prices that are established must be valid for at least a 6-month period. Printing good-quality menus is expensive and requires that price changes be made as infrequently as possible. Menu prices must include a percentage to cover increased costs between menu printings. With this increased percentage menu items will at first generate a higher profit margin that will level off over the life of the printed page. An important management key is that the increased cost percentage factor is built into the pricing structure so that profits will not become losses by the time management is ready to reprint the menu.

MENU PRICING METHODS

Depending on management's theory of food costing and the style of the restaurant operation, a variety of methods can be applied for determining a selling price for menu items:

1. Food cost percentage method

2. Actual cost method

3. Prime cost method

4. Contribution to profit method

Food Cost Percentage Method

The *food cost percentage method* is based on the management theory that the cost of food used to produce the item represents an established percentage of the selling price. This method also allows management the flexibility to price menu items individually. Menu categories such as appetizers and desserts are often priced at a different food cost percentage than main course items.

In order to calculate the food cost percentage method, two out of three primary factors must be known for the menu item:

1. Cost of food

2. Selling price

3. Food cost percentage

When any two of these factors are known, one of three pricing formulas can be applied to calculate the third. These three formulas and their abbreviations are the following:

1. Food cost ÷ selling price = food cost %
$$FC \div SP = FC\%$$
2. Food cost ÷ food cost % = selling price
$$FC \div FC\% = SP$$
3. Selling price × food cost % = food cost
$$SP \times FC\% = FC$$

For example:

The menu item shrimp scampi has a selling price of $9.50 and a food cost of $3.40. The application of formula 1 produces a food cost percentage of 0.357, or 36 percent:

$$\text{(FC) \$3.40} \div \text{(SP) \$9.50} = \text{(FC\%) 36\%}$$

The menu item breast of chicken salad has a desired food cost percentage of 35 percent and a food cost of $3.50. The application of formula 2 yields a selling price of $10.00:

$$\text{(FC) \$3.50} \div \text{(FC\%) 35\%} = \text{(SP) \$10.00}$$

The menu item broiled crab cakes has a selling price of $16.95 and a desired food cost percentage of 30 percent. The application of formula 3 finds $5.08 available for food cost:

$$\text{(SP) \$16.95} \times \text{(FC\%) 30\%} = \text{(FC) \$5.08}$$

Menu items may need to be offered at a higher or lower food cost percentage in order to be made available as specials and promotional items. If the balance of the menu has been calculated to produce a predetermined food cost percentage, then the sales of items with a fluctuating food cost percentage should be averaged into the total costs.

The food cost percentage method has the advantage of being able to be calculated on a daily or even a per-food-service basis, if a computer food service system is used. Management can immediately spot food cost percentage variances in both individual items and total sales. Figure 5-4 is a computerized printout showing variances in food cost percentages for menu items.

Actual Cost Method

The actual cost method is applied to situations in which management has already established the selling price and needs to determine what is available for the cost of food ingredients.

The actual cost method establishes desired percentages of costs based on a profit goal. Desired revenues are calculated in terms of these figures. Table 5-1 outlines the actual cost method. In this example, the profit goal is set at 10 percent of total revenues. Overhead costs are preset to represent 20 percent of total revenues and labor cost at 30 percent.

Owners and investors have preestablished a profit goal of $250,000. If profit represents 10 percent of total revenues, then desired annual revenue becomes $2,500,000. Overhead and profit are calculated as $500,000 and $750,000, respectively, bringing the total of profit and costs to $1,450,000. When this figure is subtracted from total revenues, the balance available for food cost is $1,050,000. The result of the application of the food cost percentage formula Food Cost ÷ Sales = Food Cost % is a food cost percentage of 40 percent.

TABLE 5-1   Actual Cost Method

Estimated total food sales		$2,500,000
Profit goal		
10% Profit goal	250,000	
Estimated costs		
20% Overhead	500,000	
30% Labor Cost	750,000	
Total:	1,500,000	− 1,500,000
Available for food cost		$1,000,000

(FC) $1,550,000 ÷ (SP) $2,500,000 = 40%

The available food cost for each menu item is now calculated by applying the equation

Selling Price × Food Cost % = Food Cost

Restaurants that often need to apply this method of costing are chain operations such as Bennigan's, TGI Friday's, and Chili's. The pricing range for each menu category is established by the corporate office. Company management has already set a pricing policy that requires actual menu prices to fall within certain dollar figures.

For example; appetizer prices must be priced between $3.95 and $5.95. The menu prices are established on a regional basis and management must use these prices. Management, however, is also responsible for producing no more than a 40 percent food cost, regardless of problems with local distributors and price fluctuations. Management now applies the following calculations to each menu item to establish exactly how high the cost of food can be and still produce a 40 percent food cost.

Menu item	Menu price		FC%		Food cost
Caesar salad	$3.50	×	40%	=	$1.40
Broiled scallops	$10.75	×	40%	=	4.30
Chocolate mousse	$3.75	×	40%	=	1.50

Prime Cost Method

The *prime cost method* is applied to menu programs that use a large amount of preprepared food products as ingredients. As the availability and increasing costs of labor present greater concerns to restaurant operators, preprepared food items offer cost saving alternatives.

MENU ITEM FOOD COST REPORT   MICROS 4700 VERSION 3.00 SYSTEM   02-SEP-88 05:43 PM PAGE 1
RANGE 33–154   SYSTEM   C: PRIMARY DATABASE

EXAMINE   POSTED 92-Sep-88 05:28 pm   CURRENT RESET 0002 02-Sep-88 02:32 am TO-DATE RESET 0001 01-Sep-88 02:35 am

CURRENT AND TO-DATE TOTALS

Item	Description		Prep Cost	Sales Price	Qty Prep	Qty Sold	Qty Rtrn	Total Prep Cost	Total Sales	%Food Cost	%Yield
33	FRUIT SALAD	D	1.19	4.95	7	7	0	8.33	34.65	24.04	100.00
					33	32	1	39.27	158.40	24.79	96.97
35	HOUSE SALAD	D	1.02	4.50	16	16	0	16.32	72.00	22.67	100.00
					83	83	0	84.66	373.50	22.67	100.00
38	CAESAR SALAD		3.72	10.95	6	6	0	22.32	45.70	48.84	100.00
					28	28	0	104.16	286.60	36.34	100.00
39	SALAD NICOISE		1.34	4.95	2	2	0	2.68	9.90	27.07	100.00
					2	2	0	2.68	9.90	27.07	100.00
46	TURKEY CLUB		1.68	4.95	6	6	0	10.08	29.70	33.94	100.00
					15	15	0	25.20	74.25	33.94	100.00
48	HAM & SWISS		1.87	5.50	6	5	1	11.22	27.50	40.80	83.33
					14	13	1	26.18	71.50	36.62	92.86

FIGURE 5-4   *Micros Item Food Cost Report. Courtesy Micros Pos Systems Inc.*

TABLE 5-2 Prime Cost Calculation

Menu Item	Portion Size	Raw	Preprepared	Labor Time	Labor Cost
					Recipe/pp
Clam chowder	20	×	25 min	25 min	3.25/.17
Fried oysters	10	×	35 min	45 min	5.85/.13
Chicken salad	15	×	15 min	25 min	3.25/.22
Crab cakes	10	×	30 min	40 min	3.90/.52

TABLE 5-3 Prime Cost Pricing Method

Menu Item	Food Cost	+ Labor Cost	= Prime Cost × 2	= Menu Price
Clam chowder	0.24	0.17	0.41	0.82
Fried oysters	1.33	0.13	1.46	2.92
Chicken salad	1.12	0.22	1.34	2.68
Crab cakes	2.80	0.52	3.32	6.64

Food products that are preprepared in some form include in their costs the labor for that preproduction. As some portion of the labor cost required to complete the finished product is part of the cost of the food product, management should account for that cost in calculating the selling price. When 40 percent or more of food ingredients used in an operation fall into the category of preprepared, the prime cost method should be applied to achieve more accurate pricing.

Prime cost method management begins by identifying every item on the ingredient list as either raw or preprepared. The labor time is calculated for each item, whether raw or preprepared, from the initial use of the product to final production. On the basis of hourly wage the labor time is given a value that now becomes the direct labor cost. This, added to the food cost, is the prime cost as seen in Table 5-2.

To establish a selling price, now calculate a pricing factor. The pricing factor is determined by dividing the percentage of cost into 100. Direct labor costs for a raw food product are generally calculated at 10 percent of the selling price. An established 40 percent food cost and the 10 percent direct labor cost total 50 percent. The next step is to divide 100 by 0.50 to find a factor of 2. The factor is now multiplied by the prime cost to calculate a menu price.

Prime cost × factor = menu price

Table 5-3 illustrates the calculation of a selling price using this method.

CONTRIBUTION TO PROFIT

The *contribution to profit method* is based on the selection of menu prices according to what the customer will pay for an item and the contribution that the item sales will make to the gross profit of the operation.

Each menu item is evaluated according to customer acceptability and projected sales volume. The initial selling price for each menu item is based on a desired food cost percentage as in the chart in Table 5-4. The final selling price is determined by management's estimation of what the customer will perceive as an acceptable selling price for that item.

Example

1. An 8-ounce chicken breast stuffed with cheese and ham and surrounding items will have an actual food cost of $2.29. This item, when calculated at a 35 percent food cost, has a selling price of $6.54. Management feels that customers will accept a higher selling price of $9.25. At $9.25 the contribution to gross profit on this item is $6.96.

2. A 9-ounce slice of prime rib of beef with surrounding items has a food cost of $5.18 and a selling price of $12.95 with a 40 percent food cost. Management decides that they would like to encourage volume sales of prime ribs to create a promotional menu item to increase overall sales. Volume purchasing prices will also help to lower the food cost. The selling price is dropped to $8.65, which will produce a 60 percent food cost. The contribution to gross profit on this item is $3.47. Volume sales will, however, increase this amount. If the item were left at the higher sales price, there would be resistance to pricing, resulting in lower sales. Although the individual contribution to profit would be higher, the volume increase would not occur.

3. Ravioli crevette has a food cost of $4.55. Calculated at a 33 percent food cost, the selling price of this item is $13.67. Management feels that this is a selling price that customers will find acceptable and adjusts the menu price to $13.95. The contribution to gross profit on this item is $9.40.

Table 5-4   Contribution to Profit Method

Item	Food Cost	(FC%)	Selling Price	Menu Price (MP)	Contribution to Gross Profit (GP)
A	$2.29	35	$6.54	$9.25	$6.96
B	$5.18	40	$12.95	$8.95	$3.77
C	$4.55	33	$13.67	$13.95	$9.40

Combined Menu Pricing Methods

The four menu pricing methods discussed in this chapter can often be used in combination with one another depending on the type of food service operation and management's abilities to identify effective combinations and carry them out in daily operations.

A combination of menu pricing methods is effectively developed to achieve managements' specific profit objectives by the Melrose Diner in the case study at the beginning of this chapter. Of the four pricing methods discussed in this section only the actual cost method is not applied by the management of the Melrose Diner.

When profit goals and objectives are clearly stated and management is capable of effectively determining how to apply pricing methods to their operation, a combination of pricing methods can be successful.

MAINTAINING SUCCESSFUL PRICING

Establishing selling prices that effectively meet the needs of an operation takes careful research and planning. Achieving the goals that these prices are calculated to meet requires daily monitoring of fluctuating food costs and food cost percentages. Listening to customers daily becomes an important part of reacting to their needs and demands. The production sheet, sales mix, and menu reevaluation are control systems that keep management abreast of changes on a daily and a weekly basis. These control systems are discussed in detail in Chapter 8, "Food and Beverage Cost Control Systems."

SUMMARY

Menu pricing is a management skill that combines accurate pricing procedures with marketing techniques. The marketing techniques associated with menu pricing evaluate the competition's prices, analyze the sales mix, forecast customer responses to menu pricing, and balance overall pricing on the menu.

The four components of pricing—food cost, labor cost, overhead cost, and profit—together represent 100 percent of the selling price. Pricing formulas use food cost, labor cost, and profit to calculate food cost percentage and selling price.

Once either food cost, food cost percentage, or selling price is known, a number of pricing methods can be applied to establish selling prices. Four pricing methods are offered in this chapter as examples of different management techniques of menu pricing.

Selecting a pricing method to apply to a restaurant operation often results in a combination of different aspects of two or three pricing methods. Each restaurant has goals of gross profit and customer satisfaction that must be reached through its selling prices.

CHAPTER QUESTIONS

1. How do profits relate to revenue?

2. What two major factors must management be aware of to develop effective menu pricing?

3. Define the term *pricing formula.*

4. Explain the four basic formats for menu pricing, giving a short explanation of the use of each.

5. Discuss the difference between marketing skills and accounting skills as it relates to establishing selling prices.

6. Why should menu pricing keep within an established range of dollar amounts?

7. Identify the three pricing formulas offered in this chapter.

8. List the four menu pricing methods discussed in this chapter and give a short definition of each.

9. Identify the four components of pricing, giving a short definition of each. Discuss how they relate to the total selling price.

10. What are some of the techniques and controls that management must apply to daily operations to maintain successful menu pricing?

ACTIVITIES

1. Survey the restaurants in your community and identify four separate operations that apply one of the four basic pricing formats.

2. Select one of the marketing techniques discussed in this chapter. Review and critique a restaurant menu as to how effectively management has applied the selected marketing technique to their menu pricing.

3. Using a restaurant menu from an operating restaurant, analyze the pricing structure and identify the different menu pricing methods that have been applied.

4. Calculate the following unknowns by applying one of the three pricing formulas offered in this chapter.

a. The selling price is $10.50 and the food cost percentage is 35 percent.

   The food cost is

   Formula

b. The food cost percentage is 30 percent and the food cost is $2.75.

   The selling price is

   Formula

c. The food cost is $3.25 and the selling price is $9.95.

   The food cost percentage is

   Formula

d. The selling price is $16.75 and the food cost percentage is 27 percent.

   The unknown factor is

   The correct answer is

e. The food cost percentage is 40 percent and the food cost is $15.50.

   The unknown factor is

   The correct answer is

f. The selling price is $12.75 and the food cost is $3.35.

   The unknown factor is

   The correct answer is

6 Beverage Management

OBJECTIVES

1. To understand the contribution of beverage sales to the profit margin of a restaurant operation.

2. To be aware of standards and procedures that are required for effective beverage management.

3. To be able to discuss beverage purchasing techniques.

4. To understand the importance of establishing and maintaining a safe drinking and driving policy.

CASE STUDY: RESTAURANT ALCOHOL CONSUMPTION

Alcohol consumption in the United States fell dramatically in the 1980s (Table 6-1). Awareness of the effects of alcohol on general health caused many consumers to reevaluate their drinking patterns and switch from liquor to wine or nonalcoholic beverages. National campaigns against drunk driving have also reduced alcohol consumption outside the home. Evidence of these drinking trends can be seen in a report issued by the National Restaurant Association: "The volume of all alcoholic beverages consumed in table service restaurants increased 17% between 1987 and 1990 with beer leading the way with a 30% increase over a three year period. The volume of wine consumed over the same period rose 6%, while liquor experienced a 10% decline in volume consumed."

TABLE 6-1   Percent Change in Alcohol Consumption at Tableservice Restaurants

Period	Beer	Wine	Liquor	Total
1980 to 1982	−13%	−6%	−18%	−12%
1982 to 1984	−16%	2%	2%	− 9%
1984 to 1986	14%	−3%	− 7%	6%
1986 to 1987	7%	−2%	12%	− 3%
1987 to 1990	30%	6%	−10%	17%
1980 to 1990	1%	− 3%	−21%	−3%

Source: National Restaurant Association; NFO Research, Inc., Share of Intake Panel. *Washington Weekly*, August 1991.

Beverage management, when incorporated into a restaurant operation, can have a major impact on the overall profitability of the business. Properly managed, beverage services can provide excellent opportunities for increasing revenues and profits by enhancing food sales, entertainment, and private functions. The inclusion of beverages in dining, entertainment, and catering packages can increase customers' perceived value of the package price.

The relationship of food sales to beverage sales is called the *sales mix*. Menu item sales may contribute 60 percent of sales to gross profit, while beverage sales can contribute as much as 80 percent, depending on the pricing strategy management selects.

Effective beverage management requires that strict standards and procedures be established to ensure that controls are in place to

1. Assist management in controlling beverage revenues

2. Ensure total quality management of beverage service

3. Reach beverage sales and cost percentage objectives

4. Control beverage theft

5. Meet state and local liquor service requirements

6. Maintain a responsible policy regarding safe drinking and driving concerns

Beverages are classified into two major types: alcoholic and nonalcoholic. Alcoholic beverages are generally identified as beer, wine, and liquor (distilled spirits) such as vodka, gin, and whisky. Alcohol in spirits is the result of the fermentation of the ingredients used to produce different types of spirits. Proof is the amount of alcohol found in a distilled spirit. In the United States, proof is identified by doubling the percentage of alcohol by volume: 80 proof scotch, for example, is 40 percent alcohol by volume.

Nonalcoholic beverage consumption has increased significantly in restaurant patron popularity since the 1970s. As consumer awareness of both health concerns and the effects of drunk driving has increased, restaurant patrons are seeking alternatives to traditional alcoholic beverages. Perceptive managers are responding by introducing nonalcoholic beverage selections on all sections of their menus. Management has also found that nonalcoholic beverages can be more profitable than alcohol-based beverages.

CONTROLLING BEVERAGE REVENUES

Three major areas of beverage management control beverage revenues: purchasing, bar setup, and service. Revenue control ensures that the greatest amount of revenue possible is generated by the sale of each individual drink or bottle of wine. Effective control begins with purchasing guidelines laid down by management.

The opportunities for beverage purchasing by restaurants in the United States are often limited by controls imposed by the individual states. In states such as Maine, New Hampshire, and Pennsylvania, liquor stores are state-owned and offer a limited discount to restaurant operators. Liquor and wine distributors are also restricted in the type of promotions and discounts that they can offer managers in these states. Liquor must be purchased through the state system, and importing alcohol from other states can result in the loss of an operator's liquor license. In nonregulatory states, management is free to negotiate prices.

INVENTORY TURNOVER

The most effective method of beverage purchasing is inventory turnover. Management determines the appropriate inventory of beverages needed for established periods of time. By determining how often beverage inventory is turned over during the year, ideal times for quantity purchases of certain types of beverages can be identified and inventory stocked at par levels, keeping operating costs as low as possible. Although beverages are regarded as nonperishable and large-quantity purchases may seem attractive, it may take months to sell off the inventory while monies could have been used more effectively in other areas of the restaurant operation.

Inventory turnover is determined by dividing the cost of all beverages sold for the month by the value of the inventory.

Inventory value is determined by adding the value of inventory at the beginning of the month to the value of inventory at the close of the same month and dividing it by 2.

$$\text{Inventory value} = \frac{\text{beginning inventory} + \text{closing inventory}}{2}$$

$$\text{Inventory turnover} = \frac{\text{cost of monthly beverage sales}}{\text{inventory value}}$$

Cost of monthly sales = Total costs − Closing inventory

Total costs   = Beginning inventory + Cost of monthly purchases

For example, if the beverage inventory at the beginning of the month is $6,300, the closing inventory for the same month is $2,300, and the cost of sales is $10,500, inventory turnover is determined as 1.5, or one and a half times per month, or approximately every 20 days.

$$\text{Inventory value} = \frac{6300 + 7500}{2} = 6,900$$

$$\text{Inventory turnover} = \frac{10,500}{6900} = 1.5$$

By using charts such as Figure 6-1 management can determine what types of alcohol are being consumed at different times of the year, planning purchases and promotions around these dates. Figure 6-1 offers management the opportunity to record beverage sales by category on a monthly basis, identifying periods of the year where advance quantity purchases would be justified.

Future purchases can now be planned in terms of these consumption percentages.

BAR SETUP

Depending on the variety of services offered by a restaurant, three types of bars can be used:

1. *Front bar:* a direct customer service area located in the public area of the restaurant

2. *Service bar:* generally located adjacent to the kitchen for table servers' use

Period	Beer	Wine	Liquor	Nonalcoholic	Total
January					
February					
March					
April					
May					
June					
July					
August					
September					
October					
November					
December					
Total Annual Sales					
Total Annual %					

FIGURE 6-1   *Annual Beverage Sales Category Chart. Courtesy National Restaurant Association.*

3. *Special-function bars*: generally portable and setup for private parties and group functions

Each type of bar will have an established par stock regardless of its application within the restaurant. *Par stock* is the established selection of beverages that will be served from the bar and the exact quantities of each that should be on hand at all times. This includes alcoholic and nonalcoholic beverages as well as mixers. Management must establish the par stock as an important function of controlling beverage revenue.

It is generally the responsibility of the bartender closing down a front or service bar to submit a requisition for beverages needed to establish bar stock for the next service. The opening bartender is responsible for picking up requisitioned beverages and bringing the bar stock up to par. An example of a bar requisition is seen in Figure 6-2.

By involving both bartenders and a formal requisition, a cross-check is established to ensure theft control. Special function bartenders are issued a bar stock based on the established needs of the party. If drinks are sold on a cash basis, then the amount of beverages returned at the end of the function must tally with the amount consumed.

BAR SERVICE

Bar service involves a number of functions which can affect beverage revenue. Pouring, mixing drinks, customer relations, and cash transactions are the major functions that have established standards and must be strictly supervised.

Beverage service involves the pouring and mixing of drinks. In order to establish both quality control and revenue control management must determine a pouring policy and provide drink recipes for mixed drinks.

Pouring is the way in which alcoholic beverages are measured from the bottle. *Free pour* allows the bartender to pour from the bottle without an established measure. Often a pouring cap is placed in the bottle top to indicate measure by ounce. *Measure pour* requires the bartender to use an established measuring

Bar Requisition   Date _____
Location

Item	Unit #	Unit Cost	Total Cost

Requisitioned by:
Issued by:
Received by:

Date: _____

FIGURE 6-2 *Bar Requisition*

glass, depending on the amount of beverage to be mixed. Most alcoholic beverages are measured by the ounce and indicated as 1, 1.5, or 2 ounces.

Effective pouring control involves using the established glass size for each drink. Drinks which are poured straight on ice use 5-ounce rock glasses. Drinks which require added ice and nonalcoholic mix use 8-ounce highball glasses. Specialty drinks can use a wide variety of glass sizes. Wine glasses are designated by shape and size according to the type of wine being served. Figure 6-3 shows the wide variety of bar glassware used in most full service bars.

Creating high-quality mixed drinks consistently requires standard beverage recipes. Beverage recipes, like standard food preparation recipes, should list a yield, ingredients, and complete directions and designate the style of glassware. An example of a beverage recipe for a single serving is seen in Figure 6-4.

The beverage recipe in Figure 6-4 is for a mixed beverage yielding 12 portions. This preparation method is effective for bars where seasonal or specialty drinks are popular. Premixed beverages are time-saving and ensure consistent quality.

BEVERAGE SALES OBJECTIVES AND COST PERCENTAGES

The ratio of food sales and beverage sales to total sales is called the *food and beverage mix*. This is often expressed as a 60/40 or 70/30 relationship: of 100

FIGURE 6-3　*Bar Service Glassware. Courtesy Libby Glass Inc.*

Beverage Name: Bloody Mary   *Portion Size: 8 oz.*
Yield: 12

Ingredients	Measure	Directions
Vodka	18 oz.	
*Mix ingredients		
Tomato Juice.	36 oz.	Mix Tomato juice, lemon juice,
Lemon Juice.	2 tsp.	worcestershire sauce, and tabasco
Worcestershire sauce	6 tsp.	sauce. Add salt and pepper to
Tabasco Sauce.	1 TB	taste. Add vodka and stir to
Pepper & Salt	to taste	blend. Refrigerate.

To serve, shake container to blend mix and vodka. Pour over ice. Garnish with lemon or lime wedges or a celery stalk.

Glass: Tall Highball or Specialty glass—10 oz.
*Bloody Mary Mix may be substituted.

FIGURE 6-4   *Beverage Recipe Format*

percent of sales, 60 percent is from food sales and 40 percent from beverage sales, or 70 percent from food sales and 30 percent from beverage sales. Most full service restaurants try to maintain food and beverage mixes within these percentage ranges. When the beverage percentage is equal to or greater than the food percentage, the operation is more a bar or lounge than a restaurant.

Food and beverage sales also reflect different contributions to gross profit. The ratio of food costs to selling prices is always higher than that of beverage costs to selling prices; as a result, beverage sales contribute more to gross profit than food sales.

Establishing a beverage pricing method for a restaurant operation is often dependent on the available staff to keep purchase and sales records on the implementation of a computer food service system. Beverage prices must be more standardized than menu item prices. Neither customer nor servers want to think about the difference in price between a gin and a vodka martini. Prices must be standardized to a certain extent within brand label levels. This is often done by classifying alcoholic beverages as well brands, call brands, and premium brands. For example, in Table 6-2, a listing of the brands of scotch available on a front bar of a full-service restaurant offers a wide variety of qualities. These qualities are designated by P (premium), C (call), and (W) well.

Prices are established for all drinks within a classification. This encourages customers to buy up into a higher-quality price range. Creating an established price within the pricing groups causes an averaging of beverage prices. This

Table 6-2   Beverage Price Classification

Scotch	Unit Size	Par Stock	Drink Selling Price
Glenfiddich (P)	25.6	1	$4.50
Glenlivet (P)	25.6	2	$4.50
Chivas Regal (P)	25.6	2	$4.50
Johnny Walker Red (C)	25.6	4	$3.75
Johnny Walker Black (C)	25.6	4	$3.75
Dewars White Label (C)	25.6	3	$3.75
J & B (C)	750 ml	4	$3.75
King William (W)	750 ml	5	$2.50

averaging does not generally create problems in maintaining beverage cost percentages as bottle prices per group are usually within an acceptable range.

BEVERAGE PRICING METHOD

The most common method used to price beverages for restaurant operations is based on management's desired beverage cost percentage. For example, $18.50 is the purchase price paid for a fifth (750 milliliters) of bourbon. The desired beverage cost is 50 percent. Beverage sales must total $37.00 for the contents of the bottle. If 1.5 ounces is the standard measure for the bar, then this 750-milliliters bottle will yield 16 drinks. If drinks are sold at $2.00 each, total revenue for the bottle will be $37.00.

Bottle Cost		*Beverage Cost*		*Bottle Selling Price*
$18.50	÷	50%	=	$37.00
Bottle Size		*Drink Portion Measure*		*Yield*
25 ounce	÷	1.5 ounce	=	16 drinks
Bottle Selling Price		*Yield*		*Price per drink selling price*
$37.00	÷	16	=	$2.00

By averaging drink prices in this category at $2.50 per drink, management can absorb a range of bottle prices from $18.50 to $22.00 and maintain an overall 50 percent beverage percentage.

Beverage prices must also reflect the costs of mixes and condiments in order to control overall costs effectively. For example, a martini uses 1.5 ounces of gin and 0.5 ounce of vermouth for a total of 2 ounces. To this is added the cost of bar olives or onions, totaling approximatly 12 cents. In terms of the 50 percent desired cost percentage this cost must be valued at 24 cents. If the beverage cost for 2 ounces is based on $15.00 for a 750-milliliter bottle of call gin, then pricing must be calculated as follows:

Bottle Cost		Beverage Cost %		Bottle Selling Price
$15.00	÷	30%	=	$45.00
Bottle Size		Drink Portion Measure		Yield
(750 milliliter) 25 ounce÷		2 Ounces	=	16 Drinks
Bottle Selling Price		Yield		Per Drink Selling Price
$45.00	÷	16	=	$3.00 ($2.81)
Per Drink Selling Price		Food Cost		Adjusted Selling Price
$2.00	+	0.50	=	$2.50

Management can make significant changes in the contribution of beverage sales to gross profit by decreasing the beverage cost percentage to 25 or 30 percent.

Bottle Cost		Beverage Cost%		Bottle Selling Price
$15.00	÷	50%	=	$30.00
Bottle Size		Drink Portion Measure		Yield
(750 milliliter) 25 ounce	÷	2 ounces	=	16 Drinks
Bottle Selling Price		Yield		Per Drink Selling Price
$30.00	÷	16	=	$1.90
Per Drink Selling Price		Food Cost		Adjusted Selling Price
$2.00	+	0.50	=	$2.50

CONTROL OF BEVERAGE THEFT

Controlling theft in alcoholic beverage serving settings presents unique problems for management. The opportunity for theft presents itself in many ways in both front and service bars. Computer food service management systems have greatly reduced theft as drink sales are recorded and purchasing requisitions reconciled against sales. However, opportunities still exist in the service segment of beverage functions.

The most common methods of beverage theft are the following:

1. *Overcharging customers*: Employees ring up a lesser amount on the register and pocket the difference between the price paid by the customer and recorded on the sales tape.

2. *Undercharging customers:* Employees overpour drinks or substitute premium for call brands.

3. *Overpouring:* Employees pour a measure greater than specified for a drink.

4. *Underpouring:* This is often done to cover up overpouring and may be accomplished by either overpouring or charging for house brands and giving call brands.

5. *Diluting bottle contents:* Employees pour off a certain amount of the bottle contents and replace it with water. Charges for drinks made from the poured-off liquor are not entered into the register.

6. *Charging for drinks not served:* Employees resell a drink previously paid for by a customer who did not receive it.

Bar situations that involve a limited number of employees are often subject to many of these practices. Larger operations where supervision can be provided can limit opportunities for theft.

CUSTOMER RELATIONS

Customer relations in beverage service is primarily aimed at establishing and maintaining a responsible policy regarding safe drinking and driving. Increased public awareness of the number of deaths and severity of injuries caused by alcohol-related automobile accidents has resulted in increased pressure to limit the consumption of alcohol in public facilities. As community organizations such as MADD (Mothers against Drunk Driving) and SADD (Students against Drunk Driving) have lobbied at national and state levels, involvement by national organizations and state governments has increased. The Division of Alcohol and Drug Educational Services in the state of Maine issued the table tent in Figure 6-5 to all Maine restaurant owners for the holiday season in 1991.

At the same time, the Maine Restaurant Association distributed the decal in Figure 6-6 for use throughout the year.

As the pressure from social and business organizations and costs of liquor liability insurance increase, food service operators are initiating training programs and policies. The primary training programs focus on helping servers of alcoholic beverages to identify customers who are on the verge of becoming intoxicated and handling those customers who are visibly so.

TIPS (Training for Intervention Procedures) is a nationally recognized program that has been effectively training servers for a number of years:

Your
Holiday Spirit
is not
what you
drink

Division of Alcohol
and Drug Education Services
Stevens School Complex
State House Station #57
Augusta, Maine 04333
207-289-6500

Maine Department of Education
Bureau of Instruction

FIGURE 6-5   *Table Tent. Courtesy Maine Department of Public Transportation.*

"TIPS" training helps participants to understand how what's going on inside the body influences what's going on outside. Alcohol serving professionals develop a "sixth sense" about customers who are on the verge of becoming intoxicated. TIPS training shows them how to use intuition as a spring board to action, teaching strategies that can stop an overdrinking problem before it has a chance to start. TIPS demonstrates how the total environment of a bar or restaurant can help customers drink more responsibly. TIPS training can be especially valuable, teaching participants how to prevent a customer from becoming intoxicated with firmness, concern and respect.

The Educational Foundation of the National Restaurant Association released SERVESAFE—Responsible Alcohol Service in 1991. This program trains managers in formal seminars or home-study plans. By combining written materials with video programs, managers learn how to train servers in their own operations. Managers are also encouraged to promote premium brands and the sale of food with drinks. A certificate of completion is awarded when managers and servers pass a written exam.

To identify server training programs and establish customer relations policies effectively, management should research state and local liquor laws. Insur-

FIGURE 6-6   *Drunk Driving Decal. Courtesy Maine Department of Public Transportation.*

ance companies should also be consulted regarding state and local laws which must be adhered to in order to meet safety and handicapped standards and regulations more effectively. Liability is decreased as safety awareness increases among both management and servers.

SUMMARY

Effective beverage management can provide increased revenues and profits to a restaurant operation. Strict standards and procedures must, however, be established in order to ensure control in beverage revenues, high-quality beverage service management, beverage cost percentage objectives, and beverage theft and meet the requirements of state and local liquor service agencies. Determining inventory turnover is a method of beverage purchasing that identifies the rate at which beverages should be ordered to ensure that par stock levels are maintained. Management can also determine which types of beverages are more popular during which periods of the year.

Standards of bar service include beverage measurement, standard glassware selection, and standard beverage recipes. By establishing and implementing these three standards, total beverage quality management can be ensured.

Beverage pricing methods must take into account cost percentage objectives. Prices should be based on the amount of revenue that management wants to see earn from the sale of the bottle contents. Prices must be classified into three primary segments: well brands, call brands, and premium brands. Prices must also reflect the cost of mixed drink ingredients as well as straight liquor.

Customer relations in beverage service require management to establish a safe drinking and driving program. Server training programs help servers to identify customers who are becoming intoxicated and handle those who have become so. Reacting to this significant area of public awareness creates community goodwill while decreasing liability through safety awareness.

CHAPTER QUESTIONS

1. Discuss the impact of nonalcoholic beverage consumption on overall beverage management.

2. Identify the three major areas of beverage management that control beverage revenues.

3. What is the most effective management method for beverage purchasing? How does this method help management to maintain par stock consistently?

4. How is inventory turnover determined?

5. If the beginning inventory is $3,500, the closing inventory $2,500, and the cost of sales $3,500, what is the inventory turnover?

6. Identify and define the three types of bar setups.

7. Define the term *par stock.*

8. If the bottle cost of a 750-milliliter bottle is $17.25 and the desired beverage cost percentage is 30 percent, what is the bottle selling price? For a measure of 1.5 ounces, what is the per drink price for this bottle?

9. If a mixed drink has a bottle selling price of $45.00, a drink yield of 16 drinks, and a nonalcoholic ingredient cost of 0.45, what is the per-drink selling price with a 25 percent desired beverage cost percentage?

10. Identify the three classifications of pricing segments for beverage pricing.

ACTIVITIES

1. Using the beverage sales category chart in Figure 6-1 as a guideline, interview a local restaurant manager to determine periods of the year when

beverage consumption of each category is highest. Identify the heaviest consumption periods for each beverage category.

2. Create a beverage recipe pamphlet, following the suggested format in this chapter. Develop recipes for both alcoholic and nonalcoholic beverages.

3. Identify four common methods of beverage theft. Offer ways in which you would reduce employee thefts of these types.

4. Identify the safe drinking and driving programs in your community. Gather public awareness materials and present them, giving an analysis of the specific objectives of each.

7 *Purchasing and Distribution*

OBJECTIVES

1. To understand the goals of management in the establishment and direction of a purchasing program.

2. To be able to outline the four basic requirements for an accurate and effective specification.

3. To be able to define the difference between an order giver and a purchaser.

4. To be aware of technological advances in both communication and food manufacturing technology that can reduce costs and waste as well as increase product quality.

CASE STUDY: PREPREPARED, PREPORTIONED FOOD PRODUCTS
INCREASE PROFITS

As costs of raw food products and labor for food preparation increase, management is faced with the dilemma of shrinking profit margins. Production waste costs add to the drain on the bottom line, creating three primary concerns for profitable purchasing: food cost, labor cost, and waste cost.

High-quality food products that present management with solutions to rising costs can make a significant contribution to profits. The product page featured in Figure 7-1 presents three preprepared veal items available in a variety of portion sizes. The base product can be garnished and sauced according to the recipe specifications of the individual menu item.

BREADED VEAL PATTIE
Code #225200
Selected lean milk-fed veal, chopped and fortified with a minimum of soy protein, then breaded with our single-dip process—*more veal in each meal.* A pattie with flavor you'll be proud to serve. Also available Unbreaded (Code #219200).
Breaded: Deep fry, pan fry, oven bake.
Unbreaded: Grill, pan fry, oven bake.
Portion Sizes: 3, 4, 5 and 6 oz.

VEAL STEAK
Code #216100
Selected milk-fed veal, sinew and gristle removed, chopped and formed into portions. Delicate in color—rich in flavor. *The steak to use when pure veal is a must.* Perfect for use in Health Care facilities. Also available Breaded (Code #222100).
Breaded: Deep fry, pan fry, oven bake.
Unbreaded: Grill, pan fry, oven bake.
Portion Sizes: 3, 4, 5 and 6 oz.

BREADED VEAL CORDON BLEU
Code #230100
Twin pure veal steaks concealing a delicious center of sliced *Canadian bacon and real Swiss cheese*—lightly coated with our crispy single-dip breading. Formerly a time-consuming specialty item—now a quick and delicious entree.
Deep fry, pan fry, oven bake.
Portion Size: 6 oz.

FIGURE 7-1   *Veal Specialty Product Page. Courtesy Colonial Beef Products.*

The veal pattie and veal steak are available breaded and unbreaded in portion sizes of 3, 4, 5, and 6 ounces, making them highly adaptable to appetizer, snack, luncheon, and dinner menus. Both items can be prepared by a variety of cooking methods, further increasing menu development flexibility.

The 6-ounce preportioned veal cordon bleu is a menu item that is generally labor-intensive. Preproduction costs are included in the purchase price but are significantly lower than if the item were fully prepared in a restaurant kitchen. Quality sources such as the manufacturer of this product offer purchasing agents and chefs the opportunity to combine preportioned, preprepared food product with raw product to produce a menu item which is high in quality, low in labor cost, and free of production waste.

Management's goals in establishing and directing a purchasing program are to:

1. Purchase the quality of product available necessary to fulfill the production requirement at a price that will meet established food cost guidelines

2. Minimize the cost of waste realized by loss of product in receiving, storage, or distribution

These goals can be achieved by

1. Developing step by step procedures for receiving, storage, and distribution that maximize the shelf life of the product

2. Following purchasing procedures that utilize communications technology for product pricing, helping to ensure that management purchases the desired quality of product at the best available price

Managing purchasing is one of the most important cost control functions in any food service operation. Planning, production, and service are preliminary steps in a product's creation and delivery. How well these functions are carried out can affect the final cost of the product. The actual purchase price and quality of the materials needed to produce the product are the major costs against which profits are calculated.

Managing purchasing requires establishing a series of functions that, when consistently followed, ensure that

1. The product will be purchased at the best available price

2. The product will be purchased within the optimum period for use at the point of highest quality

3. The cash flow of the operation is as efficient as possible

These functions are as follows:

1. Establish written purchasing specifications for every product that is purchased

2. Select purveyors who can best supply product, following the established guidelines for quality, pricing, delivery, and payment.

3. Determine the ordering periods that will satisfy inventory needs to keep product at a par stock level

PURCHASING FUNCTIONS

The value of product in inventory is a cost that management is constantly striving to keep as low as possible. Product, once received and put into inventory, remains a cost until used in production and sold. Management's ability to control purchasing so that a minimum amount of inventory is held for any length of time can directly influence the cash flow and overall profitability of an operation.

Waste is a major cost factor in a food service operation. Waste is classified into two major types: Preventable and uncontrollable.

Preventable waste is waste that is caused by overproduction due to inaccurate forecasting. One of the major problems facing commercial restaurant managers is the inability to plan accurate customer counts. Sales history forms and past production sheets can supply information on which to base planning decisions. In order to forecast customer counts in an ongoing operation, management must take into account historical information, current customer attendance trends, and community and world events. The closer management comes to actual customer counts with production planning, the less waste will result.

Uncontrollable waste is waste that is the result of problems over which management has no control, such as loss of electricity that results in food spoilage or unexpected storms that keep customers away.

Management must control purchasing to minimize preventable waste, instituting controls for theft and production waste. Controlling both of these areas will allow management to absorb uncontrollable waste costs such as food spoilage due to overproduction or power losses.

PROFESSIONAL PURCHASING SKILLS

Management must develop the following skills to be a purchaser, not an order giver:

1. Specification development

2. Ordering methods and techniques

3. Receiving methods and techniques

4. Product content knowledge

5. Supplier knowledge

6. Product yield knowledge

Specifications

The key to successful purchasing is well-developed specifications. *Specifications* are detailed descriptions of every item used in an operation. Detailed and accurate specifications clearly identify the quality and quantity of a product as well as the specific purpose for which it is to be used. This identification forces management to

1. Analyze the final product thoroughly, setting goals for quantity as well as quality of taste and presentation.

2. Create a level of expectation for the product and its use by management, production staff, and service staff.

3. Identify the purpose for which the product will be used to distributors and purveyors. A well-defined specification leaves no doubt as to management's exact requirements for that product.
The four basic requirements for a good specification are

    A. Use an accurate name for the food product to be purchased.
Example: whole peeled apples, 2 1/2 inch diameter packed in light syrup

    B. Establish purchase quality for the product.
The United States Department of Agriculture (USDA) has established standards for 90 percent of foods available on the American market.

        i. Purchasing specifications should establish USDA quality classifications
Example: grade A, prime, choice

        ii. Indicate a name brand that ensures an established level of quality
Example: turkeys can be indicated on a specification by the brand name: Swift's Premium, Armor Star, Perdue, Weaver

    C. Identify the intended use of the product.
Management must establish exactly how this product will be used on both a primary and a subprimary basis.

Example:
Primary: Whole turkey to be roasted, sliced, and served as an entrée item
Subprimary: Legs and other dark meat along with leftover white meat to be reconstituted for club sandwiches, turkey stew or pot pie, and turkey salad
The subprimary uses indicate the number of additional functions that a particular brand product should serve.

D. Establish information that will properly identify the product.
Example:
Potato: whole, 70 count, 11 to 13 ounces

The result of establishing these four categories of specification will be a product that is purchased in the *proper quality* for its intended use in the *proper quantity* to ensure its speedy consumption at the *proper price* to meet food cost requirements.

Food manufacturers and distributors often offer product information sheets, such as the one in Figure 7-1, that give management the required information regarding classifications, descriptions, packaging information, product yield, and suggested product use.

The specification form in Figure 7-2 outlines a format that incorporates the four categories of information to ensure successful purchasing.

ORDERING

A skilled purchasing agent is a purchaser, challenging the market (distributors and purveyors) to provide the quality, quantity, and price that will meet the specific needs of the restaurant. Effective ordering begins with a well-planned call sheet listing all of the items needed for production. Figure 7-3 is the format for a call sheet that allows space for two to three price comparisons of each item.

After receiving the required number of quotes for an item, the purchaser should circle the price on the call sheet and fill out a purchase order sheet.

The application of advances in technology has provided opportunities for alternate call sheet formats in the form of computerized spread sheets. Tie-ins to purveyors via modems allow daily price and product availability updates. Purveyors are also using FAX systems to advise customers of specials and daily price changes.

WHOLE BAKED APPLES
18-20 Count
FACT SHEET

General Product Information

Description

LUCKY LEAF® and MUSSELMAN'S® Whole Baked Apples are carefully selected from prime processing varieties, such as Golden Delicious, Stayman Winesap, Jonathan and Rome Beauty, which are chosen for their symmetry, shape and superlative baking characteristics.

Processing/Quality Assurance

After initial inspection, each apple is closely size-graded to ensure portion control. Following grading, the apples are again inspected, partially peeled, cored, and reinspected prior to vacuumization in syrup. The prepared apples are placed on trays for baking in specially designed ovens equipped with electronically regulated heat controls and uniform baking cycles. After baking, the apples are filled into the containers, topped with hot spiced syrup, sealed under vacuum, sterilized, and rapidly cooled to retain flavor, texture and color.

Ingredients

Oven baked apples, water, corn syrup, cane syrup, brown sugar, cellulose gum, citric acid, sodium citrate, natural and artificial flavors. Color added.

Packaging

- UPC/Product Code 33009
- 112 oz. net weight
- 18-20 apples per can; average 114 apples per case; each apple is approximately 2½"-2¾" in diamter.
- Dry storage is recommended between 40° and 80° to yield 18-month shelf life
- Special double enamel can lining with side seam striping
- Available in 6 #10 containers per case

Recommended Product Usage

- As a garnish for meats, fish and poultry
- Dumpling for dessert
- Breakfast fruit or appetizer
- As a dessert by filling the core with pudding, pie filling or a cinnamon stick
- Steam table for breakfast or dessert bars
- Alternative for vegetable side dish
- As a salad by filling the core with tuna fish or other low calorie items
- As a breakfast garnish by vertically cutting the baked apple in half and placing a link of sausage across the cored portion of the apple

Apples Baked and A Whole Lot More

FIGURE 7-2 *Specification Format: Whole Baked Apples. Courtesy Knouse Foods Quality Products.*

VENDOR CALL SHEET					
ITEM	UNIT	CURTZE	JORDANS	WELLS CO	CYSCO
MEAT:					
POULTRY:					
Chickens, roaster					
Chicken breasts					
Chicken wings					
Ducks, roasters					
PRODUCE:					

FIGURE 7-3   *Call Sheet Format*

The decision to purchase should be based on knowledge that a *certain quality or a certain price* will be delivered by the distributor/purveyor.

Ordering systems are the basis of a well-developed purchasing program. Ordering systems combine established operational forms with an ordering schedule that reflects the daily needs of a restaurant operation. The purchasing agent sets up separate ordering periods for both perishable and nonperishable goods. The primary goal is to have enough product in par stock to fulfill production needs without creating a large inventory which can affect the cash flow. Par stock is the maximum amount of product that needs to be in inventory to satisfy production needs for a given period.

In order to develop ordering systems, purchasing agents must establish the par stock and its rotation pattern. To establish par stock and rotation, the following information is needed for a given inventory period:

Item name

Opening inventory

Closing inventory

Par stock is established by reviewing the use of the product over a period. The amount of product that is turned over in inventory on a consistent basis establishes the par stock. An example for establishing par stock for eggs is: Specification: EGGS: Grade A, white, medium. Restaurant A has a combined product requirement for eggs of one case per day. The restaurant operates 6 days per week. Eggs are ordered on a weekly basis and have a shelf life of 21 days. Deliveries are made weekly. Par Stock is seven cases of eggs, allowing for one extra case.

To establish both rotation and par stock value, the following information is needed for an inventory period:

Opening inventory

Closing inventory

Cost of food purchased

The basic formula commonly used for accounting purposes to calculate the rotation ratio is called the *inventory turnover equation:*

$$\frac{\text{Food cost}}{\text{Average inventory value}} = \text{Turnover rate for}$$

MONTHLY FOOD INVENTORY

Opening inventory: $7,200.00

Closing inventory: $6,800.00

Food cost for the month:* $6,500.00

To calculate the food cost for the month, subtract the closing inventory ($6,800) from the combined total of opening inventory ($7,200) and food cost for the month ($6,500):

$$\$7,200 + \$6,500 = \$13,700 - \$6,800 = \$6,900$$

By dividing the total of value of monthly opening inventory ($7,200) and closing inventory ($6,800) by 2, you can find the average inventory value on a daily basis for the month:

$$\frac{\$7,200 + \$6,800}{2} = \$7,000$$

By dividing monthly food cost by the average food inventory, you can find the monthly inventory turnover rate:

$$\frac{\$6,900 \text{ (Food cost)}}{\$7,000 \text{ (Average inventory)}} = \frac{\text{Inventory turnover}}{0.95}$$

The answer, 0.95, indicates that 95 percent of the inventory turns over during the month, or approximately every 28 days.

$$30 \times 0.95 = 28.5$$

To calculate how many times per year these items should be ordered, multiply 0.95 times 12 months:

$$0.9 \times 12 = 11.45$$

Nonperishable inventory should be ordered 11.45 times per year. To establish an ordering period, divide 52 weeks by 11.45.

$$\frac{52 \text{ (weeks)}}{11.45} = 4.54$$

---

*To calculate food cost on a monthly basis, total the cost of monthly purchases of both perishable and nonperishable products for the period.

Nonperishable inventory should be ordered every 4 ½ weeks. Management decides to establish an ordering period of every 3 ½ weeks to ensure that par stock will be maintained. Perishable products are usually ordered on a daily basis, depending on availability of products and distributors' delivery schedules.

Receiving

Receiving is the point in the purchasing program where most loss can occur. Loss is categorized as

Loss of quality

Loss of product in storage

Loss by theft

Loss of quality occurs when the distributor sends product of lesser quality than was promised or implied. It is a common practice among less reputable food distributors and purveyors to substitute product by the case in large orders, hoping that the differences will not be noticed before the product has been distributed for production. Receiving agents must check every case for product quality and quantity, referring to the original purchase orders as a guideline.

Loss of product in storage is directly related to the temperature and conditions at which different products, both perishable and nonperishable, are stored. Every perishable food product has an ideal holding temperature that will ensure maximum shelf life for a desired quality. A strong purchasing program identifies these temperatures and assigns specific storage areas which can maintain these temperature levels.

Nonperishable products require storage areas that provide a dry atmosphere and storage on racks or flats to keep product off the floor, away from walls, and out of direct sunlight.

Loss by theft can occur in every area of an operation. Product is most vulnerable to theft in the period between checking the product in and distributing it to storage. Purchasing originally checks the product or receipt and notes that it coincides with the invoice. On the loading dock product can easily be moved to an ajacent area and removed at a later time. The total quantity of the product order is usually never checked again, making this an excellent point for theft.

Product Knowledge

Purchasing skills include a thorough knowledge of the products that are being ordered. It is important for management to know the origin of the product, how it is packaged, and the expected yield from either the raw or the packaged product form.

Understanding how the geographical origin of a product can affect the yield and taste is a professional purchasing skill that influences the quality of product that a restaurant uses.

An example of the effect of geographical origin is the variation in the quality of strawberries and potatoes. California strawberries have a sweeter taste and a longer shelf life than strawberries from Florida, which are blander in taste and break down faster because of water content. Potatoes from Idaho are denser and have a higher cooked yield factor and better taste quality than potatoes from Maine because of soil content.

Identifying the best price quote for a product requires a knowledge not only of product quality but of the variety of forms in which product is packaged. Food manufacturing technology has developed methods of production which are making fresh products available in a variety of preprepared stages of readiness for production. Purchasing agents can consult chefs to select the stage of readiness which best meets the needs of the restaurant.

Preproduction labor is often one of the most costly areas of food production. The labor force of the 1990s presents problems in ongoing availability and inconsistent skill levels for food service preparation. By making selections which reduce labor and provide a high-quality food product with a good shelf life, labor costs can be reduced.

Four Seasons Produce in Denver, Pennsylvania, is a distributor of fresh fruits and vegetables to wholesalers and food service operations in a seven-state area. This company provides their customers with a wide variety of ready-to-use preprepared cuts of vegetables. A recent analysis of cost comparisons of whole product versus preprepared product produced the results in Figure 7-4.

A manager's understanding of the brand names of produce suppliers can affect quality and yield. Cauliflower offers an excellent example of how product knowledge affects purchasing yield. Cauliflower is generally packaged in cases of 12 heads with an average weight of 23 pounds per case. The yield from the case depends, however, on how much base leaf and stem is included in the case weight versus the whole head. This is controlled by the packer and indicated by brand name. An examination of two separate heads of cauliflower, one slightly trimmed of excess leaves and one head with leaves off and stem trimmed, indicates that the yield will be much higher on the fully trimmed head. A difference in price between the two brands without brand name product knowledge could cause management to order the case with the lower cost. The higher yield on the other brand would actually produce an equal or lower cost.

Broccoli offers the following comparison in comparing the cost of florettes processed from the whole head and purchased in preprepared form:

Broccoli: whole head

Packaging	Weight	Price
Case/ whole head	23 lb	$16.00 case

Shelf handling yields:

Florettes	10 lb

Time to handle: 1 ½ hours at an hourly rate of $7.50

Cost to handle: $11.25

Total cost for raw product and labor: $16.00 + $11.25 = $27.25

Price per pound based on florette yield of 10 lb: $2.73/lb

Broccoli: Precut Florettes

Packaging	Weight	Price
4 3 lb bags	12 lb	$18.75

Price per pound based on packaging weight of 12 lb: $1.56/lb
Precut product is available processed without sulfites or preservative and has a shelf life in unopened bags of 5 to 7 days from receipt if held in refrigeration at 34° F/1° C. Product in this form provides consistent quality and size of cut. Precut product generally has a more stable pricing structure over a period of months. Management knows exactly what to expect in regard to yield, quality, and cost from this product on an ongoing basis.

FIGURE 7-4 *Raw Product versus Preprepared*

Supplier Knowledge

To understand thoroughly how product is available in today's market, a purchasing agent must know what distributors and wholesalers are capable of providing. The selection of suppliers should be based on a complete inspection and analysis of their facilities, product, and customer services. Managers and purchasing agents who have professional purchasing skills conduct on-site inspections of suppliers to assess storage capabilities and conditions under which products are handled and stored. This also allows suppliers to educate management on product availability. After the inspection visit it is advisable to evaluate the supplier in writing as a reference and record of capabilities and performance. The form presented in Figure 7-5 outlines the four major areas of a supplier operation that should be evaluated. These forms should be updated regularly with visits scheduled to the supplier on a 6-month basis if possible.

PLANT FACILITY	ABOVE AVERAGE	AVERAGE	GOOD	POOR
VENDOR EVALUATION FORM				
VENDOR _____ DATE _____				
ADDRESS _____				
TELEPHONE _____ FAX _____				
CONTACT _____				
Location _____				
Storage Capability _____				
Refrigeration Capacity _____				
Storage Condition _____				
Refrigeration Condition _____				
PRODUCT				
Availability _____				
Quality _____				
Product Variety _____				
Information _____				
Competitive Pricing _____				
SERVICE				
Billing Procedures _____				
Delivery Schedule _____				
Credit Policy _____				
Ordering Systems _____				
Customer Services _____				
SALES REPRESENTATIVES				
Professional _____				
Knowledgeable _____				
Responsive to Complaints _				
Follow Through _____				
COMMENTS				

FIGURE 7-5 *Supplier Evaluation Form*

Product Yield Knowledge

Product yield versus cost is a highly influential factor in the profitability of a restaurant. Management's ability to purchase product that will yield the highest number of established quality portions in production with the least amount of waste is a professional purchasing skill.

A knowledge of product yield is gained by

1. Investigation of suppliers and distributors

2. Experience with produce

3. Yield tests

Cooking loss yield tests are the most effective type of yield tests. Product is tested a minimum of three times under the same conditions, using the same method of preparation to measure the amount of cooked product yielded. This gives management a measure against which to compare it with similar products.

The decision to purchase should be based on knowledge that a *certain quality or a certain price* will be delivered by the distributor/purveyor.

SUMMARY

As purchasing is one of the most important cost control functions of any food service operation, management must establish goals by which to establish and direct a purchasing program. Achieving these goals requires developing procedures for receiving, storing, and distributing product. An important part of effective purchasing is establishing written specifications for every product. A good specification accurately identifies the product by name and intended use, establishes the purchase quality, and supplies information to identify the product properly.

Ordering systems are the basis of a purchasing program. Ordering periods establish the purchasing pattern by which management maintains par stock levels that satisfy production needs without creating high inventory levels that affect the cash flow of an operation.

Management must understand the role of receiving in the purchasing program. The greatest amount of loss, in quality, spoilage, or theft, can occur during receiving.

Professional purchasing skills require management to have a thorough knowledge of the products that they are ordering. Preprepared product is available in a wide variety of ready-to-use forms that can reduce labor costs and provide consistent, quality product.

CHAPTER QUESTIONS

1. Identify the major management goals for a purchasing program and discuss how these goals can be achieved.

2. List the three purchasing functions and give a short explanation of each.

3. What are the two types of waste and three types of loss discussed in this chapter? How does purchasing waste relate to purchasing loss?

4. Identify and define the professional purchasing skill that management must develop as the key to successful purchasing.

5. Outline the four basic requirements for a good purchasing specification.

6. Why is it important for a purchasing agent to establish ordering periods?

7. At what point in the purchasing program can most loss occur?

8. What factors should be known before a decision to purchase is made?

9. Discuss how preprepared products can affect yield and cost.

10. Product yield knowledge is based on what three factors?

ACTIVITIES

1. Using the specification format example in Figure 7-2, select one item from each of the following categories:

   Fresh fruits and vegetables

   Dairy products

   Poultry and eggs

   Meats

   Beverages

   Draw up a written specification for each item, using textbooks and other research material as the basis for product information.

2. Select one of the professional purchasing skills discussed in this chapter. Discuss in detail how you would develop that skill.

3. Visit a large distributor of fresh food product and investigate product that is offered in some form of prepreparation. Conduct a supplier evaluation after your visit. Present your findings to the class.

4. Calculate the ordering period for each of the monthly inventory situations in this problem, using the formula offered in this chapter.

   a. Monthly inventory

   Opening inventory $12,575

   Closing inventory 8,950

   Food cost 7,645

   b. Monthly inventory

   Opening inventory $10,650

   Closing inventory 9,865

   Food cost 6,335

   c. Monthly inventory

   Opening inventory $9,380

   Closing inventory 8,665

   Food cost 7,305

8 *Food and Beverage Cost Control Systems*

OBJECTIVES

1. To emphasize the importance of established systems procedures to effective food and beverage cost control.

2. To be able to outline food and beverage control systems and identify their importance in a successful restaurant operation.

3. To understand the importance of menu reevaluation to the continued success of a menu program.

4. To be able to apply a theory of menu analysis to the reevaluation of a menu program.

CASE STUDY: FOOD AND BEVERAGE COST ANALYSIS

The results of the application of food and beverage cost controls to the daily operations of a restaurant business are data, figures, and percentages that reflect the well-being of the operation. Daily and/or weekly food and beverage cost reports can be compiled from the results of the control reports to produce an analysis of total costs, total sales, and their respective percentages of operational costs and effect on the overall profit margin. Figure 8-1 is an example of a weekly food and beverage cost report form for a restaurant operation. When completed, this report form offers management the ability to assess the success of the purchasing program, identify possible waste and overproduction problems, recognize sales trends, and track forecasted revenues and cost percentages.

Date:

Period: From: _____ To: _____

Overall food cost: _____ Food cost %: _____
Overall beverage cost: _____ Beverage cost %: _____
Average daily food cost: _____ Food cost %: _____
Weekly food cost: _____ Food cost: _____

Food cost month to date: _____
Food cost % month to date: _____

Actual food cost month to date: _____ Forecasted month to date: _____
Actual food cost year to date: _____ Forecasted year to date: _____

Actual beverage cost month to date: _____ Forecasted month to date: _____
Actual beverage cost year to date: _____ Forecasted year to date: _____

Day:	Sun.	Mon.	Tues.	Wed.	Thurs.	Fri.	Sat.
Sales:							
Food:							
Beverage:							
Total F&B:							

Total weekly sales: Food: _____ Beverage: _____

Average daily sales: _____

Day:	Sun.	Mon.	Tues.	Wed.	Thurs.	Fri.	Sat.
Costs:							
Food:							
Beverage:							
Total F&B:							

Total weekly costs: Food: _____ Beverage: _____

Average daily combined food & beverage cost: _____

FIGURE 8-1 *Food and Beverage Cost Control Report*

Food and beverage cost control systems are a series of forms and procedures that, when applied in a restaurant operation on a consistent basis, help to ensure profitability. Control systems are operational guides for the major areas of a restaurant that create cost and produce revenue. These operational guides give managers standard operating practices to produce product, control costs, and track sales. The control systems discussed in this chapter are *production controls* and *menu sales controls*.

Production controls help to ensure that a food product is consistently produced to yield an established number of portions at a predetermined cost. These controls include the standard recipe card and the standard cost card.

Menu sales controls provide management with a standardized means to control menu production, track menu sales, and evaluate server sales efforts. These controls include the following:

Production sheet

Sales mix

Server sales evaluation

Production Controls

To control costs, management must identify the most cost-intensive areas of the operation and institute controls that serve as guidelines to controlling costs. The most cost-intensive area of a restaurant operation is food production.

The labor market of the 1990s has become one of the chief concerns of the food service industry. The lack of availability of skilled labor for food preparation and service creates major problems for management, particularly in food production areas. In order for a kitchen to be able to purchase a food product that has consistent quality and yield, guidelines must be provided to assist the chef in dealing with a constant turnover of food production staff.

Standard Recipe Card

To produce a product of a determined quality to yield an established number of portions consistently, management should develop standard recipe cards: "Standard recipe cards present a formulated set of instructions that have been systematically tested and proved to result in a product of consistent quality, when produced under a given set of conditions."[1] The recipe card format in Figure 8-2 provides a well-organized and highly readable outline of

---

[1] Nancy Scanlon. *Marketing by Menu, 2nd Ed.* (New York: Van Nostrand Reinhold, 1990). p. 98.

STUFFED POTATO JACKETS THE STORE

FROM: THE STORE RESTAURANT BASKING RIDGE, NJ JACK WELSH, OWNER

YIELD: 24 SERVINGS
PORTION: 3 JACKETS WITH 2 OUNCES FILLING EACH

Ingredients	Weight	Measure
JACKETS		
Idaho® Potato Skins, fresh or frozen	12 pounds	72 pieces

Method

1. Use prepared fresh or frozen skins. Fill each skin with 2 ounces filling using #24 scoop (fill with Bacon & Cheddar or Dilled Seafood fillings). Place filled skins on sheet pans, cover tightly with plastic wrap and refrigerate until ready to serve. To prepare single serving, place 3 filled skins on sizzle platter and bake in 350°F convection or 400°F conventional oven 10 to 20 minutes or until cheese melts and skins heat through. Serve skins cut in half lengthwise on bed of greens, if desired.

CHEDDAR & BACON FILLING: 1 1/8 gallons—filling for 72 skins

	Weight	Measure
Bacon, diced	4 pounds	2 quarts
Cheddar cheese, grated	6 pounds	1 1/2 gallons
Parmesan cheese, grated	2 pounds	2 1/2 quarts

1. Cook bacon until crisp and brown; remove from heat and drain thoroughly.
2. Combine bacon with Cheddar and Parmesan cheeses; mix well. Place in covered container and refrigerate until ready to use. Serve Cheddar-Bacon Jackets with a horseradish-sour cream sauce.

DILLED SEAFOOD FILLING: 1 1/8 gallons—filling for 72 skins

	Weight	Measure
Cream cheese, softened	3 pounds	1 1/2 quarts
Swiss cheese, grated, divided	2 1/2 pounds	2 1/2 quarts
Mayonnaise	2 pounds	1 quart
Scallions, chopped	1 pound	1 quart
Fresh dill, minced	4 ounces	1 1/2 cups
Salt		1 tablespoon
Ground red pepper		1 teaspoon
Surimi, roughly chopped	3 pounds	2 quarts
or		
Canned salmon, drained	3 pounds	2 quarts

1. In bowl of mixer equipped with paddle, combine cream cheese, 1 1/2 quarts Swiss cheese, mayonnaise, scallions, dill, salt and pepper; blend thoroughly on medium speed.

2. Stir in surimi or salmon and continue to mix until blended. Place in covered container and refrigerate until ready to use.
To serve: Fill each skin with 2 ounces filling and top with remaining grated Swiss cheese (1 1/2 tbsp. per skin).
Other filling possibilities: Black bean chili; smoked chicken salad; brie and chutney.

FOR MORE INFORMATION OR ADDITIONAL RECIPES, CONTACT THE IDAHO POTATO COMMISSION, P.O. BOX 1068, BOISE, ID 83701.

FIGURE 8-2 *Potato Recipes. Courtesy Idaho Potato Commission.*

the ingredients and directions for preparing 72 pieces of stuffed Idaho potato jackets. The accompanying photograph of a suggested plate presentation helps the kitchen to display the food items in a colorful and appetizing design presentation.

Food production costs often represent the largest percentage of costs in a food service operation. Controlling food cost is a management skill that is concentrated in the areas of purchasing and production. Food cost is one area of an operation where management controls can significantly impact overall profitability. Management must produce food product at an established cost that can be sold at a menu price which is both competitive and acceptable to the customer and will generate a desired profit.

Standard Cost Cards

"The standard cost card for each recipe provides a cost breakdown for each ingredient as well as the total food cost for each recipe. From this information, portion costs can be established and the final prices of all menu items fixed."[2]

To realize a consistent profit from a menu item the costs of the food product must be constantly reviewed so that either the food product or the menu price can be adjusted. In order to monitor food costs, management should develop standard cost cards. With accurate cost cards, management can establish prices for menu items that will generate the amount of profit necessary to the ongoing success of the restaurant.

Menu Sales Controls

Monitoring the sales of menu items can give management a constant overview of the day-to-day business of a restaurant. Customer counts, sales volumes, and preferences in the selection of menu items are factors that influence purchasing and staffing as well as future planning for the restaurant.

By understanding both daily overall sales volumes and individual item sales volumes, management can plan food purchasing and staffing more cost-effectively.

The Production Sheet

Product has been purchased, received, and stored on the basis of the customer demand that management forecasts. The *production sheet* is a listing of each menu item that is to be served during a given meal period. The estimated

---

[2] Nancy Scanlon. *Marketing by Menu, 2nd Ed.* (New York: Van Nostrand Reinhold, 1990) page 196.

numbers of items to be served are the basis on which purchasing and management plan for product and labor. In order to complete a production sheet it is necessary to know the food cost, selling price, and food cost percentage of every menu item. These factors are basic to the calculation of actual food cost, revenue, and cost of waste, three important types of information provided by completed production sheet (Figure 8-3).

The findings from the production sheet now give management the information to analyze the sales of each individual menu item in detail. Menu item analysis is an important management skill for successful restaurant operation in the 1990s. The identification of menu items that have low-volume sales figures allows management to adjust the menu program appropriately. Items with high food costs that cannot be reconstituted and create waste can be eliminated from the menu to be replaced by items that will generate greater customer response and lower food costs.

The Sales Mix

The *sales mix* represents the sales of each individual menu item over the period of one month in detail (Table 8-1). This will give management the ability to compare the sales of menu items with one another as well as to review the day-

Total estimated customer count:						Service:			Actual # served:		
Date:	Time:						Chef:				
Item	# of item to be served	Food cost	Total food cost	Actual # served	Actual food cost	Selling price	Total rev- enue	F.C. %	Over- age	Value	Waste F.C. %

FIGURE 8-3   *Production Sheet. Source:* Marketing by Menu, 2nd Edition.

by-day sales of each item. This information, combined with a sales history for the same period, gives management the basic information for future planning.

The two primary factors that control the effectiveness of sales are production and service. By applying the production sheet as part of the menu control system, management can monitor the daily sales of menu items and track their food cost percentages. Periodic review of the sales mix identifies menu items with high or low sales volumes, allowing management to direct server sales efforts to areas of the menu and/or specific menu items that need to increase sales volume.

Server Sales Evaluation

The *server sales evaluation* format records the daily or weekly menu sales pattern of each server. The most effective format for this control is a computer food service systems report that carries information generated from the sales check to a separate computer file for each server. The server sales profile is then compiled by the computer for management to review. By hand this is a lengthy, time-consuming process. Reports of this type are generally overlooked by restaurant managers who do not operate with a computer food service system. The information generated by this effort is, however, extremely important to the sales program of any restaurant operation. The server is the most important sales tool in any restaurant. Servers have a direct impact on menu item sales by the way in which they knowingly or unknowingly direct customer response. Management's ability to analyze server sales patterns can provide an effective tool in increasing menu item sales and profitability.

Before developing a server sales evaluation format, management must identify the area of information that needs to be analyzed. Management must also determine how much information can be handled if a computer food service system is not being applied to recording the control system. The format for a server sales evaluation form shown in Figure 8-4 has been developed for recording by hand. Figure 11-12 illustrates the computer system method of recording and analyzing this control system.

The information being analyzed in this report is broken down into three general areas:

1. Overall sales: month to date/year to date

2. Average sales per check

3. Major menu category sales

Section 1 in this report format concentrates on the breakdown of net sales (sales after tips) on a per check/per guest basis to identify (1) the server's total average check and (2) the server's average sales per guest.

TABLE 8-1 Sales Mix

Items: Appetizer, Soup, Entrée, Dessert *Time period: 18 Days*

Compiled by:

Month: October

	T	W	T	F	S	S	T	T	W	T	F	S	S	T	T	W	T	F	S	S	T	T	W	T	F	S	S	T	T	W	Average #
	1	2	3	4	5	6		8	9	10	11	12	13		15	16	17	18	19	20		22	23	24	25	26	27		29	30	
Appetizer:																															
1. Oysters	54	47	68	83	156	191	499																								
2. Escargot	32	31	37	49	75	52	276																								
3. Melon & Pros.	25	20	31	37	54	35	202																								
4. Artichoke	29	30	38	52	65	60	274																								
Soup:																															
1. French Onion	45	49	42	54	78	61	329																								
2. Carrot	13	10	8	15	28	20	94																								
3. Cream of Mushroom	32	38	36	46	59	48	259																								
Entrée:																															
1. Veal Cordon Bleu	26	20	38	54	66	55	259	21	25	27	35	41	37	186	27	29	32	60	63	42	253										39
2. Tournedos	38	43	52	62	78	66	339	33	38	45	48	56	47	267	32	40	47	54	68	54	295										50
3. Prime Rib	45	40	47	68	80	61	341	42	40	48	55	61	42	288	49	45	54	60	72	58	338										54
4. Scampi Shrimp	12	15	25	30	44	32	158	18	15	20	26	32	30	141	21	18	23	32	39	31	164										26
5. Salmon Steak	8	9	12	18	25	19	91	5	8	11	15	19	20	78	7	6	15	20	24	20	92										15
6. Scallops	21	17	22	31	48	33	172	17	21	23	27	31	26	145	23	32	25	30	35	30	175										27

138

7. Filet of Scrod	18	22	28	30	27	25	96	17	19	21	26	29	31	143	20	27	25	33	31	28	164	25
8. Lamb Chops	9	12	11	15	18	12	77	8	10	12	16	19	15	80	8	17	13	18	20	14	90	14
9. Chicken Forestiere	4	2	6	7	9	6	34	2	3	5	9	12	8	39	12	10	8	13	9	12	64	7
10. Roast Breast Capon	30	28	41	62	68	54	283	29	32	40	49	61	52	263	31	40	51	54	62	50	288	46
Dessert:																						
1. Mousse	30	24	35	51	108	58	306															
2. Apple Pie	21	20	29	47	96	51	264															
3. Hazelnut Torte	41	35	39	48	112	48	323															
4. Sherbet Bombe	18	25	34	52	78	50	257															
5. Fresh Fruit	11	21	28	35	47	38	108															
Total Entrée:	211	208	282	377	463	363	1850	192	211	252	306	361	308	1630	230	264	293	374	423	339	1923	
Total Appetizer:	140	128	174	221	350	238	1251															
Total Soup:	90	97	86	115	129	682																
Total Dessert:	123	125	165	233	441	245	1332															

SERVER NAME: _____ ID # _____		
DATE: _____		
SECTION 1	MONTH TO DATE	YEAR TO DATE
*NET SALES SALES PER CHECK (average check) *after tips		
SECTION 2	MONTH TO DATE	YEAR TO DATE

SALES PER MENU CATEGORY
 	
     LIQUOR
     BEER
     WINE
     *BEVERAGES
     APPETIZERS
     SALADS
     MAIN COURSE
     DESSERTS
*includes coffee, tea, soda		

TOTAL SALES		

FIGURE 8-4   *Server Sales Evaluation Form*

A running record of sales per check allows management to track fluctuations in overall sales over a prescribed period. The *average check* figure provides a means of comparing the individual server's sales per customer to the total average check for the restaurant. This comparison will give management an accurate assessment of how one server's sales compare with overall sales for the operation as well as with other servers' sales.

The *sales per menu* category records server sales in each section of the menu. This analysis allows management to identify which major categories of the menu the server concentrates his or her efforts on selling. Conversely, this also identifies areas of the menu in which the server has weak sales, indicating either a lack of confidence in selling these menu items or an aversion to the menu category. Management can now take steps to give servers product knowledge and influence their attitudes toward menu categories. The availability of this control system allows management to conduct server sales incentive programs, tracking the results of each server's efforts. Wine sales incentive programs or dessert sales incentive programs are areas management often targets for increased sales.

MENU REEVALUATION

Menu reevaluation is the menu control system that uses information from the production sheet and sales mix to maintain constant monitoring of the sale of individual menu items. Menu reevaluation is necessary to the continued success of a menu program once it has been put into operation.

The primary information that the production sheet provides in relation to menu reevaluation is the daily food cost analysis of individual menu items. This information allows management the ability to identify menu items that are experiencing increases in food cost quickly. Although adjustments such as an immediate price change or removal from the menu may not be possible, management is made aware of problem items and can track their sales and food cost percentages accordingly.

The *sales mix* is the most important menu sales control format, providing sales information on each individual menu item over a month's time. Ability to analyse the sales of menu items in relation to the balance of total menu items allows management to identify those items which are experiencing strong or weak sales.

Menu reevaluation requires that management establish the relationship that menu items have to one another in terms of sales and profit within specific menu categories. A number of established methods are used throughout the food service industry to conduct this analysis. Some of these can be carried out manually, and others require a computer software program. The two methods of menu analysis that are discussed in this chapter are contribution to profit and menu item evaluation.

Contribution to Profit

Contribution to profit is a method of menu analysis that calculates whether sales of individual menu items are profitable to the overall menu program. Menu items with high-volume sales may actually be reducing profits by their high food cost. These items may be experiencing volume sales due to customer reactions to price, content, and/or quality. Management must base the decision to maintain or increase prices on these items on an evaluation of the sales and profitability of the overall menu. The following information is necessary to calculate contribution to profit:

1. Number of menu items sold

2. Selling price

3. Item food cost

4. Food cost percentage

In Table 8-2 ten main course menu items are reviewed, using the contribution to profit method of menu reevaluation.

Menu item number 10, veal medallions, is shown as an example of how these figures and percentages are calculated:

TABLE 8-2   Contribution to Profit Menu Analysis

Date:

Menu Item	Total Sold	Food Cost	Total FC	Selling Price	Total Sales	FC%	CP
1. Prime rib	25	6.75	168.75	12.95	223.75	52%	$55.
2. Breast capon	15	3.50	52.50	10.50	157.50	33%	$105.
3. Shrimp scampi	10	4.25	42.50	11.75	117.50	36%	$75.
4. Pork chops	6	4.00	24.00	10.00	60.00	40%	$36.
5. Fettucine Alfredo	12	2.50	30.00	9.50	114.00	25%	$84.
6. Swordfish steak	10	5.80	58.00	14.50	145.00	40%	$87.
7. Seafood pie	8	4.20	33.60	13.95	111.60	30%	$78.
8. Steak teriyaki	5	4.50	22.50	12.50	62.50	36%	$40.
9. Sirloin tips	11	5.25	57.75	14.00	154.00	37%	$57.75
10. Veal medallions	7	5.60	39.20	13.95	97.65	40%	$58.45

1. *Total food cost is calculated* by multiplying total sales (7) times food cost ($5.60):

$$\$5.60 \times 7 = 39.20$$

2. *Total sales is calculated* by multiplying items sold (7) times selling price ($13.95)

$$\$13.95 \times 7 = 97.65$$

3. *Food cost % is calculated* by dividing total food cost ($39.20) by total sales ($97.65)

$$\$39.20 \div \$97.65 = 40\%$$

4. *Contribution to profit is calculated* by subtracting total food cost ($39.20) from total sales ($97.65)

$$\$97.65 - \$39.20 = \$58.45$$

5. *Contribution to profit percentage* is calculated by dividing contribution to profit ($58.45) by total sales ($97.65)

$$\$58.45 \div \$97.65 = 6\%$$

Management studies the figures presented in the contribution to profit analysis and selects three menu items that represent the high, middle, and low of menu sales and contribution to profit to review.

The leader in total sales volume is item number 1, prime rib, with total sales of $223.75 (Table 8-3).

The food cost percentage on this item, however, is 52 percent. When total sales are compared to total food cost, $168.75, the contribution to profit (CP) is only $55.00.

TABLE 8-3   Contribution to Profit: Prime Rib

Menu Item	Total Sold	Food Cost	Total FC	Selling Price	Total Sales	FC%	CP
1. Prime rib	25	6.75	168.75	12.95	223.75	52%	$55.00

TABLE 8-4   Contribution to Profit: Fettucine Alfredo

Menu Item	Total Sold	Food Cost	Total FC	Selling Price	Total Sales	FC%	CP
5. Fettucine Alfredo	12	2.50	30.00	9.50	114.00	25%	$84.

In comparison, item number 5, fettucine Alfredo, has total sales of $114.00, representing only 9 percent of total sales but offering a contribution to profit (CP) of $84.00 with a 25 percent food cost (Table 8-4).

Item number 2, breast of capon, has total sales of $157.50, representing 13 percent of total sales, with a 33 percent food cost and a contribution to profit (CP) of $105 (Table 8-5).

A management analysis of these three menu items could provide several findings: Prime rib, menu item 1, is being offered at a lower selling price as a promotional item to increase customer counts. Ideally sales of appetizers, desserts, and beverages will help to balance the loss of profit on this item. Sales volume figures indicate that the promotional price is receiving positive customer response. Further investigation is needed to determine whether customer counts have actually increased or whether customers have merely shifted their menu item preference in response to the promotional pricing.

Breast of capon has high average sales, with a 33 percent food cost percentage and a contribution to profit of $105, or 10 percent of total profit. The item receives strong customer response and is priced properly to produce a desired profit. This item should be maintained at its current price level to balance menu items with higher food cost percentages. If increased food costs are experienced on this item, then the content should be adjusted to maintain the 33 percent food cost.

Contribution to profit is an effective method of menu reevaluation because it presents all of the available information on a menu item to help management to draw appropriate conclusions. As profit is the goal of every restaurant operation, the profitability of a menu item should be the major consideration in the reevaluation process.

TABLE 8-5   Contribution to Profit: Breast Capon

Menu Item	Total Sold	Food Cost	Total FC	Selling Price	Total Sales	FC%	CP
2. Breast capon	15	3.50	52.50	10.50	157.50	33%	$105

Menu Matrix Analysis

A second theory by which to conduct menu reevaluation, *menu matrix analysis*, is based on the premise that menu items can be classified into four areas within the menu sales profile, based on their volume of sales, food cost, and profit margin. Items are placed in the matrix according to the relationship of item sales to item costs. This theory is the basis for a computer menu analysis program developed by Michael Kasavana of the University of Michigan that is discussed in Chapter 11 in relation to computer systems applications.

The following information is needed for the menu matrix analysis:

1. Item food cost

2. Number of items sold

3. Percentage of profit

The menu item information in Table 8-2 will be used to carry out the menu matrix analysis. This information would also be available from the production sheet and sales mix that includes these menu items.

The total sales for this grouping of items has a high of 25 and a low of 5. The average sales for this menu group is 10.9 per item. Menu items should be ranked high or low on the basis of this midpoint, with items selling 10 or more placed in the high range and all others in the low. There is no classification for midrange sales.

The total volume sales for this grouping of items is $1,243.50. The average sale for this menu grouping is $11.40. This figure was calculated by dividing total volume sales by the total number of items sold:

$$\$1,243.50 \div 109 = \$11.40$$

Menu items should be ranked high or low in terms of this midpoint, with items selling at $11.00 and above placed in the high range. Any item selling below $11.00 should be indicated as low.

The average food cost percentage for this group is 31.6 percent. Menu items should be ranked high or low in relation to this midpoint: items having a 31 percent or greater food cost are placed in the high range, and those having a food cost percentage below 31 percent should be indicated as low.

The percentage of profit is calculated by first establishing an item's gross profit and then calculating the percentage that gross profit represents of the selling price.

Item number 8, seafood pie, has a food cost of $4.20, which represents 30 percent of the selling price of $13.95. To establish gross profit on this item, subtract the food cost from the selling price.

$$13.95 - \$4.20 = \$9.75$$

To calculate the percentage of gross profit, divide the gross profit by the selling price:

$$\$9.75 \div \$13.95 = 69\%$$

Item number 10, swordfish steak, has a food cost of $5.80, which is 40 percent of the selling price of $14.50.

$$\$14.50 - \$5.80 = \$8.70 \text{ (gross profit)}$$
$$\$8.70 \div \$14.50 = 60\% \text{ (\% gross profit)}$$

The total food cost for this group of menu items is $528.80 and the total sales $1,243.50. The gross profit for this grouping is $714.70:

$$\$714.70 \div \$1,243.50 = 57\%$$

The percentage of gross profit for this grouping is 57 percent. Menu items should be ranked high, medium, or low in relation to this midpoint. All items with a profit percentage of 66 percent or more should be placed in the high range, those with a profit percentage of between 33 percent and 65 percent should be ranked as medium, and those below 33 percent as low.

Management now analyzes the distribution information in Table 8-6 to identify which of the four areas in the matrix in Figure 8-5 the menu item fits. It is important to note that menu items are not assigned a matrix location solely in terms of the amount of profit that they can generate.

The result of the menu matrix evaluation is a rating of each menu item into one of four categories. This ranking allows management to review each menu

TABLE 8-6   Menu Sales Analysis

Sales		Cost				
High	*Low*	*High*	*Low*	*Item*	*Profit*	*% MR*
X		X		Prime rib	M	1
X		X		Breast of capon	H	1
X			X	Shrimp scampi	M	1
	X	X		Pork chops	M	3
X			X	Fettucini Alfredo	H	1
X		X		Swordfish steak	M	2
	X		X	Seafood pie	H	3
	X	X		Steak teriyaki	H	3
X		X		Sirloin tips	M	2
	X	X		Veal medallions	M	3

High sales Low cost	High sales High cost
Low sales High cost	Low sales Low cost

FIGURE 8-5   *Menu Sales Matrix*

item on the basis of three major factors: sales volume, cost, and level of profitability. The following menu items are ranked accordingly:

1. Shrimp scampi is given a menu ranking of 1. High sales and low cost make it a leader in menu sales, balancing a medium ranking in profitability. Pricing on this menu item could be changed if food cost increased.

2. Pork chops is given a menu ranking of 3. Low sales and high costs make this an item which could present overproduction waste costs. The product should be purchased preportioned and packaged for maximum shelf life. This menu item could be removed from the permanent menu and used as a "special" if sales slipped further.

3. Seafood pie is given a menu ranking of 3. Low costs and high profit make it a potential leader. Low sales, however, indicate that a change needs to be made in the marketing of this item. Management should first look at the

item's position on the printed menu to see whether it is in a strong sales area. The name of the item could also be changed to make it more appealing. A promotion on this item following these marketing efforts would help to increase sales. The high cost on this item could create problems if management did not monitor the food cost percentage. Item content could easily be changed to adjust the food cost downward without increasing the price.

Decisions on whether to remove menu items, change item contents and/or prices, or create promotional items are based on how the individual menu item relates to the other items in the category.

Menu matrix analysis is a theory of menu reevaluation that allows management to interpret the information on the production sheet and sales mix quickly. A restaurant operation that is functioning without a computer food service system program would find this method less time-consuming than others that require lengthy calculations to draw conclusions.

SUMMARY

The application of food and beverage control systems is essential to the ongoing success of a restaurant operation. Control systems provide managers with standard operating practices to produce profit, control costs, and track sales. These systems are categorized as either production controls or menu sales controls. Production controls provide formats that help to ensure consistency in production and costing. Menu sales controls give management a daily review of menu production and sales. This review acts as a constant monitor of production costs and sales revenue that allows management to identify problem areas as quickly as possible.

Menu reevaluation is the application of the information provided by menu sales controls. It is performed by applying a theory of menu analysis in a format through which management can determine the effectiveness of both the overall sales of individual menu items and the menu program.

QUESTIONS

1. Discuss the importance of food and beverage cost control systems to the success of a restaurant operation

2. How do menu controls differ from production controls? Identify the controls discussed in this chapter.

3. How can management affect profit by controlling food cost?

4. What are the major factors that influence purchasing and staffing plans?

5. List the information headings that are presented on the production sheet.

6. Why is menu analysis an important management skill?

7. What are the two primary factors that control the sales effectiveness of a menu program?

8. Explain the value of the server sales evaluation to the sales program of a restaurant operation.

9. List the two methods of menu analysis discussed in this chapter and give a short definition of each.

10. How do you calculate contribution to profit (CP)?

ACTIVITIES

1. Create an outline of all of the food and beverage control systems discussed in this chapter. Show how information from one report is used in another by tracking the path of information.

2. Using either contribution to profit or menu matrix analysis, reevaluate the menu program of a local restaurant. Using the menu as a basis for your analysis, work with the owner/manager to identify costs and gross profit. Present your analysis to the class.

3. Calculate the contribution to profit on the items in Table 8-7.

4. Using the items listed in activity 3, develop a menu sales matrix and assign each a rating on the matrix.

TABLE 8-7   Main Course Items Contribution to Profit

Menu Item	Total Sold	Food Cost	Total FC	Selling Price	Total Sales	FC%	CP
Chicken wings	45	1.80		4.95		36	
Shish kebab	25	2.60		7.95		33	
Sirloin steak	30	4.25		12.50		34	
Broiled haddock	15	3.35		9.75		34	
Grilled chicken	22	3.10		9.50		33	
Grilled tuna	18	4.90		11.95		41	
Baked shrimp	28	5.25		11.75		45	

9 *Employee Organization*

OBJECTIVES

1. To be aware of all of the major forms of business that make up the hospitality industry.

2. To realize the variety of job positions available in food service.

3. To understand the importance of an organization chart to a business.

4. To be able to develop job descriptions which accurately outline job responsibilities and functions to management and employees.

5. To be able to differentiate between line and staff authority in any type of organization.

CASE STUDY: THE LAW OF THE WORKPLACE

The growth of the American restaurant industry in the twentieth century has been accompanied by a continuing recognition of the rights of employees and employers as a central focus of the American legal process. Most food production and food service jobs were originally, and in many cases still are, held by minority workers. With the development of unions in the industrial sector of American business, workers in the hotel and food service industries recognized the need to be represented in negotiations with management for wage increases and changes in working conditions. Union elections between 1977 and 1989 involved representation by over fifty unions. The six principal unions[1] most active in hotel and restaurant elections are the following:

HERE: Hotel Employees and Restaurant Employers

IBT: International Brotherhood of Teamsters

IUOE: International Union of Operating Engineers

SEIU: Service Employees International Union

UFCW: United Food and Commercial Workers

RWDSU: Retail Wholesale and Department Store Union

Efforts by many unions have contributed to the enactment of major laws governing such issues as minimum wage, sex discrimination, equal employment opportunity, child labor, and job safety. The following are some of the federal laws that have affected the hospitality and food service industry:

National Labor Relations Act	1935
Social Security Act	1936
Fair Labor Standards Act	1938
Work Hours and Safety Act	1962
Civil Rights Act	1964
Age Discrimination in Employment Act	1967
Occupational Safety and Health Act	1970
Vocational Rehabilitation Act	1973
Immigration Reform and Control Act	1986
American Disabilities Act	1992

The newest law, enacted in January 1992, the American Disabilities Act, gives civil rights protections to individuals with disabilities similar to those provided to individuals on the basis of race, sex, national origin, and religion. Individuals with disabilities are guaranteed equal employment opportunity in

---

[1]S. K. Murrmann and K. F. Murrmann, *Union Membership Trends and Organizing Activities in the Hotel and Restaurant Industries* (Washington, D.C.: Virginia Polytechnic Institute/State University, Council on Hotel Restaurant and Institutional Education, 1991)

employment, transportation, public accommodations, state and local government services, and telecommunications.

Food service businesses in the United States currently employ approximately 8 million people working in a wide variety of positions throughout the hospitality industry. The hospitality industry is composed of companies that are in the business of making people feel "at home" by providing high-quality food, shelter, entertainment, and leisure time activities to the general public.

Five major business areas supply these services and activities in a variety of commercial and noncommercial settings:

Hotel/resort

Restaurant

Institutional

Recreation/leisure

Travel/tourism

The major support service necessary to the success of all of these businesses is food service. The production and service of preprepared food products in a wide variety of packaging, presentation, and service are required to fulfill customer needs and demands in every area of the hospitality industry. The diagram in Figure 9-1 indicates the food service management needs of each hospitality business area.

Within each of these areas of business and food service management are an exciting range of jobs and careers. To understand the variety of positions that

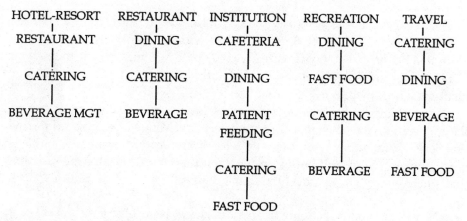

FIGURE 9-1 *Food Service Requirements in Hospitality Businesses*

are available throughout any food service related operation, it is necessary to review a variety of organization charts.

An *organization chart* is the graphic representation of job positions set out in the pattern of how work is accomplished and how authority and responsibility are assigned and delegated. An organization chart should clearly show who reports to whom throughout the line of work in a business, as well as the flow of authority. It is essential that an organization chart also indicate the breakdown of management levels, such as top management, middle management, operating management and workers.

Management levels begin with top management positions, people who are responsible for setting policy and making the major decisions that affect the ongoing success of a business. These positions make up a small percentage of the total number of jobs in a large business or corporation. Middle managers are responsible for the basic management functions: planning, directing, controlling, organizing, and coordinating. Operating managers are responsible for supervising the work flow of an organization and deal directly with workers. Workers, along with operating managers, carry out the work functions of a business. In a restaurant these functions include guest services and food preparation.

In a corporate food service organization that controls a large number of both company-owned and franchise restaurant operations the organization chart is similar to that of many other corporations. The organization chart in Figure 9-2 is for the corporate structure of a quick serve restaurant company. This chart outlines positions for top and middle management levels. The flow of authority in Figure 9-2 is broken down into two segments known as line and staff authority. It is important in food service operations to understand the difference between these two segments and their effect on a successful operation.

Managers with line authority directly influence the success of a business. *Line authority* is the ability to direct, appraise, and discipline staff. *Staff authority* is applied by those who do not directly contribute to achieving the major goals of a business. Individuals who have staff authority support other key management personnel by providing assistance, services, or advice.

Figure 9-2 indicates the major divisions that control the daily operations of the corporation: advertising, accounting services, MIS (Management Information Services, including computer and telecommunications systems), and legal departments. The second tier of positions on this chart indicates the functions that are necessary for the development and growth of the corporation.

1. The vice president of company operations is responsible for restaurant units owned by the parent company.

CORPORATE ORGANIZATION CHART

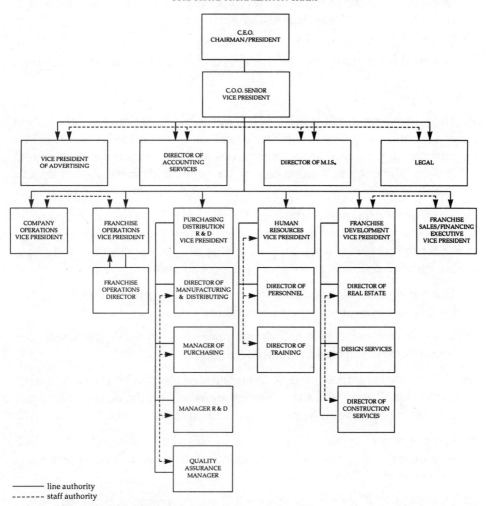

FIGURE 9-2 *Corporate Organization Chart. Courtesy Al Copeland Enterprises Inc.*

2. The vice president of franchise operations is responsible for restaurant units owned by franchisees.

3. The vice president of purchasing, distribution, and research and development (R&D) is responsible for the purchase, storage, and distribution of all material and food needs of the corporation. Research and development is new product design and development, an area that can have a great impact on the future success of the corporation.

4. The vice president of human resources is responsible for any activity involving the employees of the corporation.

5. The vice president of franchise development is responsible for the design and construction of franchise restaurant units.

The third tier includes middle management positions within the corporate structure:

A. The franchise operations director is responsible for the ongoing operations of all franchise units. This position will also call on the resources of the directors of personnel and training from the human resources department and the directors and managers of distribution, purchasing, R&D, and quality assurance.

B. The director of manufacturing and distribution in a food service corporation will be responsible for the manufacture of food products and ingredients under the corporate label. Responsibilities also include storage and distribution of all products purchased by the corporation.

C. The manager of purchasing is responsible for the buying of all materials and food products required by the corporation.

D. The manager of research and development is responsible for developing future food products and restaurant concepts.

E. The quality assurance manager is responsible for developing standards of quality for all aspects of the restaurant units and for the design and implementation of programs to meet and maintain those standards.

F. The director of personnel is responsible for the hiring and firing of all employees. This position also includes responsibility for implementing employee benefit programs.

G. The director of training is responsible for designing and implementing training programs at all levels of the corporation. Training programs are required for corporate staff and restaurant employees.

H. The director of real estate is responsible for identifying location sites and negotiating the sale and purchase of both corporate and franchise units.

I. The director of design services is responsible for developing the design package for each concept unit and restaurant. Some quick serve corporations have a number of different restaurant design concepts that require different design packages.

J. The director of construction services is responsible for overseeing the construction of both corporate and franchise units.

FOOD SERVICE POSITIONS

In order to understand the type of job positions available in most food service businesses, it is helpful to look at the job descriptions and organizational charts of restaurants and kitchens.

Restaurant operations require a total food service management team. Whether part of a hotel/resort or a restaurant chain or controlled by independent ownership, restaurants generally have the same type of organizational chart. The number of job positions in each category will depend on the size of the restaurant and the volume of business. The chart in Figure 9-3 is broken down into two separate sections. *Back of the house* refers to all areas outside public space and *front of the house* describes all areas involved with guest service.

Front of the House Positions

Restaurant Manager In an independent restaurant operation the restaurant manager works in conjunction with the chef while maintaining total authority and responsibility for the entire operation. Staffing and training are a major function of this position along with handling guest relations. In addition,

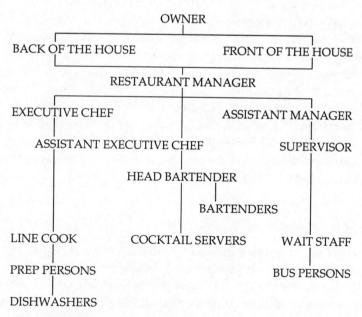

RESTAURANT ORGANIZATION CHART

FIGURE 9-3 *Restaurant Organizational Chart. Courtesy Al Copeland Enterprises Inc.*

the manager is responsible for the profitability of the operation. This involves determining food and beverage costs as well as pricing and developing the menu program. The condition of the building and surrounding property as well as the safety and sanitation practices of the operation are also major responsibilities. In a situation where there are multiple restaurants and individual managers for each unit, many of these responsibilities will be taken over by purchasing managers, house engineers, food and beverage managers, and controllers.

Assistant Manager In an independent restaurant the assistant manager is often assigned some of the responsibilities of the manager. The assistant manager is responsible for the entire operation in the absence of the manager. In many operations the assistant manager assumes responsibility for training front of the house staff. In a multiunit facility the assistant manager is often the maître d'hôtel.

Dining Room Captains The responsibility for service and guest relations within identified sections of the dining room, known as *stations*, during assigned service times is the primary function of this position. Dining room captains should have a good working knowledge of table side food perparations and be able to train other staff members. To take full advantage of this position a good knowledge of the wine list and menu is important.

Wait Staff and Bus Persons These positions are responsible for providing high-quality, professional service to guests in a friendly manner. The style of restaurant operation will identify the type of service that wait staff must be able to provide. Bus persons assist wait staff when necessary and are responsible for clearing between courses and resetting the table.

Hosts and Hostesses These positions are responsible for greeting customers, assigning seating, and backing up the wait staff whenever possible. Full-service restaurants often employ a maître'd for this position, depending on the level of formality of atmosphere and service. Casual family-style operations generally employ a host or hostess for these duties.

Head Bartender In restaurant operations with more than one alcoholic beverage outlet the head bartender is responsible for purchasing, staffing, training, and overseeing beverage costs. Bartenders, cocktail servers, and cashiers report to the head bartender.

Back of the House Positions

Executive Chef The responsibilities of the executive chef vary according to the type and size of food service operation. In a hotel facility the executive chef can manage up to four or five kitchens depending on the size of the overall facility and volume of food service related business. He or she may also supervise a number of assistant chefs (sous chefs) who are assigned to the kitchens of various food service outlets. A knowledge of the application of computer food service programs is essential in a position of this magnitude.

In a freestanding restaurant seating approximatly 250 guests the executive chef often becomes the purchasing agent as well as working on the production line.

Assistant Executive Chef (Sous Chef) The assistant executive chef is often called by the French term for this kitchen position, *sous chef.* The sous chef's responsibilities include being able to assume any of the line cook positions as well as to assume responsibility for the kitchen in the absence of the execuive chef.

Line Cooks Line cooks are assigned to various cooking stations in the kitchen. The size of the kitchen facility and variety of cooking methods used for preparation will determine the number of stations on the cooking line. The grill station, sauté station, and broiler station are features of many kitchens. Some line cooks specialize in a particular area of food preparation, such as garde manger work. Cold food displays, salad and buffet preparations, as well as ice sculptures are usually within the preparation capabilities of a garde manger chef.

Pastry Chef Pastry chefs are primarily responsible for the production of desserts rather than breads and rolls. Often, a pastry chef will become involved with highly creative display pieces for buffets and decoration. This particular area of food preparation is expected to be in greater demand by industry in the 1990s than any other. It is estimated that the need for pastry chefs and bakers will increase by 35 percent by the year 2000.

A large hotel/resort complex generally operates at least three food service outlets. The organizational chart in Figure 9-4 is for the back of the house food preparation staffing requirements for two restaurants, a cafeteria and a large banquet facility. The menu demands are such that a full pastry department, butcher shop, and garde manager station are required in addition to the production kitchens.

This guide also acts as a personnel scheduling form. The head chef for each preparation area will submit his or her personnel requirements for a given period. The executive chef's office will then determine total personnel needs for the production times in question. The station *chef de partie* is a position that is generally assigned as a section leader or 'swing chef' during periods of heavy volume when it is necessary to have one chef responsible for the production of a large function while the kitchen provides the balance of the operation's production needs.

Quick-Serve Operations

In a quick serve operation the front of the house and back of the house jobs meld into a team of individuals who are referred to as a *crew.* The organizational

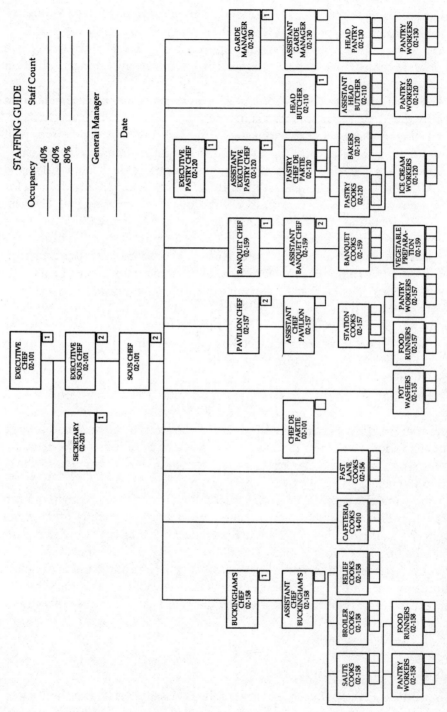

160

FIGURE 9-4 *Kitchen Staffing Guide. Courtesy Hilton Hotels Corporation.*

chart for quick serve operations often includes the positions outlined in Figure 9-5. This graphic illustration outlines the six positions within a McDonald's operation. The job descriptions for positions in quick serve operations are a blend of front and back of the house functions (Figure 9-5). The close proximity of the customer to food production stations requires a different system of allocating management responsibilities than often exists in a full service restaurant. The following job descriptions are common to store positions in most of the major quick serve restaurant chains.

Quick Serve Restaurant Job Descriptions

Store Manager   The manager, like any other restaurant manager, is responsible for overseeing the entire operation, including sales volume and profitability. Because of the 24-hour operations schedule of many quick serve operations, this position requires the ability to handle a diverse group of employees, often in a multilingual setting.

First Assistant   The first assistant actively administers the crew training program. Responsibilities of this position include monthly budget projections and all personnel functions for the store.

Second Assistant   The second assistant must be capable of operating the store. This position also requires the ability to conduct personnel interviews.

Swing Manager   The swing manager runs assigned shifts of the store operation, directing the crew and dealing with customers.

Swing Trainee   The swing trainee assists in managing the store in preparation for promotion to the position of swing manager.

Crew Leader   The crew leader is responsible for assigned areas of the store during the shift. A positive teamwork attitude and the ability to communicate that to other crew members are essential to this position.

Crew Trainer   The crew trainer is responsible for training all new hires. Leadership ability and good people handling skills are necessary for this position.

Crew Person   The crew person is responsible for carrying out the activities of the area of the restaurant to which he or she is assigned.

Job Descriptions

A *job description* lists the duties and responsibilities of a position that has been formally established in an organization. Every position listed on an organization chart should have a corresponding job description. The short explanations of the job positions discussed in this chapter are summaries of job descrip-

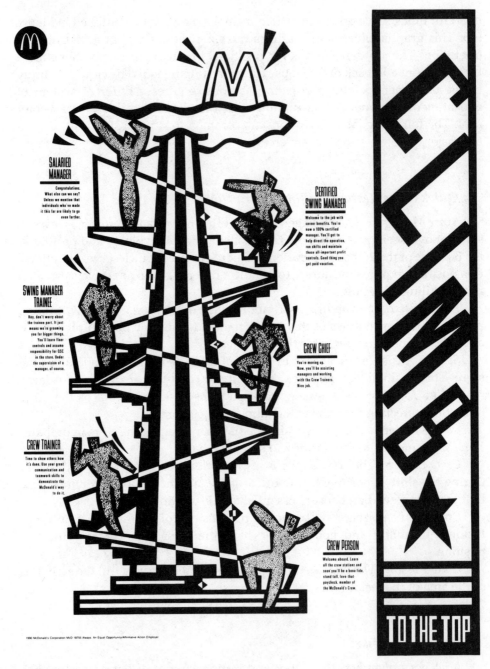

FIGURE 9-5   *McDonald's Climb to the Top. Courtesy McDonald's Corporation.*

tions. The job descriptions in Figure 9-6 are for the positions of swing manager and crew trainee. The statements regarding these positions indicate both the job function and its responsibilities.

By going through the exercise of creating an organization chart and corresponding job descriptions, management forms a much clearer picture of their organization. Lines of authority, communication, responsibility, promotion, and work are specified so that areas that have been characterized by inconsistency, miscommunication, and low productivity can be identified.

Often, management recognizes areas where authority is overlapping, causing confusion and often hostility among the staff. The line of work that has become tangled because of confusion regarding job responsibility can now be set out for the more effective accomplishment of work. Communication is a vital linking pin in any successful business. When managers and staff are unsure of exactly who is responsible for job functions and who has authority over whom, communications become ineffective. Individual job descriptions clearly identify authority and responsibility, giving both managers and staff an accurate understanding of the job.

SUMMARY

The hospitality industry includes five major areas of service industries: hotel/resort operations, restaurants, institutional services, recreation/leisure businesses, and the travel/tourism industry. Each of these industries has a demand for food service, providing an exciting range of jobs and careers.

Organization charts graphically represent the job positions in an organization in an outline of the flow of authority as well as the breakdown of management levels. A review of a variety of organization charts reveals the variety of job positions in food service organizations from corporate vice presidents of advertising to line cooks.

In any business operation it is important to outline the organization and define the flow of authority. This is especially important in food service organizations, where there is a constant turnover of both management and line staff. When management and staff are unsure of the lines of authority, the business will not function smoothly.

The variety of job positions available in the many restaurant styles of operation offer challenging career opportunities. Fine dining and full-service restaurants offer traditional preparation and service positions. Quick serve restaurant companies offer the ability to advance rapidly up their career ladders, actively participating in all aspects of an operation.

SWING MANAGER

QUALIFICATIONS:
- Verified on all stations with S.O.C.'s completed at 100%.
- Must be a minimum of 18 years of age.
- Must run all shifts effectively as the shift manager demonstrating:
  - Implementation of pre-shift checklist.
  - Prioritizing the "To Do" list.
  - Management of people, products, and equipment.
  - Track and manage hourly sales and labor.
  - Implementation of the production control system.
  - Operational knowledge of equipment/product times and temperatures.
  - Positively manage customer complaints.
  - Demonstrate proper procedures in handling emergency situations.
- Praise exceptional performance, counsel poor performance when necessary.
- Complete S.O.C.'s on crew and review them explaining areas of opportunity.
- Demonstrate proper cash handling through the use of skims, accurate drawer counts, deposits, and cash sheets.
- Complete all PMS assignments as scheduled.

RESPONSIBILITY/ JOB DESCRIPTION:
- Manage store at a high level of Q.S.C.
- Properly positions people, product, and equipment and adjusts as volume/transactions fluctuates.
- Follows store's policies & procedures in giving direction to the crew.
- Enforces security procedures to provide a safe working environment.
- Actively participates in store management meetings contributing unusual or significant events which occurred on their shift.

PROMOTABILITY CRITERIA:
- Successful Verification #2.
- Complete B.O.C. and the B.O.C. post action plan.
- Successful completion of Verification #3, completed by the Area Supervisor and Operations Manager.

CREW TRAINER

QUALIFICATIONS:
- Must maintain an above average job performance level.
- Display leadership ability, giving direction at all times demonstrating good people handling skills.
- Follows all procedures 100% and is able to teach other crewpeople the same standards.
- Appearance and dependability meets company standards.
- Maintains positive team work attitude.
- Must show a high degree of concern for the customer.

RESPONSIBILITY/ JOB DESCRIPTION:
- Assists the management team by training all new hires following the store's training program.
- Completes assigned S.O.C.'s, and reviews one on one with the employee.
- Corrects any procedural discrepancies on all employees and brings these to the attention of the manager in charge.

PROMOTABILITY CRITERIA:
- Must be verified by store manager that the trainer effectively supervises 1 person through coaching, teaching, and training.

FIGURE 9-6   *Quick-Serve Job Descriptions. Courtesy McDonald's Corporation, "Steps to Success."*

A good job description is the key to successful job placement for both management and employee. When management thoroughly reviews the functions of a job position, it becomes clear where functions and responsibilities are overlapping and unclear. Management can now define their needs and accurately assess the responsibilities and functions of each position. Positions that are redundant can be eliminated and new positions created for job functions which are not being effectively covered.

CHAPTER QUESTIONS

1. List the five hospitality businesses and discuss their food service management needs.

2. Define the term *organization chart.*

3. Discuss the importance of an organization chart to the success of a business.

4. Identify the two segments of authority discussed in this chapter. Give a short definition of each.

5. What impact does defining authority have on the daily operations of a business?

6. Discuss the four management levels that should be indicated on an organization chart. Give a short definition of each.

7. What factors determine the number of job positions in a restaurant?

8. Identify and define the two major sections of a restaurant operation.

9. Select one of the two major sections of a restaurant and list the job positions, giving a short description of each.

10. Discuss the importance of job descriptions as they relate to the organization chart and the success of a business.

ACTIVITIES

1. Select one of the five hospitality business areas and identify an ongoing business in your community supplying that hospitality service. Determine all of the food service management needs of that business and write an analysis of how those needs are being met.

2. Identify a food service related business in your community. Research the company to determine the flow of authority and all of the job positions available. Create an organization chart detailing this information.

3. When you have completed activity 2, develop job descriptions for a variety of management and staff positions. Consult the personnel department of the company to include all of the job responsibilities for each position.

10 *Employee Staffing and Training*

OBJECTIVES

1. To be able to identify the four key management segments of employee staffing and training.

2. To understand the importance of the interviewing process to the overall success of a business.

3. To be able to define the training cycle.

4. To understand the importance of a training program to the retention of employees.

CASE STUDY: ECOLAB TRAINING PROGRAMS

Successful training programs integrate visual aids with hands on application, reinforcement and continued management supervision. Well designed and systematically implemented training programs decrease costs and increase profitability.

Emphasizing the costs of poor training programs, ECOLAB, a major supplier of commercial and institutional cleaning supplies, recognizes the implications for overall profitability of employee productivity in (Figure 10-1).

Emphasizing training as the key to productivity, ECOLAB offers institutional systems to implement management's in-house training programs. Figure

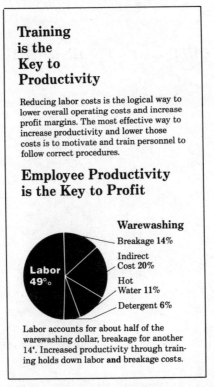

Training is the Key to Productivity

Reducing labor costs is the logical way to lower overall operating costs and increase profit margins. The most effective way to increase productivity and lower those costs is to motivate and train personnel to follow correct procedures.

Employee Productivity is the Key to Profit

Warewashing

- Labor 49%
- Breakage 14%
- Indirect Cost 20%
- Hot Water 11%
- Detergent 6%

Labor accounts for about half of the warewashing dollar, breakage for another 14¢. Increased productivity through training holds down labor and breakage costs.

FIGURE 10-1   *Training: The Key to Profitability. Courtesy ECOLAB, Inc.*

10-2 outlines the job tasks for waitresses, busboys, and dishwashers for cleaning, dish scraping, and presorting and loading of the dishwasher.

The dishwashing procedures illustrated in Figure 10-3 detail the individual steps in the dishwashing process. This combination of illustration and written instruction in both Spanish and English reflects the training needs of many workers in this job position level.

According to the Bureau of Labor Statistics, the food service industry is expected to employ over 12.4 million workers by the year 2005, up from 9.5 million in 1990.

These job positions will range from dishwashers to managers requiring diverse talents, skills, and training. The labor pool from which these employees will be drawn includes teenagers, high school and college graduates, homemakers, and senior adults. Many of these new employees will be members of minority groups for whom English is a second language.

Hiring, training, retaining, and firing employees are key management functions representing a major cost to any business operation. Employees are a

CLEAN UP

A

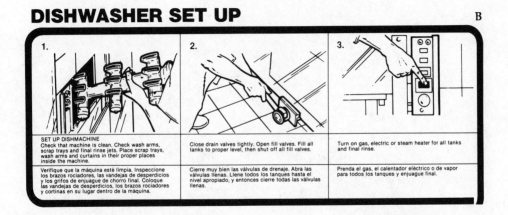

CLEAN UP
Turn off machine, heaters and electronic dispenser. Drain all tanks. Remove curtains and scrub clean with detergent and water. Inspect curtains for wear and tears. Let curtains dry overnight.

LIMPIEZA
Apague la máquina, los calentadores y el distribuidor electrónico. Drene todos los tanques. Quite las cortinas y restriegue hasta limpiarlas con detergente y agua. Inspeccione para ver si están gastadas o desgarradas. Deje secar las cortinas hasta el día siguiente.

Remove and clean scrap trays. Clean the pump screens. Check and clean overflows.

Quite y limpie las vandejas de desperdicios. Limpie las mayas de la bomba. Inspeccione y limpie los derrames.

Remove and clean prescraper, wash and power rinse arms. Set aside for inspection. Clean final rinse jets by carefully poking out obstructions.

Quite y limpie prerestregador, el lavador y los brazos de enjuague a presión. Ponga a un lado para inspección. Limpie los grifos del enjuague a presión finsl picando cuidadosamente donde haya obstrucciones.

DISHWASHER SET UP

B

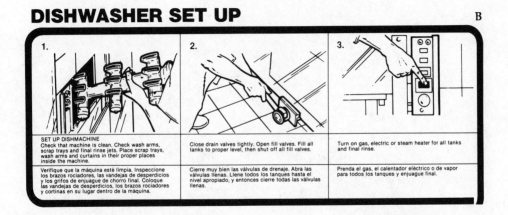

SET UP DISHMACHINE
Check that machine is clean. Check wash arms, scrap trays and final rinse jets. Place scrap trays, wash arms and curtains in their proper places inside the machine.

Verifique que la máquina esté limpia. Inspeccione los brazos rociadores, las vandejas de desperdicios y los grifos de enjuague de chorro final. Coloque las vandejas de desperdicios, los brazos rociadores y cortinas en su lugar dentro de la máquina.

Close drain valves tightly. Open fill valves. Fill all tanks to proper level, then shut off all fill valves.

Cierre muy bien las válvulas de drenaje. Abra las válvulas llenas. Llene todos los tanques hasta el nivel apropiado, y entonces cierre todas las válvulas llenas.

Turn on gas, electric or steam heater for all tanks and final rinse.

Prenda el gas, el calentador eléctrico o de vapor para todos los tanques y enjuague final.

C

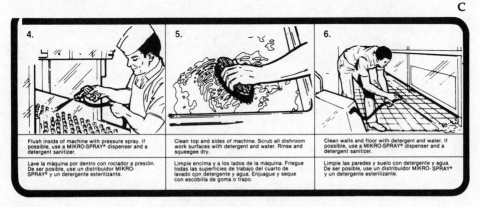

Flush inside of machine with pressure spray. If possible, use a MIKRO-SPRAY® dispenser and a detergent sanitizer.

Lave la máquina por dentro con rociador a presión. De ser posible, use un distribuidor MIKRO-SPRAY® y un detergente esterilizante.

Clean top and sides of machine. Scrub all dishroom work surfaces with detergent and water. Rinse and squeegee dry.

Limpie encima y a los lados de la máquina. Friegue todas las superficies de trabajo del cuarto de lavado con detergente y agua. Enjuague y seque con escobilla de goma o trapo.

Clean walls and floor with detergent and water. If possible, use a MIKRO-SPRAY® dispenser and a detergent sanitizer.

Limpie las paredes y suelo con detergente y agua. De ser posible, use un distribuidor MIKRO-SPRAY® y un detergente esterilizante.

FIGURE 10-2 *Loading the Dishmachine. Courtesy ECOLAB Inc.*

DISHWASHING PROCEDURES

A

1.

DISHWASHING OPERATING PROCEDURES
Scrape food soil from plates. Sort and stack dirty dishes on dish table. Remember, the warewashing machine is not a garbage disposal.

Quite todos los desperdicios de comida de los platos. Acomode y coloque la loza sucia en la mesa de loza. Recuerde que la máquina lavaplatos no es un eliminador de basura.

Rack dishes of same size together in straight rows. Do not overload or overlap. Place cups, glasses bowls, etc. upside down in racks. Do not mix. Do not stack. Place only one layer in each rack.

Coloque los platos del mismo tamaño juntos en filas derechas. No sobre carge o encime la loza. Ponga las tazas, vasos, cuencas, etc., boca abajo en las rejillas, no revuelva, no amontone. Por favor ponga solo una capa en cada rejilla.

3.

Presoak all flatware 15 to 20 minutes. For machine washing, place flatware with handles down, eating end up, in the silverware baskets. Knives, forks and spoons should be mixed so that spoons do not nest.

Preremoje todos los cubiertos de 12 a 15 minutos. Para lavarlos en la máquina, ponga los cubiertos en las cestas para cubiertos con mangos para abajo, el lado por el que se come para arriba. Los cuchillos, tenedores y cucharas deberán mezclarse para que las cucharas no se aniden.

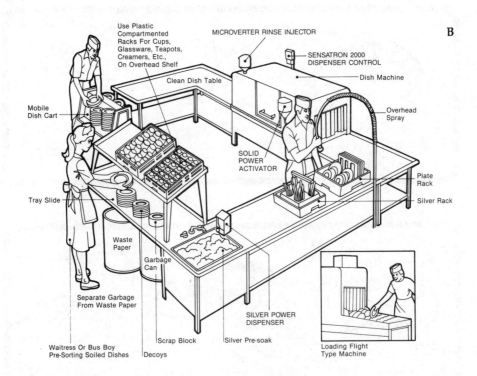

B

Bussing Dishes • Loading the Dishmachine

FIGURE 10-3 *Dishwashing Procedures Courtesy. ECOLABS Inc.*

significant part of overall operating costs. In addition to the hourly wage or salary, employers can expect to add 25 percent to an employee's pay as the cost of benefits. The operational costs of hiring, training, and firing can average as much as an additional $600.00 per employee.

Good interview skills improve the quality of the hiring practices of an organization. The ability to access an applicant's attitudes and personality accurately can help to identify potential employees for designated job positions. When the right person is hired for the right job, the employee performs to the employer's expectations. Satisfied employees stay in job positions, absorb training, become part of a team, and contribute to an organization.

Training is an integral part of the continued success of a business. Well-developed training programs include job orientations, instruction, evaluations, and development training. Employees who are continually given the initiative and skills to take on new and better paying positions stay and grow within an organization.

The staffing and evaluation process outlined in Figure 10-4 breaks down the steps that management must complete in the successful hiring and training of employees.

HIRING

Hiring employees for designated positions is the final step in a selection process that begins with a recognized need for labor. This labor shortage can be generated by a vacancy created by the loss of an employee or a growing demand for employees.

Recruiting

The method applied to recruit new employees is dependent on the level of the job position to be filled. Worker and staff positions are usually posted in the personnel office or appropriate locations in an operation. They are also listed in the classified Help Wanted section of local newspapers. The Equal Employment Opportunity Commission and the Fair Employment Practices Commission have laid down strict guidelines that must be followed in the announcement of the availability of any job position.

Employment agencies and advertisements in appropriate newspapers and trade journals are used to recruit employees for middle and upper management positions. Large food service companies have professional recruiters on staff who visit schools and colleges and other sources of employees, conducting formal recruiting programs. To interest prospective applicants, companies issue

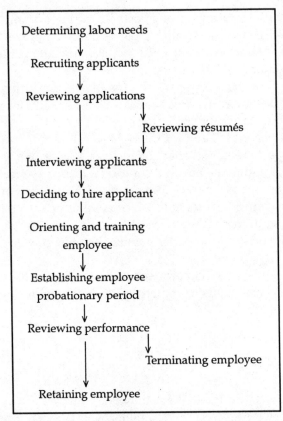

FIGURE 10-4   *Staffing and Evaluation Process. Source: Helen Delfakis, Nancy L. Scanlon, Janis B. VanBuren,* Food Service Management *Cincinnati: South-Western Publishing Co., 1992, p. 302.*

recruitment announcements and job descriptions that outline the job opportunity and benefits. Figure 10-5 is the initial recruitment advertisement that could be used for newspaper and magazine advertisements, handouts, and enclosures as well as bulletin boards in college career development offices and other locations. This format outlines the educational qualifications for applications and company benefits and is used to create general interest in the company.

Figure 10-6 and Figure 10-7 detail the job requirements for similar positions in two large quick serve corporations. Both of these companies are looking for assistant manager candidates to help operate units located on U.S. military bases worldwide. Each format states the criteria for the position, salary range, and benefits of working for the company.

The applications generated by these recruiting efforts form the applicant pool from which management can identify job candidates. For middle and

A rewarding career can be yours...

Come GROW With Us!

We're looking for graduates with Bachelors and Associate degrees in restaurant or food management (Business and other majors considered), or experienced food managers/supervisors who:

- enjoy active work in the food field
- have outstanding interpersonal skills
- are willing to relocate periodically and accept overseas assignments

It's up to you. Our ladder to success is challenging, but it's a rewarding climb. Opportunities to move up quickly are excellent. We offer a great benefits package, too.

Our Fringe Benefits Include:

medical insurance	shift differentials
moving expenses	Sunday Premium Pay
shopping privileges	retirement plan
savings plan	paid holidays
educational opportunities	vacation leave
training allowances	sick leave

If you're interested in a future with AAFES, please send your resume to:

HQ AAFES
ATTN: Burger King Executive Recruiter
    P.O. Box 660202
    Dallas, TX 75266-0202

FIGURE 10-5   *Recruitment Announcement. Courtesy Burger King Corporation.*

DEPARTMENTS OF THE ARMY & THE AIR FORCE
Army & Air Force Exchange Service
P.O. Box 660202
Dallas, TX 75266-0202
(214) 780-2011

POSITION	ASSISTANT MANAGER - AAFES BURGER KING
WHAT IS AAFES?	The Army & Air Force Exchange Service (AAFES) is a worldwide Retail, Food, and Service Organization devoted to serving the men and women in the Armed Services of the United States.
OUR NEEDS	We need Assistant Managers and Store Managers that are goal-oriented, enthusiastic, and motivated to serve in a fast-paced environment. Our 12 week, expense paid training program helps prepare you for a management position in one of our 130 plus Burger King stores located on military installations worldwide.
QUALIFICATIONS	Associate of Arts Degree in Food Service, Hospitality related fields, Business or Liberal Arts majors. Previous food service experience. Willingness to relocate periodically and accept overseas assignments. Ability to work in a demanding and high volume environment.
SALARY	Starting salaries are $18,900 to $24,500 per year, with promotions based strictly on performance.

BENEFITS		
	Moving Expenses	Vacation Leave
	Education Assistance	Sick Leave
	BX/PX Shopping Privileges	Retirement Plan
	Sunday Premium Pay	Savings Plan
	Night Shift Differential	10 Paid Holidays
	Medical Insurance	Training Allowance

CONTACT	Reginald C. Neely Executive Recruiter AAFES-BURGER KING HQ AAFES, ATTN: Recruitment Branch P.O. Box 660202, Dallas, Tx 75266-0202

FIGURE 10-6   *Job Requirements: Burger King. Courtesy Burger King Corporation.*

THE INTERNATIONAL OPPORTUNITY

We're looking for Assistant Manager trainees to serve Popeye's products to US military personnel and their families at overseas locations. Those interested in this unique opportunity should possess these qualifications:

- A two or four year college degree or recent food service management/supervisory experience
- Ability to relocate to overseas locations. All positions are located on US military installations throughout Europe and the Far East.
- A work history of stability and integrity
- Desire and potential to assume management responsibilities in a high-volume environment

We offer:

- Entry level salaries between $18,000-$23,000 based on experience and education
- 9 weeks of paid comprehensive training
- Major Medical and Dental insurance coverage
- Sick leave and vacation leave
- Educational assistance
- Relocation benefits
- And more

Send resume and letter of interest to:
Popeye's Executive Recruiter
Army & Air Force Exchange Service
P.O. Box 660202
Dallas, Texas 75266-0202

AAFES is an Equal Employment Opportunity, Affirmative Action Employer

AAFES★
Army & Air Force Exchange Service

FIGURE 10-7 *Job Requirements: Popeye's Famous Fried Chicken. Courtesy Al Copeland Enterprises Inc.*

upper management level positions resumes are also submitted with applications. Resumes provide a detailed breakdown of an applicant's employment history as well as information about education, professional associations, and achievements.

Having determined a set of criteria or guidelines for the position, management selects for interviews those applicants who qualify to the extent that they would like to assess their attitudes, personality, and personal characteristics. From the results of these interviews, management then selects the person to whom they will offer the position.

Interview

The interview process allows the employer to assess prospective employees on a one to one basis. There are two basic interview formats known, the direct interview and the indirect interview.

Direct Interview The direct interview is a highly structured situation with preplanned questions asked of the candidate in a set pattern. These questions have been designed to elicit specific information regarding experience, capabilities, and other factors that the employer feels are necessary to indicate the eligibility of the candidate.

Indirect Interview The indirect interview combines a planned format with a flexible question and answer scenario. Questions are designed so that the candidate can respond more spontaneously, often revealing personality traits and attitudes.

Interview Questions

Managers who are developing interview questions should be aware of what they may and may not ask a prospective employee under the laws and guidelines set down by federal antidiscrimination laws. The following are general guidelines concerning information that an interviewer may not attempt to elicit in an interview. The interviewer may not ask questions in the following categories to which the applicant must supply information which will reveal the information indicated:

Name: National origin, marital status or original name if applicant has legally changed his or her name.

Birthplace: Birthplace of applicant or applicant's parents.

Religion: Applicant's religious preference or affiliation as well as what church or parish is attended and religious holidays observed.

Age: Age, or date of birth except where such information is necessary in order to satisfy state or local laws as well as guidelines governing apprenticeship programs and employee benefit programs.

Sex: Sex, marital status or number of dependents of the applicant.

Race or color: Applicant's race or skin color.

Marital status: Whether an applicant is single, divorced, married or widowed as well as the number of children or the intent to have children.

Education: Applicant's race, nationality or religious preference.

Citizenship: Applicant and applicant's families citizenship or date of U.S. citizenship or status of naturalization.

Military record: Draft classification or eligibility for military service or date and conditions of discharge.

Arrest record: Arrest record unless directly related to the responsibilities of the job.

Handicaps: Whether a handicap exists and the extent of that handicap.

The content of interview questions is determined by the type of information that the interviewer needs to evaluate the applicant. Some job positions require direct questions relating to job experience, training, and skill level. The interviewer will also ask questions that can reveal how the applicant works with others. Middle and upper level management job positions require more indirect questions aimed at assessing the applicant's personal characteristics, personality, and attitudes as well as technical information. Applications and resumes for these positions have already provided in-depth work experience, education, and training information.

Guidelines for Job Orientation

1. Present a complete job description for the position.
2. Outline each specific job task for the position.
3. Divide each job task into a series to instructional steps.
4. Establish a training method for each instructional step.
5. Determine the amount of time for each instructional step.

6. With the employee, establish a training schedule for each instructional step.

7. Execute the first instructional step using the designated training method.

8. Evaluate the employee's job performance.

9. Proceed to the second instructional step only when both you and the employee are satisfied that the task can be completed successfully.

Law in the Workplace

As seen in the Case Study, Law in the Workplace, in Chapter 9, federal laws that govern major employment issues in the hospitality and food service industry have been enacted. The most recent of these laws, the American Disabilities Act (ADA), protects the rights of individuals with disabilities. These protections include hiring practices as well as the ability of disabled persons to function within the workplace. Because a restaurant requires a variety of physical activities to be performed in many job positions and good communications skills in others, understanding of the requirements of this law is important for managers at every level of an operation.

Employers will be required to recognize a prospective employee's disability and how that disability may or may not limit his or her ability to perform specific job tasks related to job positions. The ADA defines the term *disability* as follows:

- An impairment that substantially limits one or more major life activities, such as walking, hearing, speaking, seeing, learning, or working

- A record of an impairment that substantially limits major life activities from which the individual is recovering or has recovered

- An assumption by others that an impairment exists which in actuality does not, such as the presence of hearing aids and severe scarring from accidents or burns

The American Disabilities Act: *Questions and Answers* (Washington, D.C.) p. 2, Office on the Americans with Disabilities Act, U.S. Department of Justice, states that an employer may not discriminate against a qualified disabled person who can perform the necessary functions of a job position:

A qualified individual with a disability is a person who meets legitimate skill, experience, education, or other requirements of an employment position that he or she holds or seeks, and who can perform the "essential functions" with or without reasonable accommodation. If the individual is qualified to perform essential job functions except for limitations caused by the disability, the employer must consider whether the individual could perform these functions with a reasonable accommodation. If a written job description has been prepared in advance of advertising or interviewing applicants for a job, this will be considered as evidence, although not necessarily conclusive evidence, of the essential functions of the job.

Reasonable accommodation includes making existing facilities accessible to and usable by disabled employees, changing specific job functions, adapting equipment, or modifying educational programs and training materials. Under this act, accommodation must also be made to allow any disabled person to enjoy goods and services in public accommodations fully and equally.

Employers are required to meet the following specific requirements in their job hiring, training, and firing practices:

- Reasonably accommodate the disabilities of qualified applicants or employees unless to do so will cause undue hardship.

- Not discriminate against a qualified individual with a disability simply because they do not want to make reasonable accommodations. .

- Not use employment tests to screen out people with disabilities unless the tests or criteria are job-related and consistent with business necessity.

- Make only those preemployment inquiries concerning medical conditions that are strictly job-related.

- Not require preemployment medical exams. Conditional offers of employment may be made pending the results of medical exams if all new employees must have such exams. An applicant may not be rejected because of medical exam results unless the reasons for rejection are job-related and consistent with business necessity.

- Not discriminate against a qualified individual because of a known relationship or association with an individual with a disability.

Employers are given specific rights under the Americans with Disabilities Act:

- To counter discrimination charges by proving that the alleged discriminatory standards are job-related and consistent with business necessity and that the worker could not have done the job without reasonable accommodation.

- To reject applicants or fire employees who pose a significant risk to the health and safety of other individuals in the workplace.

- To use traditional risk assessment considerations when designing health benefit plans. Some restrictions do apply to this area.

In job interviews employers may not ask the following questions which relate to disabilities:

1. Whether a prospective employee has a disability.

2. Whether a prospective employee has a physical problem limiting his or her ability to carry out specific job tasks.

3. Whether a person has a history of drug or alcohol abuse.

4. Whether a person has filed for worker compensation claims and on what basis.

5. Whether there is a history of health problems.

Interview questions in these areas should be focused on the prospective employee's ability to perform specific job tasks. Managers should be particularly sensitive to this act and make every effort to be fully knowledgable about accommodations that must be made to an operation's physical facilities as well as employee practices.

The Americans with Disabilities Act is legislation that recognizes the contributions that persons with disabilities can make to the workplace as both employees and customers, restricting the ability of both employers and operators of public accommodations to prejudge their abilities to perform, participate, and enjoy.

Job Orientation

Once the position has been offered to an applicant and accepted, the most important stage in the hiring process, job orientation, must take place. To train an employee effectively, it is necessary for management to state the tasks and responsibilities of the job position clearly in a job specification or analysis. These guidelines assure that management knows exactly what functions the worker will serve. After presenting and discussing these specifications with the employee, job instruction begins.

Instructions for each position should be developed to establish a standard orientation to the job as well as to allow management to assess the skills and abilities of new employees.

Often, worker and staff positions employ the buddy system, pairing the trainee with an experienced worker who carries out the same job effectively. This system can be a direct introduction to the job or a method for reinforcing training.

Training

Training is a management skill which is most effective when a variety of training techniques and methods are applied in a wide range of situations. Effective trainers must have the capacity to listen as well as to instruct. There are established training methods that can be adapted to achieve an organization's training goals for individual positions. Management's training goals will change at each level of job authority and responsibility.

Worker Level   At the worker level management's overall goal is to produce an established quality of product or service in a harmonious setting. Training is primarily task oriented with an emphasis on team compatibility if the task is to be completed by a group.

Staff Level   The staff level positions often require a leadership role as either a crew leader, foreman, or supervisor. In addition to job task orientation, training methods are employed to teach management skills in group dynamics and leadership. Effective training methods provide role playing situations in which prospective managers learn how to react and interact with workers.

Middle Management   The middle manager enters his or her position with the required skills and training to carry out a large portion of the job's responsibilities. Job orientation for this management level requires a thorough indoctrination program into the organization's goals, history, policies, expectations, and benefits. Organizational systems will have to be explained as well as standard operating procedures that affect the job position. Training for these positions is ongoing as an integral part of the job. Middle-level managers should consistently be exposed to training programs that will increase their effectiveness as leaders and coworkers. Training is also necessary to keep middle-level managers current on changes in techniques, developments, and advancements in their area of business.

Upper-Level Management   New employees in upper-level management positions follow the same orientation pattern as middle-level managers. The depth of their orientation into company goals and policies will depend on the impact that their decisions have on the future success of the business.

Training Cycle

All training programs are developed in a series of steps that, when completed, lead to the next level of training for the employee. Effective training programs are ongoing, helping employees to learn new skills that will help them to advance into better paying job positions. The following outline details the training cycle:

Planning

1. The goals and objectives of any training activity must be clearly stated.

2. The amount of time needed for each segment of the training activity must be predetermined so that scheduling will not interfere with ongoing operations.

3. The teaching methods that are to be applied to the training activity must be established. Audiovisual equipment needs, handouts, workbooks, and evaluation procedures must be determined.

Preparation

1. The trainer is required to prepare the training area effectively so that the objectives of the training method can be accomplished. Materials and audiovisual equipment should be in place and working properly.

Presentation

1. The presentation of a training activity should be conducted within the established period.

2. The training period should be broken down into time segments. Each of these segments is assigned a presentation method that will hold the trainee's attention, create interest, and effectively instruct.

3. The presentation format should always allow for the flexibility of question and answer sessions at appropriate times in the program.

Application

1. Hands-on training allows the trainee to perform the task or activity covered in the training program. It is advisable that hands-on training take place in conjunction with formal training discussion.

2. The buddy system can be integrated into this segment of the training program. Working along with an experienced employee, the trainee can be directly instructed on a one-to-one basis.

Evaluation

1. Evaluations should be made at every stage of the training process. Written and oral quizzes will reinforce material in the presentation phase of the

training program. Application can be evaluated at scheduled intervals as the employee gains confidence as well as ability to carry out the job task.

Training Programs

Training programs are based on management objectives regarding the individual position. Worker and staff positions often have a high turnover rate which makes an investment in lengthy training programs too expensive to be cost-effective for the overall operation. Training programs for such positions often have the short-range goal of getting the trainee out on the production line and effectively turning out the product or service required. The problem with short-range training objectives is that they do not include the time to provide incentives to the trainee to learn new skills and continue into higher paying positions. This can often be accomplished by establishing incentive training goals that give employees incentive to learn new skills, as suggested in the Case Study at the beginning of this chapter.

Long-range training programs have the advantage of being able to develop a plan to present skill development and information programs at scheduled times over a specific period. Initial training includes job orientation and training for the job position. Secondary training reinforces initial training and provides developmental skills and/or management techniques, depending on the position.

The financial benefits of job advancement by learning new skills and work methods give employees the incentive to

1. Maintain job interest, reducing absenteeism and labor turnover

2. Improve the overall quality of the product or service through their own performance

3. Develop company loyalty and retain their association with the company over a period of years

Although long-range planning may initially be expensive, its long-range benefits to the work system have proved highly beneficial. The R. J. Wood Co., a contract feeding company in Allentown, Pennsylvania, gives employees at all levels long-term training opportunities. The excerpts from their corporate training schedule in Table 10-1 show how the company addresses the needs of employees by offering training on a variety of dates at various locations. As this schedule is released months in advance, supervisors and managers can plan well ahead to have employees attend. The choice of dates allows managers to ensure coverage of their operation by some of their

TABLE 10-1 Corporate Training Schedule, January through June 1991

I. Management Development

Course Title	Date(s)	Location	Suggested Audience	Length	Instructor(s)	Course Contents
1. Basic Training & Coaching Skills (603S)	Feb. 5	Simpson House Belmont & Edgely Philadelphia, PA	Primarily FSD's, Assistant FSD's Dietitians & FLS	1:00 PM to 5:00 PM	Roxann Filasetta Northampton Community College	1. Purpose of Training 2. Role of Training in Improving Employee Performance and Productivity.
CEU's: ADA—3 hrs. DMA—3 hrs.	Feb. 13	Merck Training Center 485 Route 1 South Parkway Tower, Bldg. E Iselin, NJ		1:00 PM to 5:00 PM		3. Training vs. Coaching 4. Adult Learning Issues 5. Identifying Different Learning Styles: and Utilization of Diverse Teaching Modes
	May 1	Home Office Allentown, PA		1:00 PM to 5:00 PM		6. Motivation and Building Self-Esteem 7. Communicating Clear Messages 8. Case Studies 9. Application of Learning to Job and Feedback
2. First Line Supervisory Training (606S)	Jan. 23 & Jan. 30	Home Office Allentown, PA	All First Line Supervisors First Cooks, Etc.	1:00 PM to 4:00 PM	Bob Soter Karen McIntyre Bonnie Scott	Company history, motivation, corporate values, problem solving, One Minute Manager, duties of a supervisor, etc.

CEU's:
DMA—5 hrs.

Feb. 5 & Feb. 6	IBM Endicott, NY	1:00 PM to 4:00 PM
Mar. 26 & April 1	Roseview Manor 1201 Rural Avenue Williamsport, PA	1:00 PM to 4:00 PM
May 8 & May 9	Leader Bethel Park 60 Highland Road Bethel Park, PA (Pittsburg area)	9:00 AM to 12:00 PM
May 29 & June 5	Home Office Allentown, PA	1:00 PM to 4:00 PM
June 13 & June 14	University of Maryland Baltimore Campus (U.M.B.C.)	9:00 AM to 12:00 PM

employees while others attend the session. The alternate date is used by the second group.

In Schedule A, the training goal is management development. The course First Line Supervisory Training is the initial job orientation program for the supervisory positions. The course contents description outlines the issues that the training program will cover. The course Basic Training & Coaching Skills is a training program specifically designed for the middle-management positions of food service directors, assistant food service directors, dietitians, and first-line supervisors. The course contents outline specific training skills and methods that effective managers need.

In Schedule B the training goal is food skill development. The course Food Production: Show the Trainer is the skill development program for food service managers and production personnel. The course contents description outlines the issues that the training program will cover. The primary goal of this training program is to teach management and supervisory level personnel the skills and appropriate teaching techniques to train production employees. The secondary goal of this program is to develop skill proficiency at this level of supervisors and management. The third program, Waitstaff: Train the Trainer, is the skill development program for food service managers and service personnel. Much as in the Food Production program, the skills and teaching techniques appropriate to this area of a food service operation are covered by the course contents.

Training Methods

The application of a specific training method to a training program is dependent on the level of job positions included in the training session and a determination of short- or long-range goals for the skills being addressed. Training programs are generally classified as task-oriented or group and lecture.

Task-oriented training provides application of the job task as part of the direct training. In the application stage of the schedule the employee performs the job in conjunction with the training discussion. The buddy system or mentoring provides reinforced task application during actual job performance.

In group and lecture training the trainer communicates the information to a group of individuals in a passive setting where there is little or no opportunity for job application. There are, however, programs which provide the opportunity for role playing situations where managers are trained in employee management techniques and methods. Professional presenters will encourage discussion and interaction between attendees to provide the opportunity for shared information, learning, and growth.

SUMMARY

The ability to hire and train employees effectively is a management skill which can significantly contribute to the profitability of a restaurant operation. The cost of hiring, training, and firing employees can be a significant factor in an ongoing operation. Employee retention rates directly affect employee management costs. The higher the retention rate, the lower the cost of employee management.

Evaluating prospective employees through the interview process requires the development of accurate job descriptions which clearly state the criteria for the position, salary, and benefits.

The job orientation process is the foundation for employee retention. Employees who clearly understand what is expected of them and their position in the organization will be more productive and satisfied with their job.

Management should establish training goals and select training methods which will best meet the objectives of the training program. The primary goal of training programs is to increase profitability by maximizing worker productivity. Workers who understand their job positions and have the skills necessary to complete job tasks will be more likely to remain in their jobs and take advantage of additional training programs.

CHAPTER QUESTIONS

1. Identify the four key segments of employee staffing and training.

2. How do good interview skills improve the quality of the hiring practices of an organization?

3. Outline the steps in the staffing and evaluation process.

4. Identify the four levels of job position discussed in this chapter. How do recruitment techniques differ between them?

5. Explain the differences between a job description and a job instruction.

6. What are the two basic interview formats? Give a short explanation of each.

7. Why are constraints placed on the type of questions that can be asked in employment interviews?

8. Identify and discuss the training goals for the four job levels.

9. Outline the training cycle, giving a short definition of each of the six steps.

10. What are the major distinctions between short-term training programs and long-range training programs?

ACTIVITIES

1. Identify a variety of restaurant job positions and develop job descriptions and instructions for each.

2. Create a series of interview questions for a specific restaurant position. Use the interview guidelines suggested in this chapter and the Americans with Disabilities Act requirements to phrase questions within legal boundaries.

3. Develop training materials for a selected job. Determine training goals and design a variety of materials to help achieve those goals.

4. Design a training schedule for a restaurant business such as offered in this chapter. Identify levels of positions as well as short- and long-range goals. Create appropriate training program titles to meet employee needs.

11 *Computer Food Service Systems*

OBJECTIVES

1. To understand the contribution of a computer food service system to the effective management of a restaurant operation.

2. To be able to identify food service computer systems and understand their applications in a variety of restaurant operations.

3. To be able to apply computer report information to increase restaurant revenues and profitability.

4. To be aware of the marketing applications derived from the analysis of computer report information.

CASE STUDY: JONATHAN'S OGUNQUIT, MAINE—COMPUTER FOOD SERVICE APPLICATION PROFILE

- Location: Coastal resort area
- Open year round, 7 days a week
- Serving lunch and dinner daily; weekend brunch
- Seating 230 in dining areas, 50 in bar/lounge area
- Entertainment—piano bar

189

Jonathan's is a popular year-round restaurant with an average check of $17 without alcohol and $22 with, producing an annual volume of $1,500,000 in sales. The application of a computer foodservice system is essential to the profitability of this operation. During the summer months, the highest volume time of the year, a complement of 12 servers operate in three dining room areas entering beverage and food orders into 5 separate computer terminals along with guest check printers. A sixth work station in the bar area also allows the bartender to enter orders and print guest checks. Remote printers relay customer orders to the 4 members of the kitchen production line. In the back office another terminal is dedicated to credit card authorizations which are relayed to and from the server workstations.

The floor plan in Figure 11-1 illustrates the layout of the front and back of the house areas and identifies the location of server computer workstations, remote printers and the back office main computer system. Jonathan's uses the Fischer Computer Software System with IBM-compatible hardware.

The application of computer food service systems to restaurant management is essential in the volatile and highly competitive market of the 1990s.

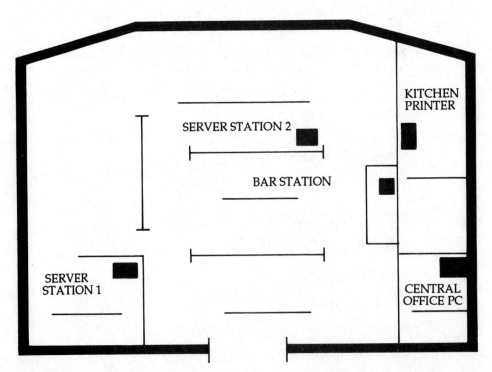

FIGURE 11-1   *Jonathan's Floor Plan. Courtesy Jonathan's Restaurant, Ogunquit, Maine.*

Eighty percent of all new restaurant operations have been experiencing failure within the first 18 months of operation. These failures result primarily from a lack of understanding of business management principles by owners and operators. The inability of many food service owners to understand or carry out the day-to-day functions of accounting and food cost management has resulted in numerous bankruptcies and closing, while the sheer frustration of working seven days a week, 12 to 14 hours a day, just to "break even", has caused many operators to sell or close their restaurants. In today's increasingly competitive market, restaurants must absorb rising costs and face shrinking customer counts.

Industry projections forecast a 30 percent growth in restaurant operations by the year 2000. The available pool of customers will, however, remain constant until well into the twenty-first century.

As we have seen in previous chapters, it is essential for management to establish operational controls that monitor the daily productivity and profitability of a restaurant business. The activities of purchasing, production, service, costing, pricing, and marketing require information to be supplied, recorded, and processed daily. The integration of a computer food service system into a restaurant operation can increase profits while providing essential time-saving recording systems.

In this chapter, computer-assisted management applications that can develop and monitor quality and operational control activities will be reviewed.

Quick-serve restaurants require different computer functions than full-service restaurants. The turnover rate and speed of customer ordering and service combined with the needs of many quick service personnel have caused computer companies to develop specific hardware and programs for this segment of the restaurant industry.

The applications of computer-generated information go beyond operational concerns. Employee management, compliance with labor laws, wage and tip reporting guidelines, and analysis of marketing data are some of the additional areas that benefit from the application of computer food service management systems.

FOOD SERVICE COMPUTERS

Food service computer hardware serves a wide range of equipment functions, depending on the individual needs of an operation. Computerized cashier stations such as the one pictured in Figure 11-2 are available with a variety of hardware designs and interface capabilities with back office computer systems.

Quick-serve operations often find the TEC server workstation pictured in Figure 11-3 an effective compromise between a cash register and a computer terminal.

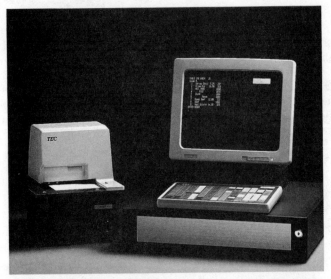

FIGURE 11-2   *The Cashier Station. Courtesy TEC Systems Inc.*

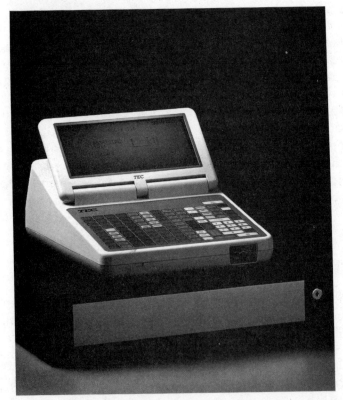

FIGURE 11-3   *TEC Quick-Serve Workstation. Courtesy TEC Systems Inc.*

The development of the digital crystal display screen gives servers a review of the order and prompts suggestive selling in enlarged characters. Multilingual programs are available. Each workstation is equipped with two cash drawers.

Casual family style and fine dining restaurants can apply a variety of modular systems, depending on the needs of the operation. Figure 11-4 features the REMANCO touch screen terminal.

The touch screen terminal displays menu categories to the server for ordering selection. Servers touch the screen at the corresponding menu item, activating the ordering system. The complete check can be reviewed on the screen for accuracy. This workstation can support four cash drawers simultaneously. Information is relayed to the back office, where the computer screen and keyboard take on a more conventional business design with a keyboard and monitor.

The TEC computer system featured in Figure 11-5 provides the server with a color-coded 124-position keyboard. This keyboard gives management the opportunity to display the entire menu with options. The screen allows for server prompting and highlighting of menu categories.

Portable electronic server pads such as in Figure 11-6 allow servers maximum flexibility in large restaurant operations. These battery-powered units are hand held and transmit information by radio signal.

Modular systems allow orders to be printed in a number of locations. Beverage orders are printed out in the bar, entrée orders on the main kitchen production line, and salad orders in the pantry. The complete order can be simultaneously printed out in the kitchen for expediting purposes and

FIGURE 11-4   *REMANCO Touch Screen Terminal. Courtesy Remanco International Inc.*

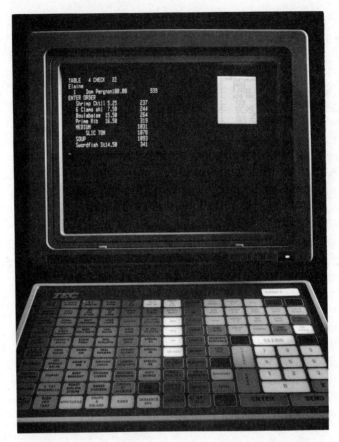

FIGURE 11-5   *TEC Computer System. Courtesy TEC Systems Inc.*

management control. Printers are available in a wide variety of designs depending on their function and location; one design is illustrated in Figure 11-7.

FRONT OF THE HOUSE APPLICATIONS

Computer-assisted management applications in the guest service areas of a restaurant begin with server orders. Information relayed to preparation stations is, at the same time, recorded on designated files in the back office computer. This applies to both quick-serve and full-service restaurant operations.

FIGURE 11-6   *REMANCO Electronic Server Pad. Courtesy Remanco International Inc.*

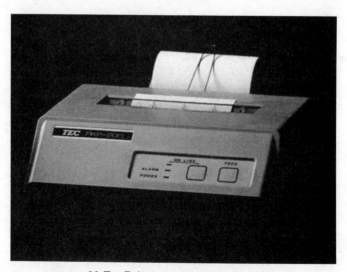

FIGURE 11-7   *Printer. Courtesy TEC Systems Inc.*

GUEST CHECK

The guest check in Figure 11-8 outlines a quick-service order. A full-service guest check includes beverages, side orders, and desserts. Information from the guest check is transferred into the assigned computer files illustrated by Figure 11-9.

SALES REPORTS

Guest checks supply the information management needs to know to evaluate the sales of individual menu items. In the menu item usage report in Figure 11-9 a record of the sale of menu items and beverages during the lunch period on January 25 provides management with a detailed overview of menu item popularity and beverage consumption. This information is taken one step further to analyze customer spending patterns and revenues per customer and per check in the average check report in Figure 11-10.

FIGURE 11-8   *Quick-Serve Guest Check. Courtesy TEC Systems Inc.*

CATEGORY REPORT
Chateau VISION – RESTAURANT
PERIOD: 01/25/91 – 01/25/91

Printed 01/26/91 03:24			Current Database			Rpt# 04 Page 1	
	Items	Voids	Waste	Sold	Net Sales	Food Cost	Cost %
OUTLET: DINING ROOM							
FOOD							
FOOD	1,154	6	0	1,148	5,177.60	1,476.40	28.5%
FOOD Total	1,154	6	0	1,148	5,177.60	1,476.40	28.5%
LIQUOR							
LIQUOR	210	0	0	210	549.75	120.97	22.00%
LIQUOR Total	210	0	0	210	549.75	120.97	22.00%
DINING ROOM Tot	1,364	6	0	1,358	5,727.35	1,597.37	27.88%
OUTLET: LOUNGE							
FOOD							
FOOD	109	5	0	104	309.54	85.53	27.63%
FOOD Total	109	5	0	104	309.54	85.53	27.63%
LIQUOR							
LIQUOR	396	1	0	395	707.79	146.88	20.75%
LIQUOR Total	396	1	0	395	707.79	146.88	20.75%
LOUNGE Total	505	6	0	499	1,017.33	232.41	22.85%
Report Totals	1,869	12	0	1,857	6,744.68	1,829.78	27.12%

FIGURE 11-9   *Menu Item Category Report. Courtesy Remanco International Inc.*

In this printout example, 284 menu items are sold for total net sales of $1535.35, representing 89.9 percent of sales between the hours of 7:00 p.m. and 9:30 p.m. 66 checks were written with an average total of $22.58 per check. 173 guests were served for an average menu sale per guest of $8.67. 148 dinner entrees were served at an average selling price of $10.37 per item. The productivity report for the same period in Figure 11-11 indicates the total amount of labor hours compared to total revenues.

A V E R A G E   C H E C K   R E P O R T
Chateau VISION – RESTAURANT

PERIOD: 01/25/91 – 01/25/91

Printed 01/26/91 03:27   Current Database   Rpt# 07 Page 1

	ITEMS		NET SALES		CHECKS			GUESTS			ENTREES		
	Count	%Total	Amount	%Total	Count	Avg.Amt	%Total	Count	Avg.Amt	%Total	Count	Avg.Amt	%Total
OUTLET: DINING ROOM													
11:00 – 2:00													
FOOD	437	93.4%	1,456.65	95.3%	79	18.44	95.3%	207	7.04	95.3%	214	6.81	95.3%
LIQUOR	31	6.6%	71.35	4.7%	15	0.90	4.7%	40	0.34	4.7%	0	0.00	0.0%
11:00 – 2:00 Totals	468		1,528.00		79	19.34		207	7.38		214	7.14	
2:00 – 4:00													
FOOD	48	100.0%	199.95	100.0%	12	16.66	100.0%	20	10.00	100.0%	20	10.00	100.0%
2:00 – 4:00 Totals	48		199.95		12	16.66		20	10.00		20	10.00	
4:00 – 7:00													
FOOD	341	78.0%	1,803.30	87.4%	87	20.04	87.4%	206	8.51	87.4%	192	9.39	87.4%
LIQUOR	96	22.0%	260.40	12.6%	42	2.89	12.6%	103	1.23	12.6%	0	0.00	0.0%
4:00 – 7:00 Totals	437		2,063.70		90	22.93		212	9.73		192	10.75	
7:00 – 9:30													
FOOD	284	80.2%	1,535.35	89.5%	66	22.58	89.5%	173	8.67	89.5%	148	10.37	89.5%
LIQUOR	70	19.8%	180.10	10.5%	31	2.65	10.5%	83	1.02	10.5%	0	0.00	0.0%
7:00 – 9:30 Totals	354		1,715.45		68	25.23		177	9.69		148	11.59	
9:30 – CLOSE													
FOOD	38	74.5%	182.35	82.8%	12	15.20	82.8%	30	6.08	82.8%	21	8.68	82.8%
LIQUOR	13	25.5%	37.90	17.2%	5	3.1	17.2%	13	1.26	17.2%	0	0.00	0.0%
9:30 – CLOSE Totals	51		220.25		12	18.35		30	7.34		21	10.49	
DINING ROOM Totals	1,358		5,727.35		244	23.47		604	9.48		595	9.63	

FIGURE 11-10   *Average Check Report. Courtesy Remanco International Inc.*

SERVER SALES RECORDS

As a security precaution against theft, each server is assigned a code number permitting him or her to enter the computer system by signing on at designated workstations. This number also allows management to track the record of server sales and to maintain surveillance on their incomplete transactions.

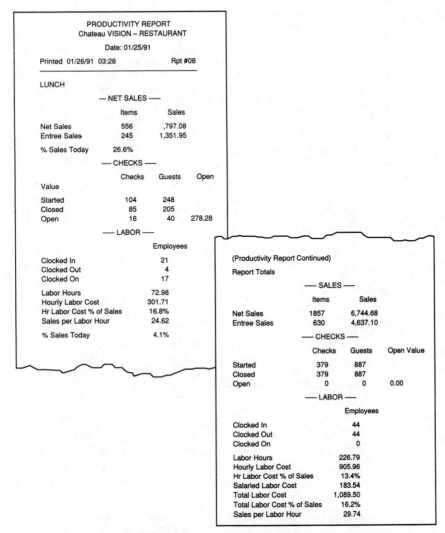

PRODUCTIVITY REPORT
Chateau VISION – RESTAURANT

Date: 01/25/91

Printed 01/26/91 03:28   Rpt #08

LUNCH

— NET SALES —

	Items	Sales
Net Sales	556	,797.08
Entree Sales	245	1,351.95
% Sales Today	26.6%	

— CHECKS —

Value	Checks	Guests	Open
Started	104	248	
Closed	85	205	
Open	16	40	278.28

— LABOR —

	Employees
Clocked In	21
Clocked Out	4
Clocked On	17
Labor Hours	72.98
Hourly Labor Cost	301.71
Hr Labor Cost % of Sales	16.8%
Sales per Labor Hour	24.62
% Sales Today	4.1%

(Productivity Report Continued)

Report Totals

— SALES —

	Items	Sales
Net Sales	1857	6,744.68
Entree Sales	630	4,637.10

— CHECKS —

	Checks	Guests	Open Value
Started	379	887	
Closed	379	887	
Open	0	0	0.00

— LABOR —

	Employees
Clocked In	44
Clocked Out	44
Clocked On	0
Labor Hours	226.79
Hourly Labor Cost	905.96
Hr Labor Cost % of Sales	13.4%
Salaried Labor Cost	183.54
Total Labor Cost	1,089.50
Total Labor Cost % of Sales	16.2%
Sales per Labor Hour	29.74

FIGURE 11-11   *Productivity Report. Courtesy Remanco International Inc.*

In Figure 11-12 the sales records of three servers are tracked for a one-day period. A total of fifty-eight items were sold with total net sales of $917.90. Fifty-eight checks were written averaging $15.83 per check. Twenty-two entrées were sold averaging $9.56 per entrée.

Tip reports, such as the one in Figure 11-13, help employers maintain records so that they can adhere to tip reporting regulations.

```
              S E R V E R   C A T E G O R Y   S A L E S   R E P O R T
                       Chateau VISION – RESTAURANT

                        PERIOD: 01/25/91 – 01/25/91

     Printed  01/26/91 08:09      Current Database        Rpt# 40 Page  1
```

		SALES		GUESTS		ENTREES			VOIDS
	Items	Net Sales	%Total	Count	AvgAmt	Count	AvgAmt	% Mix	Count
SMITH, JOHN P									
FOOD	144	513.05	97.1%	63	8.14	65	7.89	45.1%	4
FOODTotal	144	513.05	97.1%	63	8.14	65	7.89	45.1%	4
LIQUOR	8	15.11	2.9%	6	2.52	0	0.00	0.0%	0
LIQUOR Total	8	15.11	2.9%	6	2.52	0	0.00	0.0%	0
SMITHTotal	152	528.16	100.0%	63	8.38	65	8.13	42.8%	4
STARR, PAMELA J									
FOOD	76	365.00	85.3%	38	9.61	37	9.86	48.7%	1
FOOD Total	76	365.00	85.3%	38	9.61	37	9.86	48.7%	1
LIQUOR	26	62.85	14.7%	21	2.99	0	0.00	0.0%	2
LIQUORTotal	26	62.85	14.7%	21	2.99	0	0.00	0.0%	2
STARRTotal	102	427.85	100.0%	38	11.26	37	11.56	36.3%	3
LANG, DOUG									
FOOD	1	2.95	100.0%	1	2.95	0	0.00	0.0%	0
FOOD Total	1	2.95	100.0%	1	2.95	0	0.00	0.0%	∪
LANG Total	1	2.95	100.0%	1	2.95	0	0.00	0.0%	0
NEIDERT, RICHARD M									
FOOD	53	139.30	97.2%	26	5.36	22	6.33	41.5%	0
FOOD Total	53	139.30	97.2%	26	5.36	22	6.33	41.5%	0
LIQUOR	1	3.95	2.8%	2	1.98	0	0.00	0.0%	0
LIQUOR Total	1	3.95	2.8%	2	1.98	0	0.00	0.0%	0
NEIDERTTotal	54	143.25	100.0%	26	5.51	22	6.51	40.7%	0
Report Total	1857	6,744.68	100.0%	907	7.44	630	10.71	33.9%	63

FIGURE 11-12   *Server Category Sales Report. Courtesy Remanco International Inc.*

Reports such as the meal period labor report in Figure 11-14 help management to evaluate total server sales efforts in terms of net sales and number of guests served. This report indicates that labor costs for five employees during lunch periods in the week of February 1 totaled $439.06. This represented 47 hours, of which 7.5 were overtime hours. Wages totaled $351.25. Workmen's compensation and insurance were an additional cost of $87.81 for a total labor

```
            SERVER MEDIA SUMMARY RE-PRINT

        Printed  03/15/91 18:12      Rpt# 48



        ############## RE-PRINT ##############

               SERVER SUMMARY REPORT
            Chateau VISION - RESTAURANT

        Printed  3/15/91  5:29pm    Rpt# 45


              ACCUMULATED PAYMENT SUMMARY FOR

        Summary date:           3/15/91
        Last activity:  3/15/91   15:41
        Key ID          Server ID    Server Name

         15              89         LITTLE, MARK

              ACCUMULATED MEDIA ACCOUNTABILITY

        Cnt    Sales    Tip     Total


        CASH
        1      12.43    0.00    12.43
        VISA/MC/DISCOVER
        2      31.85    5.09    36.94


        TOTAL
        3      44.28    5.09    49.37
        Media to sales balance total  49.37*

        Cash Total
        1 Cash tenders              12.43

        Total cash held             12.43

        Credit card tips earned      5.09
        Service charge tips earned   0.00
        Tips received                0.00

        Total cash owed              7.34
```

FIGURE 11-13   *Tip Report. Courtesy Remanco International Inc.*

cost of $439.06. Net sales for the period were $4,200.00 representing $89.36 in sales per worker hour.

Weekly and monthly analysis of these types of reports allow management to review and appraise customer sales patterns, menu item popularity, and server sales efforts. Given advance knowledge of problems in any of these areas, management can plan menu items to meet customer needs, change the content or price of menu items, and train servers to be more effective sales people.

```
                    M E A L   P E R I O D   L A B O R   R E P O R T
                            Chateau VISION – RESTAURANT
                          PERIOD: 01/25/91 – 01/25/91

    Printed  01/26/91 06:50            Current Database         Rpt# 60  Page  1


    StaffCat        Emps  RegHrs  OTHrs  TotHrs  Wages  OverHead  LaborCost


      1:00 – 2:00
    MANAGEMENT    1    3.00   0.00   3.00   16.50   0.00     16.50
    BARTENDER     1    2.94   0.69   3.63   19.87   0.00     19.87
    KITCHEN       5   26.66   0.00  26.66  149.72   0.00    149.72
    SERVER       10   30.83   0.00  30.83   69.76   0.00     69.76
    BUSSER        1    2.05   0.00   2.05    5.94   0.00      5.94
    MAINTENANCE   1    6.07   0.00   6.07   28.83   0.00     28.83
    HOST/MOD      2    6.30   0.00   6.30   26.17   0.00     26.17

    Total        21   77.85   0.69  78.54  316.79   0.00    316.79

    Net Sales:  1,797.08
    Checks         102       Sales/Check: 17.62      Sales/LaborHr:   22.88
    Guests:        246       Sales/Guest:  7.31      Guests/LaborHr:   3.13

      2:00 – 4:00
    BARTENDER     1    0.00   0.23   0.23    1.72   0.00      1.72
    KITCHEN       6    8.50   0.00   8.50   45.71   0.00     45.71
    SERVER        8    6.86   0.00   6.86   14.91   0.00     14.91
    BUSSER        1    0.45   0.00   0.45    1.31   0.00      1.31
    MAINTENANCE   1    2.00   0.00   2.00    9.50   0.00      9.50
    COCKTAIL SER  2    0.10   0.00   0.10    0.31   0.00      0.31
    HOST/MOD      1    0.33   0.00   0.33    1.40   0.00      1.40

    Total        20   18.24   0.23  18.47   74.86   0.00     74.86

    Net Sales:   246.46
    Checks:        17       Sales/Check: 14.50      Sales/LaborHr:   13.34
    Guests:        32       Sales/Guest:  7.70      Guests/LaborHr:   1.73

      4:00 – 7:00
    BARTENDER     2    3.00   2.70   5.70   32.25   0.00     32.25
    KITCHEN       5    9.25   0.00   9.25   46.98   0.00     46.98
    SERVER        8   15.55   0.00  15.55   32.83   0.00     32.83
    BUSSER        2    2.88   0.00   2.88    8.35   0.00      8.35
    MAINTENANCE   3    2.63   0.00   2.63   12.12   0.00     12.12
    COCKTAIL SER  2    6.00   0.00   6.00   18.60   0.00     18.60
    HOST/MOD      3    4.64   0.00   4.64   20.45   0.00     20.45

    Total        25   43.95   2.70  46.65  171.58   0.00    171.58

    Net Sales:  2,555.31
    Checks:       162       Sales/Check: 15.77      Sales/LaborHr:   54.78
    Guests:       406       Sales/Guest:  6.29      Guests/LaborHr:   8.70

    Report Totals
    All Hourly         232.19   9.69 241.88  960.52   0.00    960.52
    All Salaried  18    40.85  34.60  75.45  183.54   0.00    183.54

    All Employees      273.04  44.29 317.33 1,144.06  0.00  1,144.06
```

FIGURE 11-14   *Meal Period Labor Report. Courtesy Remanco International Inc.*

BACK OF THE HOUSE APPLICATIONS

Back of the house applications for computer food service systems range from purchasing to daily food cost analysis. Recipe and cost cards as well as production sheets can help to increase menu item quality and kitchen productivity.

PURCHASING

Effective purchasing requires that at least three sources be consulted for comparative selling prices before determining which vendor to use. Computer systems provide bid and quote forms. When all bids have been received, management selects the quote that satisfies both cost and quality specifications and posts it on the bid and quote form. The application of a computer software system to this function gives management the ability to generate purchase orders based on final vendor selections. The specifications on this form detail the exact requirements for the product, identifying the grade, purchase unit, purchase unit weight, quantity to be ordered, and item file number. Carrots are listed as in Table 11-1.

The written notes specify a carrot with a minimum diameter of 1.5 inches. The carrot must be firm to the touch, not spongy or soft; the shape must be uniformly straight; and the color should be orange.

A purchase order is now generated for each vendor who has been selected. The purchase order in Figure 11-15 indicates the items that Costa Produce has been designated to provide. The term NET 10 indicates that the food service operation will pay the bill in full within 10 days. The item number, name, brand name and grade are carried over from the bid and quote form. The quantity to be ordered by purchase unit is indicated as well as the vendor order number for this item. Bananas are listed as in Table 11-2. The price per pound is listed at 0.35 per pound and the extended cost is calculated at $70.00 for 200 lbs. of bananas.

INVENTORY

Managing inventory effectively can increase operational cash flow and reduce waste. Tracking inventory from the time at which it is received through storage and production allows management to be apprised of the status of inventory on a daily basis. Variances in product use compared with projected production requirements can be identified. The ability to value inventory helps management to be aware of the financial impact of current inventory on the overall

TABLE 11-1 Sample Specification—Carrots

Item	Name	Grade	Purchase Unit	Purchase Unit Wgt	Quantity	Item Number

4" MIN LENGTH 1.5" DIA AT TOP FIRM SMOOTH UNIFORM AND FAIRLY WELL COLORED.

```
REPORT#: 248    * * * CBORD FOODSERVICE MANAGEMENT SYSTEMS * * *        PAGE:   1
OPTION : 7.3.2.4.2.    MENU MANAGEMENT SYSTEM - V4.1.35Z                NOV 05 90
                       THE CBORD GROUP TRAINING CENTER                  1506 HOURS
                                PURCHASE ORDER

Vendor : 12 COSTA PRODUCE
Address: 123 STATE STREET                              Terms    : NET 10
                                                       Lead Time:
         ITHACA        NY 14850
.................................................................................
-- Item --           Brand           Grade   Vendor    Order   Purchase    Price ------- Extended --------
Nmbr Name            Name                    Order #  Quantity Unit                    Cost    Weight
.................................................................................

406 ORANGES          SUNKIST           A     F-333___    10    88/CASE    12.50     125.00      270

409 CANTALOUPES      _____         A     F-4237__    25    LB          1.75      43.75       25

405 APPLES TABLE     RED DELICIOUS     A     F-439___   150    LB          0.68     102.00      150

408 AVOCADO          _____         A     F-654      100    AVOCADO     1.02     102.00      100

413 GARLIC FRESH     _____         A     F-890       25    LB          2.00      50.00       25

402 BANANAS          CHIQUITA          A     V-128___   200    LB          0.35      70.00      200

391 PARSLEY          _____         A     V-129___    15    LB          0.09       1.35       15

384 TOMATOES         _____         A     V-222___   300    LB          1.76     528.00      300

425 POTATOES WHOLE PEELED _____      A     V-231      120    30# BAG    12.00    1440.00     3600

386 CUCUMBERS        _____         A     V-238___   225    LB          0.90     202.50      225

379 LETTUCE ROMAINE  _____         A     V-337___   250    LB          0.61     152.50      250

380 ONIONS GREEN     _____         A     V-417       50    LB          0.28      14.00       50

374 LETTUCE ICEBERG  _____         A     V-447___   150    LB          0.51      76.50      150

 45 POTATOES SWEET   _____         A     V-539___   125    LB          0.42      52.50      125

387 CELERY           _____         A     V-542___   250    LB          0.32      80.00      250

385 PEPPERS GREEN    _____         A     V-555___   100    5 LB        3.50     350.00      500

734 MUSHROOMS WHITE  _____         A     V-655       50    LB          1.22      61.00       50

393 CARROTS          _____         A     V-870___   130    LB          0.59      76.70      130

274 TURNIP WHITE     _____         A     V-901       25    LB          1.65      41.25       25

378 ENDIVE           _____         A     V-9993___  150    HEAD        0.58      87.00      150
.................................................................................
TOTAL(S)                                                                          3656.05    6590.000
---------------------------------------------------------------------------------
```

FIGURE 11-15   *Purchase Order. Courtesy The CBORD Group.*

TABLE 11-2   Sample Purchase Order—Bananas

| Item | | Brand | | | Order | |
Numbr	Name	Name	Grade	Vendor Order#	Quantity	Purchase Unit
402	Bananas	Chiquita	A	V-128	200	lb.

operation. The inventory extension report in Figure 11-16 values current inventory and projects cash flow needs for future purchasing requirements.

The information on this report identifies the storage location as 3 Dairy Cooler in the main kitchen. The unit by which the item is purchased and stock on hand are indicated along with the item name and number. The inventory value is calculated by multiplying the price per stock unit times the number of units on hand.

Cantaloupes are listed as in Table 11-3.

To complete the analysis of purchasing and inventory, management can produce an inventory variance report that compares projected item usage with

```
REPORT#: 275   * * * CBORD FOODSERVICE MANAGEMENT SYSTEMS * * *      PAGE:   5
OPTION : 7.5.1.9.2.    MENU MANAGEMENT SYSTEM - V4.1.35Z              SEP 25 90
                    THE CBORD GROUP TRAINING CENTER                   1500 HOURS
                        INVENTORY EXTENSION

Inventory Date  : 09/25/90
Storage Location: 3 DAIRY COOLER
--------------------------------------------------------------------------------
Item Name                Item  Units    Stock     Price/    Inventory
                         Nmbr  On Hand  Unit      Stk U     Value
--------------------------------------------------------------------------------

BUTTER                   599   140.000  LBS         1.86      260.40
BUTTER PATS              3995   15.000  15 LB      26.39      395.85
BUTTER USDA              276     0.000  LBS         0.00        0.00
CHEESE AMERICAN          550    20.000  5 LB       11.00      220.00
CHEESE AMERICAN SLICED   555    14.000  5 LB       11.00      154.00
CHEESE BLEU              551    15.000  LB          1.99       29.85
CHEESE CHEDDAR SHREDDED  556    25.000  5 LB       10.85      271.25
CHEESE COTTAGE           547    20.000  5 LB        5.25      105.00
CHEESE CREAM             552    45.000  8 OZ PKG    0.63       28.35
CHEESE MOZZARELLA        553    50.000  LB          1.77       88.50
CHEESE PARMESAN GRATED   560    20.000  5 LB       14.85      297.00
CHEESE PROVOLONE         571    15.000  LB          2.13       31.95
CREAM HEAVY              604    15.000  QT          1.90       28.50
CREAM IND                3155    3.000  500/CASE    6.98       20.94
CREAM SOUR               559    15.000  QT          2.00       30.00
EGGS FRESH               548    25.000  DOZEN       0.94       23.50
MARGARINE                642    56.000  LBS         0.34       19.04
MILK HOMOGENIZED         567    15.000  GAL         2.30       34.50
MILK SKIM IND            335     7.000  48/CASE     5.76       40.32
MILK WHOLE IND           3158    5.000  48/CASE     5.76       28.80
                                                            -----------
     GROUP TOTAL                                             2107.75
                                                            ===========
--------------------------------------------------------------------------------
```

FIGURE 11-16 *Inventory Extension Report. Courtesy The CBORD Group.*

TABLE 11-3 Inventory Valuation

Item Name	*Item Number*	*Units On hand*	*Stock Unit*	*Price Stku*	*Inventory Value*
Cantaloupes	409	10.000	lb	1.51	15.10

actual production usage. Production waste or employee theft can be readily identified by this report form.

RECIPES

The standardization of all recipes used to produce established menu items is important to produce a consistent quantity and quality of food production. Computer-generated recipes allow management the production flexibility to increase or reduce production volumes on demand. Standard recipes are also the basis for purchasing requisitions and forecasted production estimates. Standard recipe formats, as discussed in Chapter 8, consistently produce a product of determined quality to yield an established number of portions.

The computer-generated recipe format in Figure 11-17 produces a yield of fifty portions. By applying the functions of the computer, the recipe portion yield can be quickly adjusted. Ingredient weights and measures are automatically changed to meet the production needs of the required portions.

1008-BEEF STEW

COOKING UTENSIL: 09	COOKING TIME: 2.5 HR	COOKING TEMP:	PREPARATION TIME: 1 HR	
		YIELDS 2.75 GAL	5.50 GAL	8.25 GAL
SERVICE UTENSIL: 8 OZ LADLE	10.00 OZ ( ) 1 CUP	50 PORTIONS	100 PORTIONS	150 PORTIONS
SERVICE PAN : FULL STEAM PAN 4"	15.00 OZ ( ) 1 1/2 CUP	33 PORTIONS	67 PORTIONS	100 PORTIONS
STEWING BEEF	--------	15 LBS	30 LBS	45 LBS
1. BROWN BEEF IN TILTING SKILLET.				
WATER	--------	2 QT	- TO TASTE -	1 1/2 GAL
SALT	--------	2 TBSP	1/4 CUP	2 TBSP
BLACK PEPPER	--------	2 TSP	2 TBSP	2 TBSP
WORCESTERSHIRE SAUCE	--------	3/4 CUP	2 CUP	3 CUP
BAY LEAVES	--------	2 LEAF	4 LEAF	6 LEAF
GARLIC MINCED	--------	2 CLOVES	4 CLOVES	6 CLOVES
2. ADD WATER AND SEASONINGS TO MEAT. COVER AND SIMMER 1 HOUR. ADD MORE WATER IF NECESSARY.				
POTATOES DICED	--------	4 LBS	8 LBS	12 LBS
SLICED CARROTS	--------	3 LBS	6 LBS	9 LBS
ONIONS DICED	--------	1 LBS	2 LBS	3 LBS
CELERY DICED	--------	1 LBS	2 LBS	3 LBS
CRUSHED TOMATOES	--------	1 #10 CAN	2 #10 CAN	3 #10 CAN

FIGURE 11-17 *Recipe Format. Courtesy The CBORD Group.*

```
-----------------------------------------------------------------------------------
MENU ITEM FOOD COST REPORT          MICROS 4700 VERSION 3.00 SYSTEM    02-SEP-   05:43 PM   Page   1
RANGE 33 - 154                               SYSTEM                             C: PRIMARY DATABASE
-----------------------------------------------------------------------------------
```

					CURRENT AND TO-DATE TOTALS				
Item	Description	Prep Cost	Sales Price	Qty Prep	Qty Sold	Qty Rtrn	Total Prep Cost	Total Sales	%Food Cost	%Yield
33	FRUIT SALAD D	1.19	4.95	7	7	0	8.33	34.65	24.04	100.00
				33	32	1	39.27	158.40	24.79	96.97
35	HOUSE SALAD D	1.02	4.50	16	16	0	16.32	72.00	22.67	100.00
				83	83	0	84.66	373.50	22.67	100.00
38	CAESAR SALAD	3.72	10.95	6	6	0	22.32	45.70	48.84	100.00
				28	28	0	104.16	286.60	36.34	100.00
39	SALAD NICOISE	1.34	4.95	2	2	0	2.68	9.90	27.07	100.00
				2	2	0	2.68	9.90	27.07	100.00
46	TURKEY CLUB	1.68	4.95	6	6	0	10.08	29.70	33.94	100.00
				15	15	0	25.20	74.25	33.94	100.00
48	HAM & SWISS	1.87	5.50	6	5	1	11.22	27.50	40.80	83.33
				14	13	1	26.18	71.50	36.62	92.86
53	TUNA MELT	1.45	4.25	10	10	0	14.50	42.50	34.12	100.00
				24	24	0	34.80	102.00	34.12	100.00
54	REUBEN SANDWICH	1.53	4.50	39	38	1	59.67	171.00	34.89	97.44
				70	69	1	107.10	310.50	34.49	98.57
62	CHEESE OMELET	1.53	4.50	9	9	0	13.77	40.50	34.00	100.00
				24	24	0	36.72	108.00	34.00	100.00
65	SPANISH OMELET	1.70	5.00	12	12	0	20.40	57.50	35.48	100.00
				28	28	0	47.60	137.50	34.62	100.00
94	CHICKEN KIEV	5.76	16.95	12	12	0	69.12	203.40	33.98	100.00
				45	45	0	259.20	762.75	33.98	100.00
151	FRESH FRUIT	0.85	2.50	5	5	0	4.25	12.50	34.00	100.00
				5	5	0	4.25	12.50	34.00	100.00
152	CHEESECAKE	1.19	3.50	3	3	0	3.57	8.75	40.80	100.00
				19	19	0	22.61	64.75	34.92	100.00
153	STRAWB CHCAKE	1.45	4.25	2	2	0	2.90	6.37	45.53	100.00
				29	29	0	42.05	121.12	34.72	100.00
154	STRAWB PARFAIT	1.34	3.95	1	1	0	1.34	3.95	33.92	100.00
				6	6	0	8.04	23.70	33.92	100.00
	Totals			640	635	5	586.79	1,926.03	30.47	99.22
				1,795	1,787	8	2,340.64	7,492.06	31.24	99.55

FIGURE 11-18　*Menu Item Food Cost Report. Courtesy Micros Pos Systems Inc.*

THE APPLICATION OF COMPUTER REPORT INFORMATION

Management application of information made available by computer reports can assist in cost analysis, marketing, and profitability. Menu sales controls, as discussed in Chapter 8, are developed from information supplied by reports such as the menu item category report in Figure 11-9 and the server category sales report in Figure 11-12.

```
MAJOR GROUP FOOD COST REPORT             MICROS 4700 VERSION 3.00 SYSTEM          02-SEP     05:42 PM    Page   1
ALL                                              SYSTEM                                      C: PRIMARY DATABASE
```

```
                                 CURRENT AND TO-DATE TOTALS
```

Grp	Description	Qty Prep	Qty Sold	Qty Rtrn	Total Prep Cost	Total Sales	%Food Cost	%Yield
1	APPETIZERS	66	66	0	76.67	242.29	31.64	100.00
		208	207	1	252.69	824.16	30.66	99.52
2	LIGHT ENTREES	123	120	3	198.19	593.50	33.39	97.56
		338	334	4	540.50	1,743.35	31.00	98.82
	Subtotal	189	186	3	274.86	835.79	32.89	98.41
		546	541	5	793.19	2,567.51	30.89	99.08
5	DINNER ENTREES	12	12	0	69.12	203.40	33.98	100.00
		86	86	0	502.78	1,479.40	33.99	100.00
	Subtotal	12	12	0	69.12	203.40	33.98	100.00
		86	86	0	502.78	1,479.40	33.99	100.00
11	DESSERTS	11	11	0	12.06	31.57	38.20	100.00
		101	101	0	112.65	327.07	34.44	100.00
	Subtotal	11	11	0	12.06	31.57	38.20	100.00
		101	101	0	112.65	327.07	34.44	100.00
15	LIQUOR	86	86	0	60.24	229.38	26.26	100.00
		212	212	0	160.93	591.20	27.22	100.00
16	BEER	205	205	0	106.39	396.92	26.80	100.00
		455	455	0	236.68	852.53	27.76	100.00
17	WINE	46	46	0	30.62	133.47	22.94	100.00
		117	117	0	228.34	769.25	29.68	100.00
18	BEVERAGES	91	89	2	33.50	95.50	35.08	97.80
		240	237	3	90.61	261.00	34.72	98.75
	Subtotal	428	426	2	230.75	855.27	26.98	99.53
		1,024	1,021	3	716.56	2,473.98	28.96	99.71
	Totals	640	635	5	586.79	1,926.03	30.47	99.22
		1,795	1,787	8	2,340.64	7,492.06	31.24	99.55

FIGURE 11-19 *Menu Group Food Cost Report. Courtesy Micros Pos Systems Inc.*

Food cost analysis of menu items informs management of individual item cost percentage fluctuations as well as the status of menu group food cost percentages. Figure 11-18 reviews individual menu items. This report also includes information from a production sheet regarding quantities of menu items that are prepared, sold, and returned. The sales mix in Figure 8-2 is the destination report for this information to analyze menu item popularity and sales patterns.

Menu marketing efforts use the information from the major group food cost report in Figure 11-19. By identifying which menu groups have the highest sales volumes, management can identify customer needs. Low sales volumes indicate menu category areas that will benefit from changes in menu items as well as marketing promotions. Food costs will often fluctuate markedly between menu

PIZZA TOPPINGS								REGULAR PRICE			
TOPPING NAME	SLICE	PERSONAL	SMALL	MEDIUM	LARGE	EXTRA LARGE					
1 Cheese	20	30	45	60	80	100					
2 Sauce	20	30	45	60	80	100					
3 Pepperoni	20	30	45	60	80	100					
4 Sausage	20	30	45	60	80	100					
5 Onion	20	30	45	60	80	100					
6 Green Pepper	20	30	45	60	80	100					
7 Jalapeno Pep	20	30	45	60	80	100					
8 Italn Sausge	20	30	45	60	80	100					
9 Ham	20	30	45	60	80	100					
10 Hamburger	20	30	45	60	80	100					
11 Mushroom	20	30	45	60	80	100					
12 Black Olive	20	30	45	60	80	100					
13 Salami	20	30	45	60	80	100					
14 Pineapple	20	30	45	60	80	100					
15 Candian Bacn	20	30	45	60	80	100					
16 Green Olive	20	30	45	60	80	100					
17 Anchovy	20	30	45	60	80	100					
18 Shrimp	20	30	45	60	80	100					
19											
20											
21											
22											
23											
24											
25											
26											
27											
28											

FIGURE 11-20   *Pizza Topping Ordering Form. Courtesy TEC Systems Inc.*

groups if management develops pricing strategies to attract customers to particular menu items as a promotion for higher volume sales. In the report in Figure 11-19, all food groups are averaging the same range of food cost percentages.

Marketing applications of computer food service systems have resulted in the development of a variety of guest check and ordering system innovations for quick-serve operations. The pizza topping ordering form in Figure 11-20 is part of a specialty quick serve software program. Order takers can maximize pizza sales by accurately calculating topping prices on a variety of pizza size selections.

The guest check for the pizza order in Figure 11-21 breaks down the pizza order specifications and indicates additional sandwich orders. As a further customer service marketing technique the computer retrieves a customer history and, using a telephone number as a code, provides delivery and check acceptance information. Figure 11-21 is the customer information printout.

FIGURE 11-21   *Customer Information Printout. Courtesy TEC Systems Inc.*

SUMMARY

Computer food service systems are an essential part of successful restaurant management in the 1990s. Increasing competition and rising costs require constant monitoring of purchasing, production, service, costing, and pricing.

Computer hardware designs for food service systems provide for a range of both quick serve and full service restaurant functions. Computerized cash registers, quick-serve workstations, touch screens, color-coded menu keyboards, and battery-operated hand-held units are some of the innovative forms of equipment that provide profitable and time-saving services.

Operational reports generated by computer food service systems assist management in gathering and analyzing information from both the front and the back of the house of a restaurant operation. The guest check is one of the key information sources for computer system reporting. Server sales and tip information, menu item sales popularity, table turnover rates, average check totals, and customer profile data are provided by this one report.

Purchasing reports increase the productivity of purchasing activities and assist in calculating inventory value. Computer-generated recipe formats reflect variable production requirements on demand.

QUESTIONS

1. What is the primary factor that results in restaurant closings?

2. What can the integration of a computer food service system accomplish in a restaurant operation?

3. List the operational activities that require information to be supplied, recorded, and processed on a daily and/or weekly basis.

4. What management information do quest checks supply?

5. What computer report does the information from the menu item category report help to complete and how?

6. How many sources should be consulted for competitive selling prices before determining which vendor to use?

7. What information does the specification on the bid and quote form include?

8. How is inventory value calculated?

9. Explain how computer-generated recipes allow management production flexibility.

10. Which operational report is the destination for information recorded from the menu item food cost report?

ANSWERS

1. The primary factor that results in restaurant closings is the inability of many food service owners to understand or carry out the day-to-day functions of accounting and food cost management.

2. The integration of a computer food service system into a restaurant operation can increase profits while providing essential time-saving recording systems.

3. The activities of purchasing, production, service, costing, pricing, and marketing require information to be supplied, recorded, and processed on a daily and/or weekly basis.

4. Guest checks supply the information management needs to know to evaluate the sales of individual menu items.

5. The information from the menu item category report helps to analyze customer spending patterns and per customer and per check revenues in the average check report.

6. Three sources should be consulted before determining which vendor to use.

7. The specification on the bid and quote form details the exact requirements for the product, identifying the grade, purchase unit, purchase unit weight, quantity to be ordered, and item file number.

8. The inventory value is calculated by multiplying the price per stock unit by the number of units on hand.

9. Computer-generated recipes give management production flexibility to increase or reduce production values on demand. Ingredient weights and measures are automatically changed to meet the production needs of the required portions.

10. The sales mix is the operational report that is the destination of information from the menu item food cost report.

ACTIVITIES

1. Identify the distributor of a major computer food service system in your area. Interview a person knowledgeable about these systems in the company and evaluate the effectiveness of their systems and operational report forms for a table service operation.

2. Select a quick-serve or full service restaurant operation in your community that currently uses a computer food service system in its operation. Interview management to determine which operational reports are being generated for management analysis.

3. Collect a variety of computer-generated guest receipts. Determine what information provided on the guest checks can be used to generate operational reports.

12 *Restaurant Marketing*

OBJECTIVES

1. To be able to outline and discuss the marketing cycle.

2. To understand the importance of the service component in the food service marketing mix.

3. To be able to identify market research data that can impact on the success of restaurant marketing efforts.

4. To be able to create a food service marketing campaign.

CASE STUDY: BRICK ALLEY PUB & RESTAURANT

The in-house promotional materials for The Brick Alley Pub & Restaurant in Figures 12-1 through 12-3 represent the identification of a marketing opportunity to satisfy customer needs for both alcoholic and nonalcoholic beverages. The combined beverage and dessert menu in Figure 12-1 features a wide variety of beverages that respond to both traditional and specialty drink customers.

The summer beverage promotion cards featured in Figure 12-2 are inserted in Plexiglas table stands. Panel A reinforces the printed menu. Panel B is a summer promotion for an outdoor courtyard area.

The owner of the Brick Alley Pub & Restaurant added a marketing technique to the back of the business card in Figure 12-3. The free beverage promo-

Potable Spirits & Desserts MENU

Desserts

Soft Serve Vanilla Ice Cream

Chocolate Sundae

Strawberry Sundae

Pineapple Sundae

Ice Cream Parfaits
With your favorite liqueur, priced accordingly.

Chocolate Fudge Cake
By Itself or
A la mode

Carrot Cake
By Itself or
A la mode

New York Cheesecake

Warm Kentucky Derby Chocolate Chip Cookie Pie
Topped with Vanilla Ice Cream.

Milky Way Cake
Heavenly . . . and yes, it is made with Milky Way bars. Limited availability

Peach Melba

Chocolate Heaven
Chocolate fudge cake, vanilla ice cream, chocolate syrup, sliced almonds, whipped cream and shaved Ghirardelli chocolate.

Chocolate Mousse Cake
Thick and rich. A chocoholics fantasy.

Sherry & Port

PORTS

Founders Reserve
Sandeman, aged Ruby

Cadima Port
Cockburn, Tawny, served chilled

Late Bottled Vintage
Taylor Fladgate, Vintage taste

Baron De Forrester
Offley, Single Vineyard

Ficklin Port
California's Finest

SHERRIES

Harveys Bristol Cream
mellow

Dry Sack
toasty

Harveys Tico
dry

Royal Corregidor
Sandeman, very rare

Dessert Wines

Piesporter Goldtrepchen Spatlese
Madrigal, Late Harvest Riesling

Chateau Lafaurie Peyraquay Sauterne
Lucious, like honey

Use our Billiards room located in the rear of the pub for your next company function.

Frozen Libations

Strawberry Daiquiri
Strawberries, rum and lemon juice.

Dirty Banana
A Jamaican favorite. Kahlua, rum, creme de banana, fresh banana and pineapple juice.

Chi Chi
Vodka, tropical fruit juices, coconut and orange curacao.

Panini
Fresh bananas, rum and orange juice.

Slow Train to Mazatlan
From the most notorious cantina in all of Mexico, Tommy D's in Mazatlan. A frosty concoction of fresh strawberries, banana, peach brandy, light and dark rum. Served in a pint Mason jar.

Blue Hawaiian
Rum, Blue Curacao, pineapple juice.

Pub Potables

Bloody Mary
Brick Alley's Bloody Mary was voted the "1st Place-People's Choice" Award at the 1988 Smirnoff Vodka RI Bloody Mary Contest.

Brick Alley "Mudslide"
Bailey's Irish Cream, dark creme de cacao and vodka, a quick shake and served in a pint shaker glass.

Sangria (Red or White)
Spanish recipe by the glass or pitcher.

Dark & Stormy
Goslings Bermuda Black Rum & Old Tyme Jamaican Ginger Beer.

Mocktails
(non-alcoholic) Ask your server about selection.

Ice Cream Libations

Oreo Express
Dark chocolate liqueur, brandy, ice cream and crushed oreo cookies.

Strawberry Short Cake
Amaretto, kahlua, strawberries and ice cream, topped with whipped cream and a drizzle of Marie Brizard Strawberry.

Creamy Navel
Vanilla ice cream, Peachtree Schnapps and O.J. This cocktail was invented right here at the Brick Alley Pub & Restaurant.

Black Cow (non-alcoholic)
Coca Cola with a float of soft vanilla ice cream.

Fruit Smoothie
(non-alcoholic) Strawberries, pineapple, coconut, vanilla ice cream and orange juice lusciously blended to creamy perfection.

Blueberry Cream Pie
Winner 1988 DeKuyper Cup Bartenders' Challenge. Invented by Brick Alley Bar Manager Dave Huggins.

Tequila Selections

Sauza Silver
Sauza Gold
Sauza Hornitos
Sauza Commemorativo
Sauza Tres Generaciones
Juarez Gold

Jose Cuervo 1800
  - a super premium tequila
Jose Cuervo Gold
  - a premium tequila
Dos Gusanos (2 worms)

Frozen Margaritas

Jumbo Rita
Our extra large frozen margarita.

Strawberry Margarita
Strawberries, Triple Sec and lime.

Banana Margarita

Blue Margarita
Blue Curacao, Triple Sec and lime juice.

Peach Margarita

Gold Margarita
Cuervo Gold and Grand Marnier.

Special Coffees

All of our International Coffees are made with our own special blend of coffees to give a special taste to your favorite cordial. Each is topped with whipped cream and shaved Ghirardelli chocolate.

Irish Coffee—The Best
Brick Alley Pub & Restaurant Irish Coffee. Winner 1983, 1985 and 1987 Jamesons Irish Whiskey Cup. The only Irish Coffee in New England inducted into the Jameson Irish Whiskey Hall of Fame and retired from competition.

Keoki Coffee
Kahlua and brandy.

Spanish Coffee
Brandy, Kahlua and Grand Marnier.

Cafe Brick Alley
Irish Mist and Kahlua.

Espresso

Decaffeinated Espresso & Cappuccino Also Available.

Espresso
Finest Italian coffee – demitasse

Cappuccino
Espresso with steamed milk.

Cappuccino L'Amour
Creme de espresso, Half 'n Half, sugar, sweet powdered chocolate, brandy, gin, white rum, creme de cacao, steamed and topped with whipped cream.

Cordials & Cognacs

Marie Brizard
imported from France
all natural flavored.

Anisette
Strawberry
Raspberry
Cherry

Peach
Pear William
Banana
Chocolate

Hennessy V.S.
Courvoisier V.S.
Hennessy V.S.O.P.
Courvoisier V.S.O.P.
Remy Martin V.S.O.P.
Martell Gordon Bleu
Metaxa 7 Star
Courvoisier X.O.
Larressingle VSOP
Sempe Vieil 15 years old

Winter Warm Ups

(Seasonal)

Hot Spiced Apple Cider
Blended with Laird's Applejack or served plain.

Hot Apple Pie
Hot apple cider blended with Tuaca topped with whipped cream.

Hot Buttered Rum
A traditional New England favorite.

Hot Cherry Chocolate
Hot Chocolate with Marie Brizard Natural Cherry liqueur.

FIGURE 12-1 *Beverage and Dessert Menu. Courtesy The Brick Alley Pub and Restaurant, Newport, Rhode Island.*

216

Summer Courtyard Specials

Pitchers of:
Frozen Daiquiris
Bacardi Black Label Rum with fresh fruits
and juices — Strawberry, Peach, Banana

Frozen Margaritas
Gold Tequila blended with crushed ice, lime juice
and DeKuyper Triple Sec
Strawberry — Peach — Original Lime

Key Largo "Courtyard Paradise"
DeKuyper Key Largo Schnapps, Bacardi Black Label Rum,
Pineapple Juice, Cream of Coconut, and Grenadine

"Truly Groovy Nectar"
DeKuyper Peachtree, Key Largo Schnapps,
and Orange Juice. *The West Coast comes to the Courtyard.*

Desert Storm
DeKuyper Cactus, Cranberry Juice served on the rocks
with a twist of lime. *Welcome Home!*

$14.00

Pitchers of Beer
MILLER LITE   GUINNESS STOUT
BUDWEISER   BASS ALE
BECK'S   HARP LAGER

"Bucket of Rocks"
Five 12 oz. Bottles of Rolling Rock
You Keep The Bucket

Frozen Jumbo
Strawberry Daiquiri
Paralyzingly cold in our 24 oz.
Newport Hurricane Souvenir Glass.
$6.95 — You Keep The Glass
Glasses available for purchase $5.00
— 6 glasses $24.95

Bottled Beer

— American —	— Imported —
Rolling Rock	Molson Golden Ale
Longneck Bud	Molson Light
Miller Genuine Draft	Kaliber
Michelob Dry	(non-alcoholic)
Coors Light	Amstel Light
Sharp's (non-alcoholic)	Heineken
Bud Light	Corona Extra
Coors	
Harpoon Ale	
Sam Adams	

Draft Beer *Pitchers Available*

Bass Ale ~ Harp Lager ~ Beck's
Budweiser ~ Miller Lite ~ Guiness Stout

Pussers Punch
Pussers Rum, Orange and Cranberry Juice — Good Sailing.
Served in a take home souvenir beach cup.

Ice Cream Libations

Oreo Express
Dark chocolate liqueur,
brandy, ice cream and
crushed oreo cookies.

Black Cow (non-alcoholic)
Pepsi Cola with a float of soft
vanilla ice cream.

Strawberry Short Cake
Di Saronno Amaretto,
Kahlua, strawberries and ice
cream, topped with whipped
cream and a drizzle of Marie
Brizard Strawberry.

Fruit Smoothie
(non-alcoholic) Strawberries,
pineapple, coconut, vanilla
ice cream and orange juice.

Creamy Navel
Vanilla ice cream, DeKuyper
Peachtree Schnapps and O.J.

English Raspberry
Chambord, Irish Cream and
ice cream.

FIGURE 12-2 *Beverage Promotion Card. Courtesy The Brick Alley Pub and Restaurant, Newport, Rhode Island.*

tion can be used to encourage first time customers, acknowledge customer patronage, or help placate a customer complaint.

Marketing in a restaurant operation is an essential management function that directly affects the success of a business. The American Marketing Association defines marketing as "the process of planning and executing the conception, pricing, promotion and distribution of goods and services to create exchanges that satisfy individual and organizational objectives."

Restaurant businesses directly produce and provide customers goods and services that satisfy the need for food, beverage, and entertainment. The producer is directly accessible to the consumer, creating a proximity that allows restaurant management to identify and respond to customer needs.

In most retail situations, the producer of the product is far removed from the consumer. In the restaurant industry, the producer is directly accessible to the consumer, as outlined in Figure 12-4.

Please
present this card
to our bartender
and you
and your guest
will receive a
complimentary
cocktail
or soft drink

Expires 1/1/99
Limit one card per
customer per visit

Thanks,
Ralph

FIGURE 12-3 *Business Card. Courtesy The Brick Alley Pub and Restaurant, Newport, Rhode Island.*

The consumer wants to inform the producer in the retail marketing chain of needs that could be satisfied or changes that would make a product more salable (Figure 12-5). In order to do this, it is necessary either to pass backward through the chain of product distribution or to find a way of reaching the producer directly. The restaurant distribution chart gives the producer and consumer direct access to one another. As discussed in Chapter 2, at the time that a decision is made to develop a restaurant business, it is necessary to

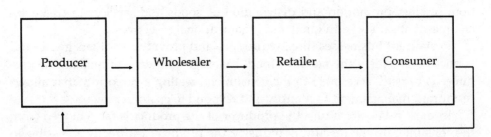

FIGURE 12-4 *Retail Marketing Distribution Chain*

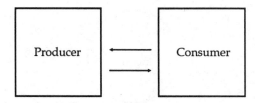

FIGURE 12-5   *Restaurant Industry Marketing Distribution Chart*

identify and understand consumer needs. In this chapter we will discuss the application of market survey information to meet the needs of the target market. Marketing methods and techniques that are essential to developing a good marketing program are the marketing cycle, the food service marketing mix, and the marketing campaign. Identifying marketing opportunities is the key to successful product/service development.

THE MARKETING CYCLE

The marketing cycle is a series of four steps that are used to create and evaluate products and services. These steps, as outlined in Figure 12-5, are the following:

1. Identify consumer needs

2. Develop products and services to meet needs

3. Generate consumer interest to purchase or use product/service

4. Evaluate financial success and consumer satisfaction

These steps must be performed in the sequence indicated to bring a product or service to market successfully.

Identify Consumer Needs

A consumer need is identified when management recognizes a service or product that is not currently being offered. Need is usually recognized when a product/service is requested by the consumer or offered by other restaurant operations.

Healthy dining is an excellent example of a customer need that has been identified by food service operations. Restaurant managers use the resources of local hospitals to create menu items which are developed to meet nutritional

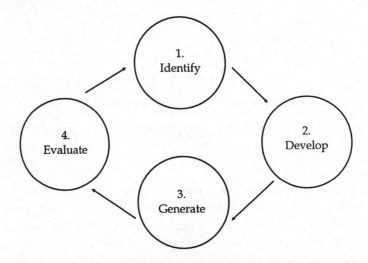

FIGURE 12-6   *Marketing Cycle*

guidelines. A number of restaurant associations across the United States have developed healthy dining programs. The menu in Figure 12-7 indicates healthy dining menu items by a heart symbol.

Develop a Product or Service

Developing a product or service to meet consumer needs requires that management thoroughly understand consumer needs and accurately identify the perceived value of the product or service.

It is essential that the selling price be determined before the product specifications are outlined. The cost of producing the product will directly affect the selling price. If consumers are not willing to pay the price, then the product will not be financially successful. Market research is an effective method of identifying perceived value.

Generate Consumer Interest

Generating consumer interest is achieved primarily by applying market research information to determine a target market at which is directed a variety of interest-generating advertising media. To achieve the desired response from the target market, it is necessary to develop a marketing campaign.

Marketing campaigns plan a series of events, promotions, and advertising placements. The objective of these activities is to reach established goals of increased revenues and/or customer counts.

THE HERBERT PUBLIC ROOM

Appetizers

Baked Mushrooms Caps with Crabmeat Suffing .... $ 4.95

French Onion Soup, with Three Cheese topping & croutons ....crock $ 3.95

Soup of the day ....cup $ 2.50 bowl $ 3.50

Seafood Appetizer of the day ....market price

Shrimp Cocktail.. $ 6.95

Chicken Satay with peanut sauce .... $ 4.50

Nothing perks up your appetite like a glass of champagne...see #1-9 on the list

We are making some suggestions on wines to accompany your dinner, in an effort to remove some of the mystique about the wines, and because we have such an extensive list to choose from. But please remember that there are no set rules about wine and there is nothing wrong with having Champagne with a steak or Merlot with fish. Our cardinal rule is: "If you like it, drink it".

Seafood Selections

Seafood Alfredo.. $12.95
Shrimp, crab & scallops with fettucini, sauteed in parmesan cream sauce with garlic.
The Italian white wines would be the perfect choice for this item, #40-42.

Shrimp and Pea Pods $13.50
Six Jumbo Shrimp sauteed with green onions, peppers, mushrooms, snow peas and finished with a garlic wine sauce.
Sauvignon Blanc would do well with the Shrimp, so see #21-26.

♥ Dilled Haddock $10.95
Haddock topped with dill, tomato, onion and baked in wine and butter.
Try one of our Australian favorites here, #32-33.

Native Sea Scallops $12.50
Baked in lemon shallot butter, topped lightly with parmesan cheese.
Try something crisp & clean from Australia, see #45-47.

Catch of the Day ....market price
Fresh from the nets of the Gulf of Maine

Children's Menu

Spaghetti with meat sauce.. $ 4.95

Herby Burger - with or without cheese .... $ 4.95

Chicken Fingers, Sauteed .... $ 4.95

Baked Haddock .... $ 4.95

NOTE: THE ♥ SYMBOL INDICATES ENTREES WHICH ARE "HEART-HEALTHY".
LOW IN SALT, FAT AND CHOLESTEROL, BUT STILL HIGH IN TASTE,
FLAVOR AND APPEARANCE. ENJOY!

Regional Maine Favorites Old and New

♥ Carrabassett Rabbit...$14.95
A native Maine treat...one-half a fresh rabbit, baked with tangy cider & apples, finished with a light cream sauce.
A California Chardonnay will go well here, so see #10-16.

Roast Spring Duckling $14.95
Slow-baked to perfection, finished with a fruit glaze.
Duck delights best when matched with a hearty Zinfandel, so see #69-72.

Venison $17.95
Today's preparation will be described by your server.
A Merlot or Petite Sirah will do this noble beast proud, so see #73-77.

♥ Sesame Chicken Sir Fry $12.50
Boneless strips of breast meat and fresh vegetables sauteed in olive oil with herbs and soy, served on rice or pasta.
The French White Burgundies will do well here, so see #27-30.

♥ Vegetarian Stir Fry ....$ 9.95
Fresh vegetables sauteed in olive oil with herbs and soy, served on rice or pasta.
A little French Loire will go well with this, so see #32-34.

Lemon Mustard Chicken $10.95
Boneless breast of chicken sauteed with shallots, white wine, and finished with Dijon cream sauce.
Chenin Blanc from California will accompany this well, so see #17-20.

♥ Chicken Trattoria $11.95
Sauteed boneless breast with Proscuitto, mushrooms and wine.
The Italian whites will be great here, so see #40-42.

Pork Cumberland $13.95
Tenderloin of pork sauteed with cream. Dijon mustard & capers.
Zinfandel will please this dish, so see #69-72.

♥ Veal Marsala 15.95
Tender cutlets of fresh veal sauteed with fresh mushrooms, garlic and marsala wine.
Veal and the French Burgundies go well, so see #87-88 or try a little Beaujolais #89-98.

Sirloin Steak $13.95
A tender cut of prime sirloin, broiled to perfection.
Our Cabernet Cabinet awaits, so see #56-63.

Steak Au Poivre, vert $15.50
Finished with green peppercorns and a brandy mustard cream sauce.
The French Bordeaux will be a perfect choice here, so see #78-86.

♥ Vegetarian Puff Pastry $10.95
With vegetables and cheese.
The wines of Chile will accompany this well, so see #48-49.

♥ Vegetarian Linguini with Roasted New Potatoes & Peppers..................$10.95
A light entree which is good for you too.
A French Loire would be the crowning touch, see #32 & 34.

All dinner selections include: cheese and crackers, salad with your choice of dressing, homemade breads and butter, choice of rice or potato, and vegetable of the day, which your server will describe.

A note about the food: We do nearly everything here on the premises, and all entrees are prepared to order. We do not use prepared or pre-cooked items. All salad dressings, breads, and pastries are made in our kitchen daily, as are all sauces, spreads and dips. We take pride in our food, and in the past years have won a number of awards for creative cuisine. We hope you will agree, and find the food worth the trip.

For your convenience a Service Charge will be added to parties of 6 or more.

Planning a party? We would love to discuss catering at your home or condominium ...we have a lot of great ideas to make you a great host.

We regret that we are unable to accommodate requests for separate checks for parties of more than four.

Smoking is permitting in the lobby area,
but the dining room is smoke-free at the request of the majority of our guests.

We accept all major credit cards — $15.00 minimum.

FIGURE 12-7   *Herbert Hotel Menu. Courtesy The Herbert Hotel, Kingfield, Maine.*

Evaluate Success

The success of a product or service is evaluated in terms of both financial and customer satisfaction objectives.

Financial success is judged by determining whether management's original financial objectives for the product were met. Customer satisfaction is gauged by analyzing customer reaction to the product or service. A good way of recording customer reactions is to provide comment cards. Cards such as the one featured in Figure 12-8 ask customers to evaluate a number of service and product factors. To use this marketing information effectively, management needs to establish a policy of sharing the comments with employees and responding directly to them. Favorable and critical comments should always be

DID WE DELIVER?

	Excellent	Very Good	Average	Below Average	Poor
1. How satisfied were you with the overall quality of services you received?	☐	☐	☐	☐	☐
2. Did our staff address you by name whenever possible?	☐	☐	☐	☐	☐
3. Was our staff friendly? Did they greet you with a smile, "good morning," "may I help you?", etc.	☐	☐	☐	☐	☐
4. Was our staff well informed, knowledgeable and professional?	☐	☐	☐	☐	☐
5. Were we responsive to your needs, solving any problems you may have had efficiently and to your satisfaction?	☐	☐	☐	☐	☐

6. We sincerely appreciate any written comments you have about our performance, including the names of staff members who were particularly helpful or friendly to you during your stay.

____

____

____

____

Hotel Location __________

Room Number ____

Name __________

Address __________

City, State, Zip __________

Telephone ______

THANK YOU!

FIGURE 12-8 *Customer Comment Card*

passed along to staff. Sharing problems identified by customers at general staff meetings often produces solutions that are employee-generated. Acknowledging customer complaints and providing an incentive to return increase the perception of professionalism and interest in the restaurant.

THE FOOD SERVICE MARKETING MIX

To set the marketing cycle in motion, three major factors regarding the product must be established. These factors, called the *marketing mix,* determine where the product will be presented to the customer, how the customer will be informed about the product, and what price the product will be assigned (Table 12-1). To address the food service industry, however, the traditional marketing mix must be adjusted to incorporate the service component that is essential to food service products.

TABLE 12-1   Marketing Mix

Marketing mix	Food Service marketing mix
Product	Product/Service service component in combination with food product
Place	Presentation theme concepts, atmosphere, location, staffing, and menu pricing scale
Promotion	Communication menu design, advertising, promotion, customer comments, and server communication
Price	

Food service products, especially in restaurant settings, require an element of service in order to reach the customer, changing the first marketing mix element to Product-Service. Presentation incorporates factors such as theme and staffing as well as location. Price is an important factor in the presentation of a food product, often determining customer acceptability. Promotion includes the application of marketing methods and the communication skills required to sell food product directly to the customer.

MARKETING OPPORTUNITIES

Successful entrepreneurs and marketing specialists are individuals who recognize an opportunity to satisfy a need or create a product or service. Their ability to do so is often aligned with circumstances that indicate the probability of success. These circumstances are primarily related to demographic or environmental issues.

The "1991 *Foodservice Forecast*" published by the Bureau of Foodservice Research states, "The final ingredient which continues to create opportunities for foodservice growth is perpetually changing demographics (population characteristics). These factors, coupled with price increases for food to be prepared at home rather than food consumed away from home, will continue to create opportunities for the industry."

The demographic issue identified as having the major impact on the food service industry will be the aging of the baby boom generation, which will increase the average age of the entire population. According to the Bureau of Labor Statistics:

Consumers in the age bracket between 34 and 54 years old spend over 30% more on foodservice than other age groups. This segment of the population will grow by 11.3 million individuals (a 32% increase) by the year 2000. The United States will experience a period of unprecedented personal wealth over the next twenty years, directly associated with this demographic transition. Services that make life easier will experience gains.

The use of restaurants and other food service operations is no longer an extravagant drain on the family budget but a necessity. In 1991 food service industry sales were over $256 billion, accounting for 45 percent of all dollars spent on food. This figure may reach 50 percent by the year 2000.

The demographics that can and are affecting the food service industry merit continual review by owners and managers, who must be able to observe, analyze, and forecast shifts and trends that will affect their customers and business.

Often referred to as external enviromental factors, demographic characteristics are of several types. In Table 12-2 all of the enviromental factors that are traditionally included in industry marketing analysis are outlined. Those factors which can have a specific impact on the restaurant industry are highlighted.

Some of the factors currently having a profound impact on the restaurant industry in the sociocultural category are life-style changes, family arrangements, and changing women's roles. Economic factors include unemployment levels as well as energy sources and costs. Competitive factors are number and strength of competitors, market growth, and market share. Radical economic

Table 12-2   External Enviromental Factors

Social-Cultural	Economic	Technological	Ecological	Competitive
*Life-style changes	Interest rates	New products	Enviromental	*Number of competitors
Life expectancies	Deficits	Patent laws	Waste management	*Strength of competitors
Birth rate	Gross national product	Industry R&D	Public image	Market entry
Growth rate	*Unemployment levels		Safety of product	Market exit
*Family arrangements	*Energy sources	Computer technology	Packaging procedures	*Market growth
Consumer activism	Inflation rate			*Market share
Shifts in population	Money supply			Foreign competition
*Changing women's roles				

*Source: Thomas C. Kinnear and Kenneth L. Bernhart, *Principles of Marketing*, 2nd ed. (Chicago: Scott, Foresman & Co., 1986).

changes in the 1990s are affecting the entire world economy. Restaurant managers should seek out and use information that interprets and indicates how these factors will affect a community to develop a marketing plan. Market survey information often provides strong indicators of how a community is reacting to national and world trends.

As demographic changes reach the community level, managers can identify opportunities to react with products or services which reflect the needs of their customer base. Market research information often provides the data to support the development of marketing opportunities.

1991 MEAL-PERIOD HIGHLIGHTS

Breakfast

- More than one out of five (20.7 percent) of all individuals over eight years old consumed a commercially prepared breakfast at least once during a week.

- On the average, individuals consumed 0.5 breakfasts away from home in a week.

- The average individual skipped 1.6 breakfasts in one week, making breakfast the most frequently skipped meal.

Lunch

- Almost six out of ten (56.8 percent) individuals ate lunch prepared away from home at least once a week. This makes lunch the meal most frequently consumed away from home.

- Individuals consumed, on the average, 2.1 lunches away from home per week.

- The average individual skipped lunch 0.6 times in a week.

Dinner

- Among individuals over age eight, 53.5 percent consumed at least one commercially prepared dinner in a seven-day period.

- The average individual consumed 1.2 dinners away from home in a week.

- Individuals skipped, on average, only 0.1 dinners in a one-week period.

MARKET RESEARCH

Market research information can be gathered from a variety of sources. Competition surveys such as seen in Chapters 2 and 3 offer information about the average check, menu items, beverage prices, and facilities of restaurants that are in direct competition for the same customer. Understanding how much the customer is willing to pay for a product or service in a competitive setting gives management a strong indication of acceptable pricing.

Charts and graphs interpret information gathered by market research firms. Figure 12-9 defines market segments by household income. The objective of this chart is to identify those segments of the market at whom restaurant marketing efforts should be targeted. The information on this chart indicates the greatest

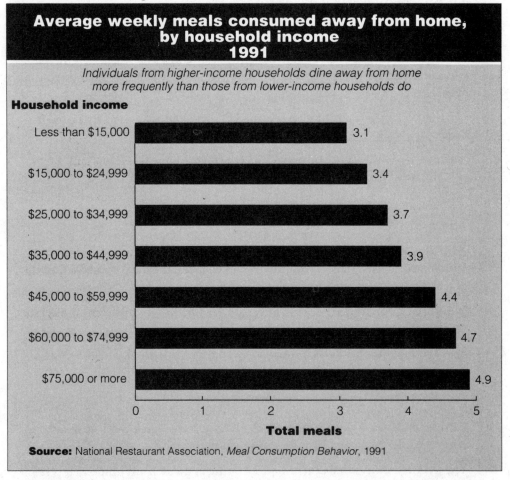

Average weekly meals consumed away from home, by household income 1991

Individuals from higher-income households dine away from home more frequently than those from lower-income households do

Household income

Household income	Total meals
Less than $15,000	3.1
$15,000 to $24,999	3.4
$25,000 to $34,999	3.7
$35,000 to $44,999	3.9
$45,000 to $59,999	4.4
$60,000 to $74,999	4.7
$75,000 or more	4.9

Total meals

Source: National Restaurant Association, *Meal Consumption Behavior*, 1991

FIGURE 12-9   *Average Meal Consumption by Household Income. Courtesy National Restaurant Association.*

use of restaurants among households having annual incomes of $35,000 to $75,000 or more.

To apply this information to an individual restaurant business, management must identify (1) the average household incomes of current customers and (2) the availability of customers within targeted income averages. Management can use market research information on average per person check totals to help identify which category of overall sales volume matches their operation. By comparing national average checks with current sales volumes, consumer spending trends can be analyzed to find out whether the customer's perceived value of menu items is higher than what is currently being charged. The results of interpreting this type of market research information could also cause management to change the focus or concept of the overall menu program.

Further analysis of the current marketplace for restaurant dollars focuses on research concerning the composition of the average American household. By understanding how households allocate food service dollars, management can identify the target market for marketing efforts for their operation. Table 12-3 indicates household spending patterns on food consumed away from home. The household segment that spends most on food away from home is Husband-Wife Only, for a total of $988 per person based on an annual income of $37,183. This is followed by single persons, with a total of $780 per person based on an annual income of $20,260.

TABLE 12-3   Household expenditures on food away from home by household composition—1989*

Household composition	Size	Income**	Average annual expenditures food away from home	Percent of food budget spent on food away from home	Annual per capita expenditures on food away from home
All households	2.6	$31,308	$1,762	42.4%	$678
Husband-wife only	2.0	$37,183	$1,977	45.1	$988
Husband-wife with children	3.9	$43,576	$2,326	41.1	$596
Single parents with children	2.9	$17,416	$1,190	34.8	$410
Single person and other households	1.6	$20,260	$1,248	46.2	$780

*Of all household groups, singles allocated the largest proportion of their total food budget to food away from home.
**Income is before taxes.
Source: Bureau of Labor Statistics, Consumer Expenditure Survey, 1989; National Restaurant Association

TABLE 12-4   Percentage of Adult Restaurant Visits

Percent of adults visiting types of establishments once a week or more, by age and marital status, 1991*

Type of establishment or service	Single, under 45 years old (%)	Single, 45 years old or older (%)	Married, under 45 years old (%)	Married, 45 years old or older (%)
Tableservice, average check $10 or more	25	17	16	21
Tableservice, average check less than $10	42	35	28	35
Fast food, eaten inside restaurant	41	17	25	19
Carryout	44	26	36	17
Self-serve cafeteria or buffet	24	13	13	19
Delivery	20	6	11	3
Supermarket, convenience store, or deli—eaten same day	28	21	12	14

*Singles under 45 years of age were the most frequent customers at almost every type of establishment or service.

Note: Check size is per adult.
Source: National Restaurant Association
Restaurants U.S.A., Washington, DC, Vol II, No. 10, Nov. 91.

If this information is matched to the information in Table 12-4, management can conclude that single persons less than 45 years of age patronize full-service restaurants with average checks of $10 or more 25 percent of the time, while single persons over 45 patronize full service restaurants with average checks of $10 or less 35 percent of the time. Married couples over 45 frequent restaurants with average checks of over $10 more often than married couples under age 45. From this information we can conclude that married couples without children spend more per capita on restaurant dining than any other market segment.

THE MARKETING CAMPAIGN

The marketing campaign is the application of the marketing cycle phase, generating customer interest. Creating promotions, planning advertising materials, and developing a formal media program are elements of a marketing campaign. The food service marketing mix provides the information that is the foundation of any marketing campaign.

The development stage of a marketing campaign requires establishing the most effective way of creating customer interest. A variety of methods for advertising and promotion are available.

Internal methods of promotion include special events incorporating holidays or specialty cuisines. In-house advertising can be accomplished by table tents and cards, posters, banners, and a server communication program.

The most effective use of advertising media for a restaurant business focuses on newspaper ads and radio time. Newspaper ads are generally timed to appear on days of the week which have been identified as those when readers are looking for entertainment information. The same principle applies to identifying radio time that reaches the established target market. An example of an interest-generating professionally produced magazine or newspaper advertisement is the one for Bookbinder's Restaurant in Philadelphia, Pennsylvania, shown in Figure 12-10.

Community goodwill is an important component in generating customer interest. A business's involvement in local activities of all types creates good public relations and often free advertising in the form of media coverage.

The final phase of the marketing campaign is the evaluation of the success of the program. Success is determined by how well management's objectives are met. If the primary objective is to increase sales, success is measured by the amount of increase in revenues. If the objective is to increase customer attendance, success is measured by the total increase in customer counts.

The customer comment card in Figure 12-8 is an effective way of recording immediate negative and positive customer reactions. However, these comments represent the reactions of only a small percentage of overall customers. In Figure 12-11 the striped areas indicate the portion of customer responses that are highly negative or positive. The remaining customers do not record their responses but represent the greatest number of returning customers.

Alternative methods must be developed to measure customer satisfaction. One of the most effective is tracking customer return rates. The number of repeat customers is an accurate indication of the satisfaction levels of customers. Management establishes a return rate target goal and methods by which to track it. If the return rate falls below the goal level, then measures are taken to evaluate product and service in order to increase repeat customers.

An effective marketing plan is generally developed around an established outline. Owners and managers who are not familiar with formal marketing plans would be advised to seek professional assistance.

FIGURE 12-10   *Bookbinder's Restaurant Ad. Courtesy Bookbinder's Restaurant, Philadelphia, Pennsylvania.*

SUMMARY

The objective of marketing a restaurant operation is to serve customers food and beverage products that satisfy their needs at a price perceived as having a fair value. In order to reach this objective it is necessary for management to follow the four steps in the marketing cycle. To set the marketing cycle in motion, the food service marketing mix must be determined. When the format for product or service, presentation, and communication has been established, marketing activities can be initiated.

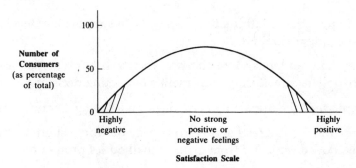

FIGURE 12-11 *Comment Card Respondents.* Source: Foodservice and Restaurant Marketing.*

Market research is a valuable activity in any marketing effort. Market research information identifies needs and opportunities in the marketplace, qualifies the target market, and provides the data to support product/service development.

The marketing campaign is the application of market research information combined with data from the food service marketing mix. The activities of a marketing campaign generate customer interest in a restaurant business, its products, and its services.

CHAPTER QUESTIONS

1. How do restaurant businesses satisfy customer needs?

2. How does the restaurant marketing distribution chain differ from the retail marketing distribution chain in allowing for customer response?

3. Outline the marketing cycle, giving a short definition of each phase.

4. What important element is combined with product in the food service marketing mix?

5. Which demographic issue will have the most impact on marketing campaigns for restaurant businesses in the 1990s?

6. Why do demographic changes tend to impact heavily on the success of restaurant businesses?

---

*Source: Robert D. Reid, *Foodservice and Restaurant Marketing*, (New York: Van Nostrand Reinhold, 1983).

7. Identify the type of information necessary to support the development of marketing opportunities.

8. Explain how understanding the way in which households allocate food service dollars can affect management's marketing decisions.

9. What phase of the marketing cycle does a marketing campaign represent?

10. Identify the most effective advertising media for restaurant businesses. Discuss how these differ from internal methods of promotion.

ACTIVITIES

1. Identify a marketing opportunity for a restaurant business. Following the marketing cycle outline in this chapter, determine a product or service, create a format to generate customer interest, and determine the level of success to be evaluated.

2. Following the guidelines in Table 12-2, determine the factors that can directly affect restaurant businesses in your community. Attempt to collect data to support your observations from the Chamber of Commerce and local town or city offices.

3. Develop a marketing campaign for a restaurant business in your community. Determine what the overall objectives of the campaign are and establish the most effective way of creating customer interest. Design promotional materials and write advertising copy as applicable. Identify advertising formats and the schedule of media placement if used.

13 *Restaurant Management Careers*

OBJECTIVES

1. To identify restaurant management career opportunities.

2. To be able to understand the characteristics of a successful entrepreneur.

3. To be aware of the opportunities for training and education for restaurant management careers.

4. To understand the importance of establishing individual career goals and objectives.

CASE STUDY: MIKE BARRETT AND DRY DOCK RESTAURANT AND THE SUNSET INN, ERIE, PENNSYLVANIA

Successful careers in the food service industry are often the result of a variety of job experiences selected from a wide range of opportunities. Mike Barrett began his food service career as a high school student working in local restaurants. After graduating from Paul Smith's College in upstate New York with a 2-year associate's degree in hotel and resort management, he received his bachelor's degree at the University of Denver's School of Hotel and Restaurant Management.

From the Pine Crest Inn in Pinehurst, North Carolina, where he had been promoted to assistant general manager, he joined Stauffers Management Food Systems in San Francisco, California, managing business and industry contract feeding accounts. With Host International he became food service director at Tampa International Airport, Tampa, Florida, and then food and beverage director at Newark International Airport, Newark, New Jersey.

Realizing the importance of management and business education, Mike returned to Erie, where he simultaneously worked on his master's degree in business and taught restaurant management courses at the School of Hotel and Restaurant Management at Mercyhurst College. As an instructor he related many of his professional food service experiences to prospective restaurant managers.

While acting as general manager of the University Club of Erie, Mike decided to try independent restaurant ownership and purchased the Dry Dock Restaurant, a combined restaurant and catering facility seating 436 guests (Figure 13-1). Today he also owns and operates the Sunset Inn, an independent catering facility which seats 300 and offers off-premise catering. These combined operations generate over $1,000,000 annually in sales.

Mike's greatest challenge today is keeping his business profitable during the recessionary economic trends that have dramatically affected the community of Erie, Pennsylvania. By keeping up with industry innovations, identifying customer needs, and offering products and services at prices that answer those needs, the Dry Dock and The Sunset Inn are successfully weathering the economic storm while other less well managed businesses are failing.

Mike is always looking toward tomorrow with the anticipation that the food service industry will offer him yet another opportunity to use his skills and talents to broaden his career path.

The food service industry offers a dynamic spectrum of job opportunities at all levels of employment, from hourly wage staff to key management. These opportunities exist in work environments that range from small independent restaurant settings to corporate offices. Locations around the United States and the world allow food service career professionals to select living environments for

FIGURE 13-1   *Dry Dock Logo. Courtesy Dry Dock Restaurant, Erie, Pennsylvania.*

themselves and their families suited to individual life-style needs. Positions are also available in a variety of workplaces ranging from 24-hour commercial food service operations to contract feeding programs that function during normal business hours, 5 days a week. Teaching positions at secondary and postsecondary schools, colleges, and universities offer the opportunity to apply industry experience and knowledge in the classroom. The operations management of the food service industry requires the skills of accountants, designers, telecommunications experts, real estate specialists, lawyers, and other professionals.

Career development is a lifelong program of personal growth toward objectives that range from financial to life-style goals. Identifying a career path in the food service industry requires a thorough understanding of all of the available opportunities. In addition, it is necessary to assess an individual's skills, strengths, and weaknesses to evaluate how well suited he or she is to meet the many and varied demands of this industry.

ENTREPRENEURSHIP

Entrepreneurs are those individuals who have identified a need, have determined a product or service to answer that need, and are willing to expend the effort and financial commitment necessary to bring that product or service to market.

The restaurant industry has historically provided an opportunity for entrepreneurs of all capabilities to fulfill their need to own their own business. Howard Johnson, Bill Marriott, Anthony Athanis, and Michael Hurst are just a few of the internationally recognized names of entrepreneurial restaurateurs. In every city and town there are entrepreneurial restaurant owners who represent a major source of employment and service in their community. Their contributions to the well-being of their communities reach far beyond financial investments.

Identifying yourself as an entrepreneur requires an evaluation of your ability to take risks. New business startups require long hours of hard work which often is not initially compensated while family and personal life is pushed aside. Entrepreneurs must be willing to accept failure as part of the process of developing ideas and concepts. Failure at one level often becomes the stepping stone to eventual success.

Entrepreneurs must have the following characteristics:

- High motivation
- Physical capability to work long hours

- Ability to accept advice
- Willingness to change direction when necessary
- Effective communication skill
- Creativity and spontaneity

Peter Drucker, a noted educator and author, identifies two theories of entrepreneurship that can be successfully applied to restaurant business development: Creative Imitation and Creative innovation. "Creative immitation satisfies a demand that already exists. "Creative innovation perfects and positions a product or service.

Marketing Entrepreneurial Ideas

As seen in Figure 13-2, the first phase of the marketing cycle is to identify a need in the marketplace. Innovative entrepreneurs create new products or services to meet these needs. Creative imitation entrepreneurs redesign an existing product or service. Both styles of entrepreneurship are particularly adaptable to food service products and services.

An example of creative innovation is the development of a ribless beef, pork, and chicken rib by Designer Foods in Wilmington, Delaware. A customer need was identified for a barbequed rib that could be eaten without using the fingers. Constant complaints were made about the problem of handling a messy product covered with sauce. Designer Foods, under the entrepreneurial leadership of

Figure 13-2 *Ribless Rib Brochure. Courtesy Designer Foods Inc., Wilmington, Delaware.*

Gene Gagliardi, developed a food processing method to shave the meat off the bone and blend it in such a way that it binds together without artificial ingredients. The blended meat is then put through a meat processor that extrudes it to form an established portion size similar in appearance to a rack of ribs. When the product is appropriately sauced, it is packaged by a process called *cryovacing*, which extends product shelf life. The ribless meat product can be microwaved, oven processed, or grilled. A marketing brochure for this product is featured in Figure 13-2.

An example of creative imitation is the Dove Bar© ice cream product. The company identified the need for a gourmet chocolate-covered ice cream product on a stick. Using a high butter fat content ice cream and an equally high quality chocolate, the company created a line of ice cream sticks boxed and priced in the range of $1.50 to $2.00 per bar.

The restaurant customer is being introduced daily to food products that have been flavored, textured, shaped, preportioned, and preprepared during the manufacturing process in ways that reduce preparation labor, waste, cooking time, and costs. The development of each of these products is part of an entrepreneurial marketing effort by food manufacturers to meet the needs of restaurateurs to reduce costs and increase profits. Figure 13-3 is a breaded veal product manufactured by Colonial Beef Company. Produced from high-quality beef in predetermined portion sizes, the lamb is frozen, ready to be put into production immediately as the main ingredient in a menu item.

Prospective entrepreneurs can prepare for a career in the food service industry through a combination of education and industry experience. After high school, an individual can identify various colleges and universities offering specific programs in entrepreneurship. Gaining job experience by working directly in the determined interest area is necessary to develop a thorough understanding of the operational activities of a business as well as the paths of work and communication that must be followed by both employees and management.

Entrepreneurs who have gained an education in their field of interest often supplement their knowledge with specific business- and industry-related courses to increase their ability to develop, market, and operate products and businesses.

FOOD SERVICE CAREER PATHS

Food service careers are broken down into three primary levels: entry, middle management, and management. Restaurant businesses classify job positions as production, service, or management. Training and educational criteria vary at

301100
LAMB SHISH KABOBS
—Gold Label—U.S. Choice

Luscious chunks of lamb cut from U.S. Choice
Legs, colorful red and green peppers, pearl
onions and quality mushrooms, all "threaded"
attractively on a stainless steel skewer.

Portion Sizes: 4, 6, 8 oz.

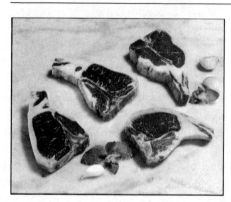

304100
LOIN LAMB CHOPS
—Gold Label—U.S. Choice

Excellent quality, cut from carefully selected U.S.
Choice young Lamb Loins. Well trimmed and
intended for better menus.

Portion Sizes: 3, 4, 5, 6 oz.

325100
LAMBETTES (Stuffed Breasts of Lamb)
—Gold Label—U.S. Choice

U.S. Choice Breasts of Lamb stuffed with lean
Ground Lamb, then shaped and cut into "chops."
Excellent for hospitals and nursing homes as
well as restaurant and cafeteria operations.

Portion Sizes: 3, 4, 5, 6 oz.

Figure 13-3   *Colonial Beef Product Page. Courtesy Colonial Beef Products.*

each level. Wages for hourly employees are often controlled by state and federal regulations. Representative salaries for management positions fluctuate regionally across the United States.

ENTRY-LEVEL POSITIONS
  FOOD PRODUCTION

      Line Cook

      Baker's Helper

      Prep Worker

      Dishwasher

  SERVICE

      Host/Hostess

      Bartender

      Waiter/Waitress

      Counter Worker (quick serve)

      Cafeteria Server

      Bus Person

MIDDLE MANAGEMENT
  FOOD PRODUCTION

      Chef

      Pastry Chef

      Kitchen Manager

      Cafeteria Manager

  SERVICE

      Beverage Manager

      Purchasing Agent

      Banquet (Catering) Manager

      Assistant Restaurant Manager

      Head Bartender

      Maitre d' Hotel (Head Waiter)

      Dining Room Captain

MANAGEMENT

    Owner/ Operator

    Food Service Director

    Personnel Director

    Controller

    Training Director

Wage rates for hourly employees are based on minimum wage regulations. In the food service industry, positions which include tips as part of employee compensation have lower minimum wage requirements than other positions. Table 13-1, compiled by the National Restaurant Association, overviews a range of hourly wages being paid to selected job positions.

Salaries for contract employees for similar job positions can vary widely between geographic regions of the United States and between food service companies. Table 13-2, by the National Restaurant Association, overviews the salaries and bonuses being paid for selected middle management and management level positions.

Now that you have been introduced to the operational aspects of restaurant management, where do you fit in? Answer the following questions yes or no:

1. Are your skills and talents applicable to the needs of a restaurant management position? _____

2. Are you able to communicate, direct others, plan, train, organize, and evaluate the work of your employees sufficiently to fulfill the responsibilities of a restaurant manager? _____

3. Are you willing to work long hours? _____

4. Do you enjoy helping other people? _____

5. Do you need a flexible work environment? _____

6. Are you creative and spontaneous? _____

If you have answered yes to the majority of these questions, then you can feel confident in investigating this career field further.

The job descriptions for many of these positions were discussed earlier. The management positions for personnel director and training director are discussed in Chapter 9 along with middle-management level service jobs and entry level food service production and service jobs.

TABLE 13-1 Survey of Wage Rates for Hourly Employees, 1990

AREA: United States

Type of Hourly Employee	Median Hourly Wage[1]	Median Lowest Hourly Wage[2]	Median Highest Hourly Wage[3]	Number of Employees	Number of Responses
Cook	$6.50	$5.50	$7.50	30479	4727
Assistant Cook	5.80	5.00	6.50	8037	2349
Short Order Cook	5.75	5.00	6.50	9467	1708
Baker	6.25	5.75	7.00	2705	1127
Food/Salad Preparation Worker	5.25	4.75	6.00	15036	2752
Crew Person (fast food)	4.25	3.85	5.00	34957	823
Crew Supervisor (fast food)	5.55	5.00	6.00	5067	753
Cafeteria Server	4.58	4.40	5.50	5592	462
Waiter/Waitress	2.60	2.31	3.50	97297	4921
Host/Hostess	5.00	4.50	5.50	17882	3289
Bartender	5.00	4.75	5.82	12557	2803
Cashier	5.00	4.50	5.50	8685	1675
Busperson	4.00	3.85	4.25	22695	3352
Dishwasher	4.50	4.25	5.00	24592	4488
Janitor/Porter	5.25	5.00	5.75	5347	1664
Driver (delivery)	5.00	4.25	5.00	5530	397

[1]Median hourly wage is weighted based on average hourly wage reported by each respondent weighted by number of employees. It is possible for weighted medians to fall outside the unweighted low to high range. See explanatory notes.
[2]Lowest hourly wage is median reported by respondents, unweighted by number of employees.
[3]Highest hourly wage is median reported by respondents, unweighted by number of employees.
Note: For tipped employees, data represent cash wage, excluding tips.
Source: National Restaurant Association survey conducted July-September 1990. Data are reflective of survey respondents and are not necessarily representative of the industry. Data should not be considered industry standards.

Table 13-2 Compensation for All Positions—All Respondents

	Base Salary				Annual Bonus			
	Total Number of Positions	Lower Quartile	Median	Upper Quartile	Total Number of Positions	Lower Quartile	Median	Upper Quartile
Owner	757	$25,000	$38,000	$00,000	335	$5,000	$15,000	$30,000
Chairman of the Board	36	30,000	95,000	204,000	18	9,000	27,500	110,055
President	304	30,000	47,500	75,000	122	5,000	16,760	40,000
Chief Executive Officer	105	29,400	46,000	75,000	54	3,850	10,000	19,250
Chief Financial Officer	78	34,000	48,000	76,500	36	3,500	10,000	15,750
Chief Operating Officer	95	34,000	50,000	70,000	52	2,000	6,000	12,000
Treasurer	109	18,600	28,000	52,000	40	2,000	6,000	14,000
Vice President								
General	30	18,100	40,000	72,500	15	1,750	8,875	34,500
Development/Real Estate	26	51,625	67,182	94,050	15	4,553	15,500	42,500
Distribution/Purchasing	33	27,250	46,000	87,510	15	4,000	7,200	30,000
Finance	31	40,875	60,000	82,750	15	11,359	19,000	39,250
Franchising	14	40,000	76,875	92,500	8	*	10,746	*
Management Information								
Systems	21	30,000	56,500	97,625	10	*	8,783	*
Marketing	58	26,500	44,200	67,000	29	1,750 6,500	25,446	

Operations	162	30,000	50,000	74,450	77	5,000	10,000	23,750
Personnel/Human Resources	54	29,000	42,000	70,000	22	3,340	6,000	16,503
Other Function	43	30,250	46,680	60,750	25	2,500	10,000	20,000
Controller	228	24,000	30,000	40,000	100	1,000	3,000	5,000
Training Director	57	24,250	30,500	42,750	30	1,000	3,000	5,525
Food and Beverage Director	305	25,000	32,736	42,000	111	1,000	2,500	5,500
Executive Chef	483	25,000	31,000	38,000	216	1,000	2,050	5,000
Banquet Manager	180	18,000	23,250	28,900	54	750	2,000	6,000
Catering Manager	157	20,000	24,000	31,000	69	1,000	3,000	5,150
Unit Manager	8,764	20,000	25,740	31,000	6,852	1,158	2,500	5,000
Assistant Unit Manager	11,873	18,500	21,600	24,600	9,378	500	1,041	2,500
Night Manager	317	15,000	18,200	23,100	155	613	1,121	2,231
Manager Trainee	2,017	16,172	18,000	22,050	69	1,013	2,000	5,875
Dining Room Manager	895	15,000	20,425	25,000	565	500	1,305	2,450
Kitchen Manager	970	18,000	22,000	27,162	390	550	1,700	3,000
Regional Manager	508	36,601	50,200	58,000	466	3,154	6,800	11,633
District Manager	887	33,950	42,000	46,400	840	2,246	4,817	7,000

Source: Survey of Wage Rates for Hourly Employees, 1990, National Restaurant Association, Washington, DC, 1990.

Compensation Packages

Compensation packages include benefits as well as salary. These benefits are often nontaxable, such as medical insurance and education. Other benefits include future income-producing opportunities such as pension plans and profit-sharing programs. Stock options also allow employees to purchase single shares of stock directly from the company without paying the broker fees normally associated with stock purchases and sales.

The value of a compensation package depends on the needs of the individual. Single persons do not need comprehensive family health and dental plans but may see considerable value in stock option benefits. Profit sharing is a benefit used by management to create employee incentive to increase quality control and profit. If the company is not highly profitable, then employees may not feel that this benefit has real value for them. On the other hand, if the company is highly profitable, this benefit could result in financial bonuses at the end of the company's fiscal year.

TRAINING AND EDUCATION

Education for food service industry related jobs often begins with high school courses in the home economics department or in a specified career track in a vocational school. These programs, combined with job experience, often give future restaurant managers their initial training and interest in the field.

Training

Training for food production jobs is often found in established apprenticeship programs in hotels and restaurants. Under the direction of certified chefs and food service directors, apprenticeship programs are administered by professional associations such as the American Culinary Federation. Through the program, cooks work with certified chefs to learn the job skills for each of the stations in the kitchen. When they have satisfactorily mastered the required skills, they are awarded a certificate of achievement that can be applied to their own professional certification. Job pay in these situations is usually less than regular wages to compensate for instruction. More information on culinary apprenticeship programs is available through The American Culinary Federation, 10 San Bartolla Rd., St. Augustine, Florida, 32084-3466, phone: 904-824-4468.

Professional certification programs available for food service management personnel include such specific areas as sanitation, food cost control, and employee supervision. These are administered as part of courses which are offered at area schools and colleges with hospitality-restaurant management programs. They are also available in correspondence form from recognized educational programs representing the food service industry. More information on this type of certification program is available from

The National Restaurant Association

250 South Wacker Drive Suite 1400

Chicago, Illinois 60606

Phone: 312-715-1010

and

The Educational Institute

American Hotel & Motel Association

P.O. Box 1240

East Lansing, Michigan 48826

Phone: 517-353-5500

Management certification programs covering broad areas of food service knowledge and experience represent industry acknowledgment and professional skill achievement. By gaining such certification an individual is accorded the privilege of using the program title initials after his or her professional name. A certified food service executive uses the initials CFE, a certified food and beverage executive CFBE, and a certified master chef CMC. Information on these programs can be obtained from the American Culinary Federation, the American Hotel & Motel Association, and International Food Service Executives Association.

Formal postsecondary education is offered by 2- and 4-year programs. In community colleges, 4-year colleges, and universities, hotel-restaurant and institutional management degree programs are available in a number of major areas.

Culinary

Culinary degree programs combine food service management and culinary arts courses with required liberal arts components. These are generally associate degree of science programs that require the completion of approximately 60 credit hours. The normal amount of time taken to complete these programs is 2 academic years. Some form of practical internship or cooperative work experience is required to complete this degree.

Restaurant Management and Institutional Food Service Management

Restaurant management and institutional food service management are the general 2-year core curriculums for both 2-year and 4-year degree programs in food service management. Students determine whether they will focus their attention on commercial restaurant management or institutional and business food service management. Depending on the course of instruction, these programs include business-related and general management courses as well as food service management and culinary arts skills. They usually require an internship or cooperative work experience component. These 4-year programs award a bachelor of science degree and require completion of approximately 120 credit hours. Additional master's degree and doctoral programs in hotel and restaurant management are available at colleges and universities throughout the United States.

CAREER CHOICES

Identifying a career path requires an individual to assess his or her skills and abilities objectively and realistically as well as to identify career and personal goals and objectives. This process of self-assessment often necessitates input from counselors, teachers, and employers, who can give considerable insight into a person's work habits, potential for achievement, and personality. Their contributions can be valuable in helping to determine whether goals and objectives are realistic.

One of the most important characteristics needed for successful self-assessment is an overall orientation toward a career field. All managerial positions require interaction with other people, particularly in restaurant businesses. Ask yourself some important questions about how much contact with other people is important to your overall job satisfaction.

1. Do you enjoy being in the company of other people the majority of the time?

2. Are you comfortable working in an environment where interaction with others is necessary?

3. Do you enjoy listening to other people's problems?

The answer to these questions will help to determine whether you are people-oriented or task-oriented. *Task-oriented* people are most comfortable when they are involved with accomplishing specific tasks where interaction with others is minimal in order to accomplish the job. *People-oriented* workers thrive in a situation where constant interaction with others is necessary to perform job tasks.

Goals and objectives are the results on which people focus their efforts, both career and personal.

1. What do you want to accomplish by working in this career field over a period of time?

2. Are you more concerned with financial reward, job title, or job responsibilities?

3. Or are you concerned with the resulting life-style?

4. Are your work environment and the type of people that you will work with important factors?

Being realistic about your real motives and goals in selecting a career goal is an important key to eventual success.

Objectives are the steps that are necessary to achieve goals. For each phase of your career, objectives should be determined. For example, it may be necessary to complete a certain level of training or education to achieve a goal of having a specific job. The objective becomes the completion of a training or educational program.

To help yourself understand which career path to follow, list your goals according to the format in Figure 13-4.

CAREER GOALS   PERSONAL GOALS

_____   _____

_____   _____

_____   _____

_____   _____

_____   _____

_____   _____

Figure 13-4   *Goals*

Evaluate the goals that you have listed in terms of the following criteria:

1. Are they realistic? Is this goal something that you honestly feel that you can accomplish?

2. Are they achievable? Have you been realistic in your ability to accomplish the necessary jobs required to achieve this goal?

3. Are they measurable? Will you be able to establish criteria by which you can measure how well you are progressing on the path to accomplishing these goals?

Now that you have been introduced to the operational aspects of restaurant management, where do you fit in? Answer the following questions yes or no:

1. Are your skills and talents applicable to the restaurant industry? _____

2. Are you able to communicate, direct others, plan, train, organize, and evaluate the work of your employees sufficiently to carry out the job responsibilities of a restaurant manager? _____

3. Are you willing to work long hours? _____

4. Do you enjoy helping other people? _____

5. Do you need a work environment that is flexible? _____

6. Are you creative and spontaneous? _____

If you have answered yes to the majority of these questions, then you can feel confident in investigating this career field further.

SUMMARY

Career development is a process that requires an individual to identify a career path and thoroughly investigate all of the available career opportunities within it. Successful career development also requires an individual to establish realistic goals and objectives for his or her career and personal life.

Food service career paths are classified by three primary levels: entry level, middle management, and management. Positions are available in each of these levels in both the production and the service areas of a restaurant operation. Compensation packages for many of these positions include benefits which increase the overall value of the job. Medical insurance, education, and pension, and profit-sharing plans offer nontaxable and future income possibilities.

BIBLIOGRAPHY

Axler, Bruce H. *Foodservice: A Managerial Approach*. The National Institute for the Foodservice Industry, 1979.

Brillat-Savarin, Jean Anthelme. *The Physiology of Taste*. Edited by M.F.K. Fisher. San Francisco: North Point Press, 1986.

Bureau of Foodservice Research. "1991 Foodservice Forecast." *Restaurants & Institutions*, 1990.

CBORD Foodservice Management Systems Report Highlights. The CBORD Group, 1990.

Coltman, Michael M. *Hospitality Management Accounting*, 2nd ed. New York: CBI Publishers, 1982.

Crawford, Hollis W., and McDowell, Milton C. *Math Workshop for Foodservice/Lodging*. New York: Van Nostrand Reinhold Co., 1980.

Delfakis, Helen, Scanlon, Nancy L., VanBuren, Janis B. *Food Service Management*. Cincinnati: South-Western Publishing Co., 1992.

Drucker, Peter F. *Innovation and Entrepreneurship*, New York, Harper & Row, 1985.

Fantetti, Donna J. *Career Directions*. Providence: P.A.R., 1987.

Kasavana, Michael L. *Computer Systems for Foodservice Operations*. New York: Van Nostrand Reinhold Co., 1984.

Kinnear, Thomas C., Bernhart, Kenneth L. *Principles of Marketing*, 2nd ed. Glenview, Ill.: Scott Foresman & Company, 1986.

Kotschevar, Lendal H. *Quantity Food Purchasing*, 2nd. ed. New York: John Wiley & Sons, 1975.

Kotschevar, Lendal H., *Management by Menu*. Dubuque: William C. Brown, Publishers/National Institute for the Foodservice Industry, 1987.

Lundberg, Donald E. *The Restaurant: From Concept to Operation*. New York, John Wiley & Sons, 1985.

Menu For Profit, N. New Portland, Maine, Profit Enhancement Programs Inc., 1991.

Millar, Jack. *Menu Pricing and Strategy*. Boston: CBI Publishing Co., 1980.

Miner, Tom. *The Business Chef*. New York: Van Nostrand Reinhold Co., 1989.

Murrmann, S.K. and K.F. Murrmann. *Union Membership Trends and Organizing Activities in the Hotel and Restaurant Industries*. (Washington, D.C.: Virginia Polytechnic Institute/State University, Council on Hotel Restaurant and Institutional Education, 1991).

Nykiel, Ronald A. *Marketing in the Hospitality Industry*, New York: Van Nostrand Reinhold, 1983.

Old Mr. Boston Deluxe Offical Bartenders Guide, Boston: Mr. Boston Distiller Corporation, 1979.

Plunkett, W. Richard. *Supervision: The Direction of People at Work*. 2nd ed. Dubuque: Wm C. Brown Publishers, 1979.

Restaurant Industry Operations Report '90. National Restaurant Association and Laventhol & Horwath, Washington, D.C.

Restaurants USA, National Restaurant Association, Vol. II, #8, Sept. 91., (Monthly), Washington, D.C.

Restaurants USA, National Restaurant Association, Vol. II, #10, Nov. 91., (Monthly), Washington, D.C.

Richman, Phyllis, "La Brasserie: Accounting for Taste" *The Washington Post*, November 26, 1990.

Scanlon, Nancy L. *Marketing by Menu*, 1st ed. New York: CBI Publishers, 1985.

_____. *Marketing by Menu*, 2nd. ed. New York: Van Nostrand Reinhold, 1990.

Sherry, John E. H. *Legal Aspects of Foodservice Management*. New York: John Wiley & Sons, 1984.

Stranger, Ila. "*Southwest Cookery—Hotter Than Ever,*" Food & Wine Magazine VII #4, p 53. AMEX Food & Wine Magazine Corp., New York, N.Y.

U.S. Department of Justice, Civil Rights Division. *The Americans with Disabilities Act: Questions & Answers*. CRD-80 Washington, 1991.

Washington Weekly, Washington D.C., National Restaurant Association, (Weekly) August 1991

Index